SOCIOLOGY AND THE SCHOOL

SOCIOLOGY AND THE SCHOOL

An Interactionist Viewpoint

Peter Woods

Routledge & Kegan Paul
London, Boston, Melbourne and Henley

First published in 1983
by Routledge & Kegan Paul plc
39 Store Street, London WC1E 7DD,
9 Park Street, Boston, Mass. 02108, USA,
296 Beaconsfield Parade, Middle Park,
Melbourne, 3206, Australia, and
Broadway House, Newtown Road,
Henley-on-Thames, Oxon RG9 1EN
Set in 10/11pt Times
Printed in Great Britain by
St Edmundsbury Press
Bury St Edmunds, Suffolk

Library of Congress Cataloging in Publication Data

Woods, Peter.

Sociology and the school.
Bibliography: p.
Includes index.
1. Sociology. 2. Social interaction. 3. Inter-
action analysis in education. 4. Teacher-student
relationships. I. Title.
HM51.W64 1983   301   82–21574

ISBN 0–7100–9342–X

For Caro, James and Becca

Contents

Acknowledgments

I have benefited from discussions with and comments from many colleagues while writing this book. In particular, I would like to thank Andy Hargreaves, David Hargreaves, Andrew Pollard, Stephen Ball, Jennifer Nias and Colin Lacey for their comments on earlier drafts of material. I am especially grateful to Martyn Hammersley for his observations on the entire manuscript. The views expressed are, of course, my own, as are any errors that remain in the text. My thanks to Meryl Baker for expert secretarial services, and to my wife and family for their moral support.

For permission to reproduce material previously published, my thanks to the editors of *Educational Review*, vol. 30, no. 2, 1978, and of the *Journal of Curriculum Studies*, vol. 10, no. 4, 1978 (parts of chapter 6); and to the Open University for the summary diagram in chapter 3 and figures 1 and 2 in chapter 5, which originally appeared in Course E202, *Schooling and Society*.

Preface

My aim in this book is to demonstrate how a particular sociological viewpoint can aid our understanding of school life. It is known as 'interactionist', for it concentrates on the small-scale detail of interpersonal relationships, what people do, and how they react to each other, the patterning of behaviours, the ebb and flow of everyday life. It takes nothing for granted about the importance of events, for that is decided by the people under study. This is their world, or more properly speaking, worlds, since there are many realities in school – the aspiring, vocational teacher, the 'nine-to-four teacher', the ambitious, career-oriented child of a middle-class family, the anti-school, truanting child of a lower working-class family from a depressed area, boys, girls, members of the hierarchy, seasoned veterans, young teachers fresh out of training college, and so on.

Given this, my focus is on how people make sense of the world, their 'frameworks' or 'perspectives', and how they change in, or are influenced by, the various situations or 'contexts' in which interactions take place; how they relate to each other, different interests and ends, and the ways and means devised to achieve them, be they teacher methods, obvious or subtle, or pupil avoidance techniques; how groups come to form, and influence their members, develop beliefs, attitudes, ways of coping and behaving; and how individuals see the course of their lives from day to day, situation to situation, and through the institution.

Over the past decade or so, interactionism has grown to become one of the leading current approaches in the discipline (Hammersley and Woods 1976, Delamont 1976, D.H. Hargreaves 1972 and 1978, Hammersley 1980c and 1983). It has produced a steady stream of research studies. The results of this continuing work form the content of this book. I hope to show its substantive and conceptual richness, and its potential both for the development of new theory within sociology and for the testing of existing theories. But interactionism has another potential – one of reducing the considerable gap between teacher and educational researcher. Because it is firmly located within the real world of teaching and its issues more obviously relate to teachers' day-to-day concerns, such as effective teaching, classroom control, and pupil deviance, interactionism speaks more clearly to practitioners than do some forms of sociology with higher degrees of abstraction and wider, system-related, concerns. But it is not unrelated to these. Thus it can serve as a bridge to more inaccessible pastures.

The book therefore is an introductory text for teachers and students of education and sociology in general, which seeks to put the many disparate studies of the past ten to fifteen years within a coherent interactionist framework. That framework is elaborated in chapter 1.

Chapter 1

Interactionism and the school

Symbolic interaction

Interactionism, by its nature, is a rather diffuse set of ideas rather than a tightly integrated body of theory, and it has spanned a correspondingly diffuse range of studies. I propose to bring these together around some central interactionist concepts, and to consider what has been achieved. In this first chapter, I will sketch what I regard as these central concepts, which will determine the structure of the rest of the book.

At the heart of symbolic interactionism is the notion of people as constructors of their own actions and meanings. People live in a physical world, but the objects in that world have a 'meaning' for them. They are not always the same objects for different people, nor are situations interpreted in the same way. To some, school is a joyful and liberating arena, to others it may appear dull and restrictive, and be compared to prison or an army barracks. To the same person, a piece of chalk might be a writing implement on one occasion, a missile on another. In other words they are symbols – they indicate to a person certain meanings which are dependent on them for their construction.

People interact through symbols. A symbol is 'a stimulus that has a learned meaning and value for people, and man's response to a symbol is in terms of its meaning and value rather than in terms of its physical stimulation of his sense organs' (Rose 1962). Language is one such symbol, as are gestures and objects. People learn through interaction an enormous number of symbols. The meaning of many of these are, of course, shared, and this enables smooth social interaction. Some even have greater constancy, to which we respond almost by instinct, and these have been called 'natural signs' as distinct from 'significant symbols' (Mead, vol. 1, 1936). The latter are learned.

What enables the construction of meaning is the individual's possession of a 'self'. We can converse with our 'selves', we can stand outside our 'selves' and look inward with 'others'' eyes. This suggests two aspects of the self – the subjective 'I', the initiator of action, the part that perceives and constructs; and the more objective 'Me', the part of self as others might see it, and as the 'I', by putting itself in the position of others, can also see it (Mead 1934, Blumer 1976). This has been called 'taking the role of the other', and it is vital for social life and cooperative activity that one learns how to do it. We are probably all familiar with the apparently selfish and egotistical young child, who wants everything his own way. He possesses only an 'I', at this stage – his social development is incomplete. But gradually he learns to put himself in the position of other people and to look in on himself from those positions. One of the chief mechanisms in socialization is play and the game, for in the game the child 'must be ready to take the attitude of everyone else involved in that game, and these roles must have a definite relationship to each other'(Natanson 1973, p. 13).

One can see one's own behaviour from the point of view of specific others, but gradually over time, one relates significant features of these perceptions together, and sees oneself in terms of generalized and abstracted norms, values and beliefs. Thus, to take the children's game again as an example, one might progress from perceiving from the vantage point of a specific mother or father, to 'mothers' and 'fathers' in general, and from there, having built up an understanding of the rules that apply to general interaction, a conception of how all other roles perceive a particular one. Hence the important concept of 'the generalized other' which makes the conceptual link between individual behaviour and society, and most clearly exhibits that behaviour as a social product.

Individuals can only develop complete selves to the degree that they are able to assume the attitude of the social group, of which they are members, towards the group's activities. Similarly, an ongoing social group or society is only possible to the degree that its members can assume the role of all other members with regard to the organized activities of the group, and can construct their own action in relation to it. Thus, the individual can only become 'whole' in the sense of a social person by internalizing the expectations embodied in 'the generalized other'; and it is through the generalized other that the community exercises influence over the individual through his very thought processes (Mead, vol. 1, 1936, p.155).

Human beings, then, are the constructors of their own actions. Since they are able to view themselves as objects, they can make indications to themselves and these they interpret. These interpretations, though guided by culturally influenced perspectives, carry the essence of individuality:

> In order to act, the individual has to identify what he wants, establish an objective or goal, map out a prospective line of behaviour, note and interpret the actions of others, size up his situation, check himself at this or that point, figure out what to do at other points and frequently spur himself on in the face of dragging dispositions or discouraging settings (Blumer 1976).

It is the interpretation that counts as far as outcomes are concerned, and therefore people's own thoughts and evaluations, not instinct, nor simply the 'objective' reality of the situation.

The 'act' is not a consequence of a sudden one-off decision, any more than the 'self' is a single component. There is continuous interaction between the 'I' and the 'Me' as the individual constructs, modifies, pieces together, weighs up the pros and cons, reconsiders, and so on. It is a continuous state of flux, or process. The act, therefore, is a succession of phases, of which the manifest behaviour is but one. It includes the initiator, the 'I', reflecting upon the various 'Mes' in the form of particular, significant and generalized others, which themselves are the product of much past interaction; taking the role of the other, making representations to oneself, interpreting, and ultimately performing the visible act.

This does not mean that interpretations are fluid to the extent that they are never actually formulated. In fact, actions need a basis on which to orient their interpretations, and to this end people first define the situation. This gives them a key to interpretation and aids the construction of their own action. Thus pupils might learn to identify what constitutes 'a proper lesson', 'a conflict situation' or 'a laugh'. Key definitions become fixed and repetitious and situations become structured because previous interaction has established common understandings of them. This is how cultures arise, and how they both form a platform for interpretation and a basis for new developments.

These habituated ways are 'roles'; not roles prescribed by society acted out mechanically, but actively constructed in accordance with the individual's generally held definition of the situation. The dynamic process, as opposed to overscripted, static conception of roles is well illustrated by Plummer:

> The interactionist starts out from the notion of men busily constructing images of how they expect others to act in giving

3

positions (role-taking), evolving notions of how they themselves expect to act in a given position (role-making), and also imaginatively viewing themselves as they like to think of themselves being and acting in a given position (role-identity) (Plummer 1975, p. 18).

The interactionist view of the relationships between the individual and society is therefore a dialectical one:

Society is a dialectic phenomenon in that it is a human product and nothing but a human product, that yet continuously acts back upon its producer. Society is a product of man. It has no other being except that which is bestowed upon it by human activity and consciousness. There can be no social reality apart from man. Yet it may also be stated that man is a product of society. Every individual biography is an episode within the history of society, which both precedes and survives it.... What is more, it is within society, and as a result of social processes that the individual becomes a person, that he attains and holds on to an identity and that he carries out the various projects that constitute his life ... (Berger 1969, p. 3).

Thus, of course, actions are rarely totally original, nor is the individual totally bound by cultural and structural constraint. Some cultural experiences are for roles rather than individuals, some are for variation rather than conformity, and cultural meanings are possibilities not pressures, and are often internally inconsistent. Thus, within these cultural meanings and influences, individuals have some possibility of innovating (Rose 1962, p. 3).

The Berlaks put it like this:

thinking is an elaborated process of adaptation of the person to the social and physical environment. It is an extension of the Darwinian concept of adaptation to include 'mind' – the capacity of the individual to examine self-consciously the problem from differing perspectives to create novel – heretofore unknown – solutions to the problem of living. The process we call in our language of entities, 'mind', is what enables homo sapiens to both adapt to the environment and alter it in order to cope with problems confronting the species (Berlak and Berlak 1981).

This view of the individual as reacting to others, and forming a self for others to react to, has been given, literally, dramatic overtones by Goffman. In *The Presentation of Self in Everyday*

Life (1959) and other works (1967; 1971), he elaborated a view with the following main tenets:

i   In interaction, individuals try to 'manage' the impressions others have of them. They put on a performance. They will try to influence the other's definition of the situation.

ii   'Others' also, of course, project definitions of the situation. Conflict is obviated and order maintained by individuals suppressing their heartfelt needs and wants and contributing to a script which all accept. They establish a 'working consensus'.

iii In projecting impressions individuals take into account their knowledge of others. As interaction proceeds, and their 'presentations' become more adjusted and refined, so they become more committed to them.

iv   When events contradict presentations, breakdown of social interaction occurs, leading to embarrassment, anger, discomfort, or shame.

Goffman puts a particular gloss on the actor's imputation of the other's self. This is seen as the product just as much of theatrical as of substantive elements in the other's behaviour. We respond to others in accordance with our 'image' of them. Others construct these 'images' in accordance with what they want us to see – i.e. they dramatize their 'selves'. Thus we manage our 'expression' so that others define ourselves as we wish them to. These expressions are made through words and actions, dress and display. All this presentation equipment Goffman terms 'front'.

> Actors have to respond to each other for meaning to emerge and they are able to respond to each other because each of them takes the necessary steps to ensure that they announce their intentions – verbally and gesturally – so that the announcement would elicit the needed responses: they dramatize their meanings and create a social act (Perinbanayagam 1974, p. 537).

This led Goffman to take a particular interest in the strategies and adaptations by which people coped with situations, as in his celebrated work *Asylums* (1961).

Focusing concepts

A symbolic interactionist approach leads one to focus on certain areas. The main ones that have been examined to date and which form the structure of this book are: contexts, perspectives, cultures, strategies, negotiation, and careers. I shall examine each, in turn, briefly here, while in the following chapters I shall discuss work that has been done in each area. In the final chapter, I shall reassess interactionism generally in relation to the school and to society.

Contexts

School consists of a number of different contexts and situations and people's interpretations have been shown to differ among them. One illustration of this is Goffman's distinction between 'front' and 'back' regions. The 'front region' is where the performance required by one's formal role is staged, while a 'back region'

> may be defined as a place, relative to a given performance, where the impression fostered by the performance is knowingly contradicted as a matter of course.... It is here that the capacity of a performance to express something beyond itself may be painstakingly fabricated; it is here that illusions and impressions are openly constructed. Here, stage props and items of personal front can be stored in a kind of compact collapsing of whole repertoires of actions and characters.... Here the performer can relax; he can drop his front, forego speaking his lines, and step out of character (Goffman 1959, pp. 114–15).

'Back regions' play an important part in sustaining impression management, providing the means whereby 'individuals attempt to buffer themselves from the deterministic demands that surround them'. Clearly the staffroom and playground might be seen in this way. The contrast between 'front' and 'back' is often evident in language, the backstage language consisting of:

> reciprocal first-naming, cooperative decision-making, profanity, open sexual remarks, elaborate griping, smoking, rough informal dress, 'sloppy' sitting and standing posture, use of dialect or sub-standard speech, mumbling and shouting, playful aggressivity and kidding (Goffman 1959, p. 129).

The situation is not simply the scene of action. It has an effect on that action, an effect which is both determining and enabling. For the situation has to be interpreted by actors. Meaning has to be attributed. Thus, different people may see different things in the situation, or interpret the same things differently. They may try to manipulate aspects of the situation to influence others' interpretations. The 'definition of the situation', therefore, is a key concern.

Situations, ultimately, are what we make them. This is the simple point behind W.I. Thomas's oft-quoted passage:

> Very often it is the wide discrepancy between the situation as it seems to others and the situation as it seems to the individual that brings about ... overt behaviour difficulty. To take an extreme example, the warden of Dannemora prison recently refused to honour the order of the court to send an inmate outside the prison walls for some specific purpose. He excused himself on the ground that the man was too dangerous. He had killed several persons who had the unfortunate habit of talking to themselves on the street. From the movement of their lips he imagined that they were calling him vile names, and he behaved as if this were true. If men define situations as real, they are real in their consequences (1928, p. 572).

The last sentence has taxed many an undergraduate examinee in recent years. But the message is simple. No matter what the objective circumstances are, or the prevailing official definition, if a person defines a situation in a certain way, that will be the context in which his plans for action are formed.

Situations, therefore, are constructed and it is the task of the interactionist to discover how they are constructed, and not to take them for granted. Work done in this field is discussed in chapter 2.

Perspectives

These refer to the frameworks through which people make sense of the world. It is through these that pupils and teachers construct their realities and define situations. People do not see one objective reality with a universal mental template. Rather, their view of reality is through a screen, or an interpretational code which they employ to understand the world. These perspectives assist in defining the situation, and identifying and locating the 'other'. The term in interactionism derives largely from Becker and his colleagues:

> We use the term 'perspective' to refer to a coordinated set of ideas and actions a person uses in dealing with some problematic situation, to refer to a person's ordinary way of

thinking and feeling about and acting in such a situation. These thoughts and actions are coordinated in the sense that the actions flow reasonably, from the actor's point of view, from the ideas contained in the perspective.... A person develops and maintains a perspective when he faces a situation calling for action which is not given by his own prior beliefs or by situational imperatives. In other words, perspectives arise when people face choice points. In many crucial situations, the individual's prior perspectives allow him no choice, dictating that he can in these circumstances do only one thing. In many other situations, the range of possible and feasible alternatives is so limited by the physical and social environment that the individual has no choice about the action he must perform. But where the individual is called on to act, and his choices are not constrained, he will begin to develop a perspective. If a particular kind of situation recurs frequently, the perspective will probably become an established part of a person's way of dealing with the world (Becker, Geer, Hughes and Strauss 1961, pp. 34–7).

As Lacey (1977) has pointed out, however, actions and action-idea systems are better subsumed under the notion of strategy, so that perspective refers more to the framework of ideas, the structure of mind from which thought processes flow. They are based on certain assumptions which are both culturally specific and context-bound. As noted, different situations may trigger different perspectives. Their connection with cultures is discussed below. Teacher and pupil perspectives are examined in chapter 3.

Cultures

Perspectives derive from cultures. They do not exist, nor are they created in a vacuum. Cultures, in turn, develop when people come together for specific purposes, intentionally or unintentionally, willingly or unwillingly. People develop between them distinctive forms of life – ways of doing things and not doing things, forms of talk and speech patterns, subjects of conversation, rules and codes of conduct and behaviour, values and beliefs, arguments and understandings. These will not be formally regulated, but heavily implicit. One's part in them may not be consciously recognized. Rather one grows into them, and may recognize them as a natural way of life. The concomitant of this, of course, is that opposing cultures (and perspectives) may be seen as unnatural or wrong.

Through ordinary processes of socialization, people are inducted into certain cultures, perhaps of a certain social class, religious, occupational, or ethnic nature. At times they might experience 'culture shock'– the term used to describe the feeling of strangeness and bewilderment when they come up against totally new cultural forms, like many children starting school, teachers beginning teaching, or those committed to prison for the first time. It is not just a matter of learning new skills and knowledge, nor even mainly that. It is more a question of learning the ropes, or tricks of the trade, finding out how to get by, discovering what the others do, settling in, finding out hierarchies and pecking orders, appropriate topics of conversation, taboo areas, what is considered important and why, acceptable work rates, leisure pursuits, typical careers.

As Lacey notes, Becker and his colleagues emphasized the homogeneity of student culture and the inexorably constraining influence of the institutional structure. They implied as a consequence, that there was little variation among student perspectives (Lacey 1977). But as Lacey's own previous work has shown, as has that of Hargreaves, student subcultures can form in opposition to the formal school culture, and exist, sometimes uneasily, sometimes comfortably, within it (Lacey 1970, D.H. Hargreaves 1967). Work since then has demonstrated the existence of many cultures within the school actively constructed by pupils and teachers (Dale 1972, Furlong 1976). I shall examine these in chapters 4 and 5.

Strategies

Perspectives, derived from cultures, are linked to action through strategies. This is increasingly coming to be regarded as the central concept in the interactionist approach, for it is where individual intention and external constraint meet. Strategies are ways of achieving goals. Invariably there are obstructions in the path leading to those goals – obstructions for the teacher that might arise from such things as inadequate resources, high pupil-teacher ratio, recalcitrant nature of some pupils, organization of the school, competition from colleagues and so on. The teacher must therefore take these into consideration and chart a course or lay a plan accordingly.

Devising and recognizing strategies is not a simple matter. Though identifiable and repeatable packages of action linked to broad, general aims, such aims cannot be taken for granted. What they appear to be may be a 'presentation of front'. In other words, the manifest aims may be part of the strategy, acting in the service of other, hidden, aims. There may be aims within aims, some deferred perhaps to await more favourable situations. Or a teacher may deploy a whole range of strategies, on which he rings the changes depending on variations either in the situation or in himself. The more complicated the goal, the more complex the strategy; and the higher the goal, the greater extension of risk. For it is the problems that intervene between intention and risk that give strategies their character. Schools are places that invite complex strategies, for ideals are strong, yet the gap between ideals and practice is large because of the problems previously mentioned.

As far as pupils are concerned, we shall find that different perspectives lead to different orientations toward school and 'work'. Definitions of the situation vary, and pupils devise different strategies to cope. These are often occluded by use of a standardized vocabulary for all activities. 'Work' for example is commonly used by all pupils, but its meaning varies. There are different realities, often behind similar façades. Often, however, different symbols are used, different forms of vocabulary or different forms of communication. These need to be identified, and their meaning divined. Clearly pupils' own vocabulary and accounts are indispensable to an understanding of their construction of meanings.

What is the relationship between cultures, perspectives and strategies? Lacey puts it thus:

> As a group of individuals develop or acquire a sense of common purpose, so the sets of strategies adopted by them acquire a common element. It is this common element that enables the common perspective to emerge. As the perspective develops, and if over a long period of time, the situations that continually face the group have a common element, then the understandings broaden and develop to produce a sub-culture. The mark of the sub-culture is that its most important elements are not immediately lost if the individual leaves the group and the common situation of the group members. Perspectives are more quickly taken up and dropped than sub-cultures. To be sure the elements of sub-culture are often suppressed and can be almost completely covered by later behaviour patterns, but

the supposition here is that these elements effect changes deep within the personality structure of the individual and are responsible for the richness, complexity and uniqueness of individual personality (Lacey 1977, p. 70).

Lacey recalls Becker's concept of 'latent culture'. This is a culture which has its origin and social referents outside the group to which the individuals currently belong. As individuals progress through life they acquire a mixture of such cultures, which are all available, to some degree or other, to translate into strategies. However, the point has been made that action is culturally specific, that is to say it is limited, as well as facilitated by culture. As Lacey points out: 'In situations, such as a school where social class is a latent culture, working-class pupils will have a limited choice of strategies and the limitations will be difficult to overcome' (1977, p. 71). I consider teacher and pupil strategies in chapter 6.

Negotiation

To study perspectives and strategies on their own is to run the risk of minimizing the interaction between people. But neither teachers nor pupils fall into these types of activity and set up camp in them. Rather, school life is a continuous process of negotiation, the subject of chapter 7. The persistent properties of the act of identifying, interpreting, reckoning, and choosing, maintain a dynamic which, in interpersonal relations of a conflict nature, makes the actual interplay between persons the most important element, as each seeks to maximize his own interests. In schools, therefore, one might expect the whole day to consist of negotiations of one sort or another.

These may be peaceful and open, and constitute working agreements. However, there are often conspiracies to disrupt, as teachers and pupils try to enforce their realities. Thus a class might attempt to transform a formal lesson into a 'laugh', or a liberationist teacher might try to undermine the authority of the headteacher. Such a community is often marked by uncomfortable truces, where embarrassment is used as a weapon in the attempt to enforce one's own version. Two things follow. First, 'negotiations' are not always peaceful, marked with goodwill and agreement to find common ground. They are often conflictual, marked by rancour, and bad feeling, not only concerned to optimize one's own concerns, but to belittle the other's. Second, in view of this, one is led to investigate the relative power of the parties to the

11

interaction. Interactionists are sometimes accused of discounting any consideration of power, but it is an essential ingredient of negotiation. There is a pronounced hierarchy amongst the teachers, amongst the pupils, and amongst various forms of knowledge. Teachers and pupils hold different positions and statuses. Teachers set the scene, make the ground rules, state the aims – basically to transform the pupil by new knowledge; while the pupil is forced to operate on the teacher's ground and by his rules, compensating only by force of numbers and certain resilient properties of their background culture.

The concept of 'negotiation' derives from the work of Strauss and his colleagues on the social relationships of psychiatric hospitals (Strauss *et al.* 1964). Their analysis includes these various elements of different cultures, different occupational ideologies and different power bases, and shows how working agreements are produced between psychiatrist and patient, and between psychiatrists themselves. These negotiations are often subtly implicit, and recognized by sophisticated and abbreviated symbols. They represent the 'hidden mechanics' that hold a working community together.

The interactionist is concerned, therefore, to discover the informal rules that underwrite the negotiation. In a sense, there are only informal rules, for the formal rules are themselves negotiated. As Strauss *et al.*, note:

> Most rules can be stretched, negotiated, argued, ignored, or applied at convenient moments. In fact, if the information, change and application of rules are examined closely, the conclusion must be that there is a 'negotiated order' within which rules fall (1964, p. 313).

It might be argued that from an 'official' position, many of these negotiated instances constitute 'deviant' cases, are anarchic and often 'meaningless'. They are meaningless, of course, only from the 'official' position. Where pupils seek more scope in interaction, the search for meaning is what it is all about. It is the task of the researcher adopting an interactionist position to uncover those meanings from the point of view of their constructors. The apparent anarchy, disorder and 'waste-of-time' that seems so typical of many schools is shown to be meaningful and rule-bound, and clearly linked to the official processes of the school (Marsh, Rosser and Harré, 1978). In other words, it is all part of the negotiative activity among teachers and pupils. 'Having a laugh', 'working', 'skiving', 'making trouble' are therefore important areas for a full understanding of school life, possibly *the* most important from the pupil's point of view; whilst from the teacher's, those snatched moments of staffroom relaxation, the interstices of the school day, also come into prominence. Further, the inter-actionist approach which develops its analysis from *within* the experiences and constructions of the inmates, raises questions about the manifest activity itself. Teaching and learning them-selves become problematic activities. What, then, are teachers and pupils doing, and why are they doing it? For a broader view of this, we need to consider teacher and pupil careers.

Careers

The commonly understood concept of 'career' is as 'a succession of related jobs, arranged in a hierarchy of prestige, through which persons move in an ordered, predictable sequence' (Wilensky 1960, p. 127). For teachers, we might conceive of one typical career structure which advances from probationer to assistant teacher, then *either* to greater specialization, to second and eventually head of department, *or* to counselling roles such as year tutor; and then to senior and deputy headteacher position, and eventually headteacher. But these are just the bare bones of a formal career structure. If we ask how people actually experience their careers, things invariably do not appear to be quite so orderly and systematic. An individual's career might not correspond to a simple, worldly progress upwards, but rather be seen 'as the moving perspective in which the person sees his life as a whole and interprets the meaning of his various attributes, actions and the things which happen to him' (Hughes 1937, p. 409). This 'subjective career' is the interactionist's focus and, as we shall see, it does offer us a means of linking the individual's experience with the institutional provision of formal careers and ultimately society at large.

Two important aspects of careers are 'commitment' and 'identity'. Commitment is described by Kanter as:

> a consideration which arises at the intersection of organizational requisites and personal experience. On the one hand, social systems organize to meet systematic 'needs'; and on the other hand, people orient themselves positively and negatively, emotionally and intellectually, to situations. Since social orders are supported by people, one problem of collectivities is to meet organizational requisites in such a way that participants at the same time become positively involved

with the system – loyal, loving, dedicated, and obedient. This requires solutions to organizational or systematic problems that are simultaneously mechanisms for ensuring commitment through their effects on individuals – their experience and orientations. Commitment, then, refers to the willingness of social actors to give their energy and loyalty to social systems, the attachment of personality systems to social relations which are seen as self-expressive (1974, p. 126).

I will take this further in chapter 8.

Commitment is closely related to identity. Individuals acquire an array of characteristics from the multifarious spread of roles available in society, and project images of selves to others in the process of 'self-lodging' whereby 'humans translate crucial features of their own identity into the selves, memories and imaginations of relevant others' (Denzin 1978). Clearly, Goffman's 'presentation of front' is closely related to this idea, as is the whole field of identity theory, which 'begins with the notion that each of us has an interest in being or becoming somebody special, sufficiently different from his fellows to save him from anonymity, and different in ways that enable him to command some admiration, respect and affection' (A. Cohen 1976).

Part of the teacher task is to influence the development of identities both in the form of individuality and initiative (as conveyed in progressive ideologies) and in the form of compliance and cooperation (as in traditional ideologies). These are not necessarily incompatible. The process of 'self-lodging' must be related to everybody else's interests, but within that general restriction, the encouragement of initiative is in the interests of the advancement of the individual and subsequently of society. However, the teacher's pedagogy in this respect also appears to be culture-bound, so that for many pupils, reared within different cultures, teachers appear to be attacking their very selves. The presentation of the desired self might become intensified as a result, together with attempts to discredit the attacker by undermining the bases of his identity.

One of the main interactionist assumptions is that people are concerned with developing, projecting and safeguarding a desired image of self. But selves are not necessarily unilinear, or unidimensional. That is to say that people may choose to project different images of self in different contexts. Some may be complementary, others may be compensatory. For example, one particular form of presentation of self may be forced, rather than self-chosen, such as the rebellious pupil forced to be dutiful, or the kind-hearted teacher forced to be autocratic. The greater the conflict within a school, the more likely this forced, false presentation of self with increasing emphasis on compensation in 'back regions'.

Inasmuch as the 'stage' of the school becomes more difficult, the 'props' remain in short supply and the audience unappreciative, the teacher will experience difficulty in presenting a fully gratifying image of self. Inasmuch as the pupils find themselves unwilling or half willing members of the theatre audience, they will not effectively perform the work necessary to construct an area of interaction productive of adequate and credible selves. But this work, none the less, must be done, if the institution is to survive. So where is it performed? One argument is that for some the main work of identity-construction is performed in the interstitial areas of the school day – between lessons, at breaks, during the lunch hour, etc. – and in the 'back regions' – staffroom, playground and corridors.

However, some undoubtedly prefer to associate their 'selves' with the institution, and their activity involves more planned and staged performances (R.H. Turner 1976). I shall take up these differences in chapter 8. For the moment, we might simply note that identity construction, projection and preservation is one of the most important concerns of the individual, that situations of heavy conflict in school represent, in a sense, battlegrounds for one's life, but that the battle may be waged half-heartedly because one's preferred identity is elsewhere. Type of investment of self depends on type of commitment; and partial investment of self aids negotiation, either by default, or because it matches pupils' partial investment.

Summary

A symbolic interactionist approach carries an emphasis on:

– individuals as constructors of their own actions;
– the various components of the self and how they interact; the indications made to self, meanings attributed, interpretive mechanisms, definitions of the situation; in short, the world of subjective meanings, and the symbols by which they are produced and represented;
– the process of negotiation, by which meanings are continually being constructed;
– the social context in which they occur and whence they derive.

15

By 'taking the role of the other' – a dynamic concept involving the construction of how others wish to or might act in a certain circumstance, and how individuals themselves might act – individuals align their actions to those of others.

These areas of social life can be illuminated by study of contexts, perspectives, cultures, strategies, negotiation, and careers, both independently, and in their inter-relationships.

With regard to school, the kinds of questions raised are:

– How do teachers and pupils interpret school processes, personnel and organization, such as lessons, the curriculum, their peers, and each other?
– What factors bear on these interpretations? What significant or generalized others have influenced them?
– How do teachers and pupils experience school processes?
– How do teachers and pupils organize their school activity? Having defined the situation (through perspectives in context) and experienced it (in relation to their identity concerns), what strategies do they adopt?
– How do teachers and pupils perceive their careers in the school? What forms of commitment do they show and what are their identity concerns?

Such questions place the centre of inquiry within individuals, as the constructors of their own action. But the locus of interaction is in neither, but between them. The most important root question, therefore, is:

– What happens among teachers and pupils in school?

A note on method

The key method of interactionist research is that of participant observation. It involves taking part in the ordinary everyday life of the group or institution under study in an accepted role, and observing both the group and one's own self. Participation enables analysis of one's own reactions, motives and intentions, and thus provides access to the intricate interplay between 'I' and 'Me' and 'others' within the self. It is not an easy role, and is fraught with dangers, such as 'going native', that is to say being taken over by the perspectives required for the role and losing the perspective of the researcher. Consequently, some have favoured non-participant observation. This, together with the informal, unstructured interview, has been the most commonly used method. Of course we shall never be able to get into another's mind to see exactly how it is working (Schutz 1967, Laing 1967), and indeed it is often difficult to analyse our own thoughts and actions. But close observation and sympathetic interviewing over a lengthy period – a popular time span is a year – and in a variety of contexts can bring us close to an appreciation of that interpretive work, that construction of meanings that is at the heart of social life. Rigorous procedures have now been devised for such work, to distinguish it as social science from purely intuitive and casual observation, and there is a growing literature to match the increasing number of research studies (Woods 1977 and 1979, Open University 1979, Hammersley 1981, Hammersley 1983).

Chapter 2

The school situation

It is reasonable to begin with the place where people work. But the interactionist is less concerned with the objective features of situations, than the sense that people make of them. This is not to say that objective features do not influence interaction. Of course they do, and I shall give some examples to that effect. But this does not alter the fact that situations are constructed, sometimes in line with the purposes and implications behind the objective features, sometimes in opposition to them. I shall consider how people make situations; how people adapt to situations, and how sometimes there are disjunctures between definitions and objective features of situations. In all of these, crucial factors like space, physical properties, time, knowledge, power, clientele and accountability are all evident. I shall go on to discuss how situations are maintained by rule-structures, and how they are operationalized. I conclude the chapter with a brief consideration of some pupil definitions and of different contexts within the school.

The construction of situations

Children are experts at the creation of situations. They need but few props – perhaps only cardboard boxes, a few articles of dress, such as a nurse's uniform, a toy gun, a blackboard – to create scenes of their own choice. Adults perhaps are less flexible, but vastly more sophisticated in the creation of effects and the translation of scenes. Some examples of recasting situations in the medical world are given by Ball (1972) and Emerson (1970). Ball shows how an abortion clinic, which otherwise might have had tones of stigma about it, was rendered 'respectable' by the setting, and the appearance and manner of the performers. One patient commented, 'I knew for the first time, really, that the whole thing might work out after all. I mean when I saw those crystal chandeliers hanging there, and all that carpeting, I thought that I would come out of it OK. It reminded me of what I imagine those clinics in Switzerland must look like' (Ball 1972, p. 72). Expensive furnishings, space, privacy, medical equipment, dress – all helped to neutralize 'the negative "butcher" stereotypes associated with abortion as portrayed in the mass media version' (ibid., p. 172), and allowed people to identify with film stars, statesmen and other notables in Swiss clinics.

Backing this luxury and cost was an emphasis on conventional medical practices and procedures; and within these, four major elements of cleanliness, competence, conventionality, and concern for the patient. All helped to tie the clinic into the normal framework of middle-class life. Thus, an organizing principle – abortion – potentially fatal for the legitimacy of the establishment was effectively neutralized. The situation was turned into something else by effective use of staging, props and script.

Emerson's study was on a not dissimilar theme – gynaecological examinations. A matter of routine for the staff, it is a potentially humiliating experience for the patient, but only if defined as a situation within her own private life-world, not as a medical examination. The staff, therefore, are at pains to sustain the 'medical' definition.

> The physician guides the patient through the precarious scene in a contained manner: taking the initiative, controlling the encounter, keeping the patient in line, defining the situation by his reaction, and giving cues such as 'this is done' and 'other people go through this all the time' (Emerson 1970, p. 29).

There are no sexual connotations in this examination, no assault on personal privacy. The staff are practising medical science, examining genitalia in the same way as they would an ear, not as *private* parts, but as *typical* ones. This reality is sustained by it taking place in 'medical space', with appropriate decor and equipment, even down to a loudspeaker calling names like 'Dr Morris, Dr Arnold Morris'. Lay people are excluded, as is anything that is likely to threaten to mix situations. There are rituals of respect for the patient, a nurse is always present, a special language depersonalizes and desexualizes the encounter, euphemisms used to avoid provoking embarrassment, eye contact avoided during the examination, and a 'brisk no-nonsense show of efficiency' displayed by the doctor.

The relevance of these studies to school should be clear. It is part of a teacher's technique to use the environment. In one school of my research, for example, the contrast between the art room and more traditional form-rooms was most pronounced. The teacher was concerned to cultivate among his pupils a feeling of freedom, informality, trust and mutual regard. Creative work had to come from 'within themselves', so they had to be oriented toward self-expression. The tables were thus arranged in a rough circle. Coffee-making apparatus was in one corner. In another, a record-player played *their* music. Around the walls were drawings, paintings, lithographs of their work. And around the sides of the room on tables and in cupboards, there were magazines, pamphlets, newspapers, materials from the *outer* world. Thus did the art teacher with his props try to mellow the hard and fast lines of the traditional classroom. Not so in the maths room, where pupils were lined up with appropriately mathematical precision in serried ranks, squared at the corners, and all facing front. The walls were bare, and pointedly uninteresting – painted a dull green – and there were no props, beyond the blackboard. In this essentially cerebral subject, traditionally taught by transmission, nothing was to distract the pupils' attention from the instructing teacher and their own thoughts.

Delamont (1976) gives some examples from similar subjects in the same school to illustrate some forms of personal adaptation of circumstances. Thus the biology teacher emphasized 'life' in her room with displays of fish, insects, birds, etc., while the physics teacher's room was 'strongly inanimate with displays of electrical and mechanical equipment'. Interestingly the atmosphere of the two laboratories corresponded, the former being light and airy, the latter small and stuffy.

One recalls rather grim pictures of nineteenth-century class-rooms, where teachers were faced with a task of 'civilizing' the masses, with moral injunctions hung round the walls. Or with the sudden transformation of classroom situations from pupil-controlled disorder, characterized by noise and 'mucking about', to teacher-controlled order, with the resurrection of all the formal rules, with the simple use of signals, like 'silence!', 'hands on heads!', or 'fingers on lips!'.

Other ready examples relate to the beginning and end of schooling. The infant 'reception' classroom is fitted out with props – toys, Wendy House, beds – that soften the transition from home to school by retaining some 'homely' elements and providing an environment to which they can individually relate. In some infant classrooms observed by King (1978) the headmistress advised, 'Make your room an exciting and stimulating place to live ... a specially devised environment which allows the children to be individuals growing at a pace and in a way most suited to their individual capacities' (p. 18). The contents of the rooms reflected this aim. In one, King made a twenty-six page inventory of the contents. Moreover, the rooms were constantly being reorganized to provide variety. Towards the end of schooling, 'work experience' is increasingly simulated for many pupils, while classrooms typically display an austere sameness.

The visual impact of a room can tell us a great deal about how a teacher wishes the situation to be defined. There may be a 'public display' when inspectors or visitors call, in which special efforts are made to approximate to the idea. On such occasions, teachers naturally wish to appear at their best, but to some pupils in a school of my research it was a nauseous practice because 'things were so rarely like that'. Dale (1972) points out that a teacher's room can reveal her view of worthwhile knowledge and who she considers to be the most worthwhile pupils. He gives an example of a display table in a primary classroom of what he calls 'American culture for tourists', consisting of objects of 'high' rather than everyday 'popular' culture.

However, situations do not necessarily need props to be transformed; it can be done in the head. An example of how people can create situations with subtle understandings occurred during my research in a secondary school (Woods 1981b). I was following the reactions of two teachers to an incident wherein the headmaster was seeking revenge on the whole school for an episode where he had suffered a personal humiliation at the hands of two boys. The headmaster's strategy was to summon a full assembly, rage at the pupils on the theme of falling standards, and order a uniform and appearance inspection for the following day. One teacher took this at face value, felt denigrated himself, refused to associate himself with the inspection, and later resigned. The other teacher, however, went through the motions of an inspection, going up the lines of pupils under his charge, pretending to inspect, but making amusing comments; and by their smiles and knowing looks, the pupils confirmed the image. Together, teacher and pupils constructed a situation that accorded with their mutual understanding, though appearances were to the contrary.

Adaptations to situations

These examples show how situations can be manipulated to produce certain definitions. Some situations, however, impose themselves upon meanings. This was so, for example, with Bittner's (1967) policemen in skid-row. They re-interpreted their role from 'law-enforcement' to 'peace-keeping', in response to their view of people living in the area as incapable of living normal lives. This, together with limited time and personnel on their part, required them to view skid-row in a special way, and to adapt their own behaviour accordingly, i.e. not employing a strict interpretation of the rules, as they might elsewhere, but to 'play by ear' and to base their discretion on their knowledge of people and places.

There are, therefore, elements in the situation that constrain behaviour. Also, it must be acknowledged that 'many physical contexts communicate powerful messages "from their makers to their users", and the traditional classroom settings have been both a symbol and a reinforcement of centrally controlled interaction' (Edwards and Furlong 1978, p. 16). The teacher's desk is at the front in such situations, often on a raised podium, with the pupils' desks in orderly lines facing it. As Edwards and Furlong point out, it is difficult for teachers in such a situation to do anything but talk at the pupils. Decentralized group work and pupil participation on their own terms is almost impossible. Westbury (1973) in fact has argued that the traditional form of teaching, known as 'recitation' in the USA is basically a coping strategy. That is, it is dictated by the context rather than any educational philosophy. '[It] secures some task attention, gives some measure of control over the activity of students, facilitates coverage of content and offers a drill and practice situation that leads to some, albeit more often than not a nominal, mastery of the facts that carefully tailored tests require as the symbols of school learning' (Westbury 1973, p. 100). What other procedures, he asks, would work as well in the circumstances? And what hope is there of achieving the goals of open education in the conventional classroom? One might compare the traditional 'chalk and talk' method in the UK. (The notion of 'coping strategy' will be discussed in more detail in chapter 6.) The dilemma for a teacher wishing to pursue his own policy with pupils, but impeded by the situational constraints is shown in this example of a probationary teacher:

> [The headmaster's] path from kindly tolerance and advice to explicit authoritarian control is well illustrated by the example of the teacher's desk. As evidence of the equality of relationships within the classroom, I had placed the desk against the wall with the drawers facing into the room for maximum accessibility and the top to be used as an additional working surface for all. Such blatant disregard for normal

classroom procedure did not pass unnoticed and Mr. H.
expressed his concern on the first day: 'It will never work. You
won't be able to see the children when you are sitting there....
I'll help you arrange it ... look, it's up to you. If you want any
help, I'll help you move it.' Several subsequent references were
made to it but I did nothing. On the third day he said: 'You
must turn this desk round you know ... you can't see the
children ... why *do* you have it like this?' and on the fourth day:
'One day you will be very tired, and you will want to set the
class off and then sit in your chair to rest while you watch them.
You don't think you will, but you will!'

But his hints, suggestions and kindness did not have the
desired effect and, after registration on the fifth day, he came
in, took over the class, and, after reorganizing the children's
tables, he pulled the desk round, established it in the centre of
the room and placed the teacher's chair behind it (Hanson and
Herrington 1976, pp. 46–7).

The organization of the room in this instance is the ideological
battleground between headteacher and probationer.

Two other aspects of definitions, heavily implicit in what has
been said, require emphasis. They are to do with resources and
accountability. One may have clearly defined aims and the primary
resource of vast knowledge of teaching, but ability to execute
plans to realize those aims is affected by other resources at one's
disposal. Several of these have already been mentioned. There are
material resources of space, furniture, textbooks, other teaching
equipment. One might expect with new developments in technology, that teaching situations would become more standardized, but
this is yet to happen. The number of teaching staff in proportion to
pupils is another resource that profoundly influences definitions of
situation. Teaching a class of forty pupils is a vastly different
matter from teaching a group of twenty. The prevailing teacher-
pupil ratio norm requires teachers to view pupils in cohorts rather
than as individuals (Lortie 1975). While some, usually extremely
good or bad pupils, may receive individual treatment, it is
impossible to handle the rest on anything other than a group basis.
The implications for how teachers then 'see' pupils will be brought
out in a later chapter. In general, we might suggest that the higher
the ratio, the greater the tendency to stereotype.

Nature of pupils is as important as numbers. They do not all
have the same abilities, aptitudes and aspirations. Teaching an
express stream for Oxbridge open scholarships is rather different
from handling a non-examination, bottom fifth-year stream with

distinct oppositional tendencies to school. It is indeed dubious whether these could both be rated as 'teaching situations'. While much of the nature of clientele is beyond the school's control, emerging from cultural backgrounds and educational decisions over which the individual school has no control (such as comprehensivization), the internal organization and policy of the school, as in streaming or mixed-ability groups, horizontal or vertical age groups, banding or setting, can clearly have an effect.

Accountability is less easily perceived, but is an equally strong influence on how teachers define the situation. In a study by Ball, 'the staff perceived "possibilities for action" available to them to be limited by a national climate of educational accountability, by the demands and expectations of parents and other members of the local community and by more abstract and generalized public or societal expectations of the role of schooling' (Ball 1981, p. 11). He quotes a headmaster as saying:

> We cannot take up the possibilities of mixed-ability at this stage because we would be doing a disservice to the kids and have their parents in uproar because they are not doing exams, we can't do that locally until the system of 16+ examinations changes nationally (ibid.).

This neatly summarizes some of the external accountability pressures. Ball also points to the 'importance of the *subject-community* as a reference group for personal values and as a source of norms delineating appropriate and acceptable teaching methods and curricular content' (ibid., p. 13). Ball gives the examples of French, which, with maths and science, was seen to have a conceptual and curricular structure that was 'linear'. That is, one must proceed in stages, not advancing to the next stage before the previous one has been mastered. Thus the nature of the subject comes to be one of the most dominant influences on the situation, requiring primarily the use of 'recitation' techniques.

Denscombe (1977, 1980a) has pointed to another form of accountability to one's colleagues. He found, during his work in four London comprehensive schools, that teachers paid a great deal of attention to the noise in their classrooms, not because high levels of this were an obstruction to their teaching aims, but because absence of noise was the basis on which their teaching competence was judged, rightly or wrongly, by their colleagues. This major orientation to their task is not an essential element of teaching, nor a result of external pressures, but a consequence largely of the organization of our schools into 'closed' classrooms. One argument for the continued prevalence of these is that 'teachers are constantly faced with new situations which oblige them to innovate and use ad hoc procedures and necessitate "deviation" from the official prescriptions for activity (such as they are)' (Denscombe 1980c, p. 14).

Physical context has for long been recognized as important in educational policy. Hence the recent experiment with 'open' classrooms, which, it was felt, would promote more active learning on the part of the pupil and less authoritarianism on the part of the teacher. But while objective features and rearrangements can exert considerable influence, they do not necessarily bring about redefinitions. Some evidence suggests that unless the prevailing definition is also transformed, the educational forms in substance will stay the same. As Denscombe writes:

> Experience of the open classroom need have no direct or concomitant effect on the strategies of pupils or teachers. Both parties bring to the situation a host of expectations and meanings based on current and previous experience of classrooms, and it is extremely unlikely that any of the participants would be willing or able to divest themselves of these orientations when operating in the open classroom, unless they came to regard the situation as routine and normal (Denscombe 1980b, p. 53).

Thus an experiment in 'open' education in one part of the curriculum only will import expectations from the rest of the 'closed' curriculum. Also, it should be noted that while the situation was altered in some ways, in others it remained the same – level of resource, teacher-pupil ratio, nature of clientele. Denscombe's own research shows how staff in a Leicestershire community college experiencing an 'open' experiment in Humanities, but subject to 'closed' teaching elsewhere, subtly tried to 'close' the ostensible 'openness' of the classroom, by, for example, breaking down the larger group of pupils into three sub-groups, and individual members of the teaching team taking responsibility for them, an implicit denial of the 'open' and 'team' approach. Pupils were also effectively limited in choices by these sub-groupings.

However, there were differences, sufficient to show the potential of context for influencing classroom behaviour. Thus, whereas in closed classrooms, 'noise' was the pupils' main armament in contesting the teacher's definition, and teachers' main concern, in open situations teachers worried less, simply because of the high observability. There were, of course, practical limits, but noise was not the central issue it was in closed classrooms. Thus, 'pupils became deprived of a well-established counter-strategy and means of negotiation for control of the classroom' (ibid., p. 59). They are not slow, however, to devise others in response to teacher adaptations, and I shall discuss these further in chapter 6. Similarly, the openness of the curriculum provided pupils with a means of influencing its content and size in ways closed situations did not. Though Denscombe's work relates to how teachers and pupils devise strategies to achieve their ends, rather than to the educational goals of open education, it does show the possibilities in constructing situations to produce forms of interaction that could profoundly influence educational forms.

The difficulty appears to be, however, that situations become so routinized (how else is the teacher to survive?) that when change is attempted, they immediately try to restore the old situation in what ways they can. Thus, Richardson (1967) has noted the tendency, when an 'old' school is moved to 'brand new' premises, for there to be not rejoicing and inspiration, but 'depression and disappointment' and nostalgia for the (now) loved old building:

> Complaints about the new one may be legion. The position of the headmaster's room and the office, the narrowness of the staircase, the inadequacy of the locker space, the mistakes in the design of the apparently splendid stage – all these may excite loud comment. Little or nothing may be said about the lightness and airiness of the classrooms, the extended laboratory and gymnasium accommodation, the pleasant views from the windows, the more spacious and attractive hall. And there may even be some envy of the school that has now taken over the old building (quoted in Eggleston 1977, p. 106).

Eggleston (1977) also noted how a large open plan integrated craft and design area in one reorganized school was immediately de-reorganized by the art, woodwork, metalwork and technical drawing specialists using the area by building walls with 'hardboard and slotted steel angles that effectively divided the area into the specialist rooms they had occupied in the previous school building' (p. 106). Wallace (1980) noticed similar moves in six middle schools:

> the first thing that teachers ask for is something to close themselves in, declared the head of school A.... In school C, the new extension had had its missing walls symbolically replaced with boundaries of cupboards, while in schools A, B and D tables and chairs had been arranged into symbolic class patterns in overspill areas.... The head of school D declared

that the opening of dividers had been tried but 'is used less and less as the supervision of children is more difficult and these children seem to need the security of four walls' (p. 133).

Wallace draws attention to two kinds of environmental data with which individuals interact. One is 'sense' data, relating to personal comfort levels of warmth, light, smell and so forth; the other is 'awareness' data, which may have aesthetic connotations, but also relates to learned symbolic boundaries as in such concepts as privacy, personal space, and territoriality. These have been learned under 'closed classroom' conditions. It seems easier, therefore, at least in these instances, to change situations rather than definitions of situations. And where the latter persist, they will endeavour to re-cast the physical environment to suit.

A strong element clearly within teacher definitions is the need for them to control the pupils in their care. While some of the problems here originate beyond the classroom, as we shall see in later chapters, some may arise through situational factors. This is well illustrated in a study by Stebbins (1970), where he compared two schools in Newfoundland and Jamaica. He shows us some consequences of school design and classroom layout, observing how certain features of the Kingston School of his study facilitated behaviours at variance with the designer's intentions. Thus, 'the combination of several buildings huddled together beneath a number of trees whose leaves darken the grounds and whose trunks obstruct vision, makes it possible for those students so motivated to be in school but not in *class*' (Stebbins 1976, p. 212). The absence of walls in a classroom allows (promotes?) exchanges between students inside and outside the room; onlookers to observe and outsiders to be present; students to learn at will; and frustrates the teacher's efforts to check punctuality and attendance. It is clear that certain constructions can promote behaviours incompatible with their designer's aims, which teachers would define as disorderly. However, it is questionable whether material alterations to context would significantly affect the definition of the situation at a stroke, as it were. What it does do is to place the teacher on firmer ground to establish *his* definition.

Rule-structures

So far I have emphasized largely physical properties of the situation, though I have pointed out that people have considerable powers of improvisation. A formal lesson can be conducted in a field or on a beach. It might present difficulties if done as a matter of routine, as Stebbins has demonstrated, but it can be done if the teacher is able to maintain the rule-structure that defines the event as a lesson.

Pollard (1979) has used the term 'rule-frame', borrowing from Bernstein's notion of framing in respect of knowledge transmission: 'Where framing is strong, there is a sharp boundary, where framing is weak, a blurred boundary, between what may and may not be transmitted' (Bernstein 1971). Pollard applies the concept to other areas, and identifies four important areas of rule-framing for any situation. These are temporal, ecological, personal and curricular. We have already seen several examples of ecological rule-frames. There are clear differences between settings such as art room and science laboratory, games field and maths room, 'open' and 'closed' classrooms, classroom and staffroom. Let us consider the other three, remembering that all work in subtle interconnections rather than separately. As Pollard concludes:

> the complex intersecting and dynamic constraints on behaviour ... evolved in classrooms ... are associated with particular times, places, purposes and personnel, and they produce situational contrasts in rule-frame and thus in the degree of support for particular teacher interests-at-hand in different contexts (1979, p. 14).

1 *Temporal rule-frames*: these apply both to the overall time frame of the institution in terms of days, weeks, terms and 'school year', with its 'markers' of events like Christmas concerts, Sports' Days, Speech Days, Parent meetings, reports and so forth; and to the sequencing of lessons. The division of time into 'periods' conditions the way a subject is taught. This has also been recognized, and experiments made with 'block' timetabling to get away from the restrictions imposed by the 40 minute period. This may work quite well with the practical subjects, which need an extended period of time to achieve their aims, and less well with intellectual subjects, where 'breaks' have been appreciated. Probably, too, teachers and pupils have welcomed 'breaks' from each other. In my own school days, both as pupil and teacher, the dreaded 'double period' was a major hurdle in the school week.

The 'period' then, as the basic temporal unit, has both instructional and control advantages. It reflects the compartmentalization of knowledge, and lends itself to strategies whereby teachers can set about getting their definitions of the situation universally accepted, and whereby pupils can generally go along with them. Hargreaves *et al.* (1975) show how the teachers of their research typically organized a lesson. They observed five principal phases: (1) entry, (2) 'settling down', (3) the 'lesson proper', (4) 'clearing up', and (5) 'exit'. Within these phases, there is a flow of tasks, interconnected by 'switch-signals'. These are signs from the teacher indicating that one task has finished and another is to begin. They consist of three components – 'attention-drawers, linking instructions and task indicators'. The authors give this example:

1st task-phase: question and answer session
2nd task-phase: written work
'Right now (attention-drawer), get out your exercise books (linking instruction) and do the first three problems (task indicator).'

The lesson is structured by rules. For example, during the 'entry' phase, there are typically three rules in play in the schools of the research: (1) Pupils must line up outside the room in the corridor. (2) Pupils must not enter the room until the teacher gives them permission to do so. (3) Pupils must enter the room 'in an orderly fashion', i.e. without running or pushing. During the 'settling down' phase, these rules generally seem to apply: (1) Pupils must go to their seats and sit down or remain in close proximity to the seat. (2) Pupils are free to talk to other pupils on any matter, but they must not shout or scream. (3) Pupils must cooperate in the distribution of equipment, if this takes place.

Such rules are immediately recognizable. They look as if they belong to lessons with which most of us are familiar. They structure the lesson along a well-worn path. We shall see, though, that other 'situations' exist alongside this official one.

2 *Personal rule-framing*: as Hargreaves *et al.* put it: 'there are some general rules that are "generally accepted" even though they are not written down. But these fuse into the individual preferences and judgements of teachers, who vary in what they will "have" or "stand for" or "tolerate" within their classroom' (1975, p. 35). There are also the individual and group preferences of pupils, where they do have some power to influence the situation. The nature of these rules is often only revealed when somebody deviates from them and exceeds the bounds of agreement – for example, a pupil 'making *too much* noise' (the point being that tolerable noise levels might differ among teachers), or a new teacher making inappropriate or unaccustomed demands on pupils, or issuing unfair punishments.

One example of what is considered by pupils an unfair

punishment is 'showings-up', which I have analysed elsewhere as unfairly invading the private sphere of the pupils' life and exceeding the bounds of the tacit agreement on rule-structures that apply in the classroom (Woods 1979). It is an interesting case, since it shows the teacher's dilemma and the pupil's vulnerability. The teacher needs to keep order, and so makes an exhibition of a pupil as a tactic towards that end. He may be believing that he is treating the pupil as a device, a cipher, as one among many, rather than as an individual, in the same way as the gynaecologist treats his patients, still regarding the rules. But this is an instance in the rules that pupils do not recognize and it is as offensive and illegitimate to them as would be a gynaecologist's indecent act or suggestion to one of his patients.

3 *Curricular rule-frame*: we have already seen some examples of this in the work of Ball and Denscombe. Subjects differ in their rule-frames, maths, for example, being more systematic, convergent and all-absorbing than art; home economics and home management being more in line with extra-curricular rule-frames than more formal subjects. There is also a pedagogical rule-frame, depending on a teacher's chosen methods of teaching. Studies of teacher language have shown how these rule-frames are embedded within their forms of talk. Hammersley (1977b), for example, shows that in seeking answers to questions, teachers are not exploring pupils' experience but merely shaping responses into 'the right answer'. The teacher, knowing the answer to the question, decides how many and what type of clues to give the pupils in order for them to discover the answer. The pupils assume that everything they need to know in order to answer the question has been provided. Thus the knowledge and skills required by pupils to show 'intelligence' in the question-answering situation may be specific to the school setting. Finding the answer requires knowledge of the conventions governing a particular kind of teaching and the ability to 'read the teacher's signs'. Selection proceeds on the basis of the pupil's ability to accept the teacher's authority and his construction of the classroom situation. I shall say more about this research in chapter 6.

Another illustration of a talk structure that sustains a particular definition of the situation is given by Torode (1977). He analysed the talk of a strong teacher, who was able to keep order in his classes, and a weak one who was not. What he discovered was that the strong teacher used pronouns like 'we' 'you' and 'I', consistently, and defined clearly the relevant persons and relationships in classroom interaction. The weak teacher was unable to sustain any typical classroom talk; 'Because his exchanges with pupils remain at the level of ordinary conversation, they lack centralized control and they display an "improper" participant-equality' (Edwards and Furlong 1978, p. 51). The distinction can at times seem a subtle one, for similar particular interactions may occur. But what may be an insult for one teacher, may be transformed by another to an appropriate part of the frame of the lesson.

These studies emphasize two important features of situation construction – knowledge and power. What one makes of a situation is strongly influenced by previous experiences and socialization and material circumstances. Hence the importance of one's own experiences of classrooms as a child and access to other seasoned teachers' experiences of real classrooms over those learnt about in teacher training (Mardle and Walker 1980). Also, for some pupils, their experiences outside school are likely to outweigh those within; and their past experiences of school will condition their attitude toward new experiments. I saw this well illustrated in one school, where a young reformist teacher tried to introduce novel techniques and information to a renegade fourth-form group. Instead of changing *their* situation, they interpreted *him* into the prevailing one. He was a 'strange teacher' with some 'peculiar ideas'. The things he told and showed them (including Swedish sex films, and nude bathing at Summerhill), were not without interest, but 'life wasn't like that'. This is similar to Denscombe's point about the predominance of 'closed' over 'open' contexts.

Power is the ability to influence others in accordance with one's own intentions. It may be that teachers can without difficulty persuade pupils to accept lessons as learning situations, especially if the pupils have had appropriate previous experiences. Alternatively, pupils may persuade teachers that it is a meaningless exercise for them, and so force a mutually agreed arrangement. The resources one can summon may be critical. The teacher has the whole weight of law, authority and tradition. The pupils have strength in numbers, and access to cultural forces replete with strategies of defence and offence.

Power has also been shown to be a strong ingredient in defining situations among teachers. A. Hargreaves (1981), for example, has shown how headteachers and deputies influence situations in the area of school-based curriculum development by the use of what he calls 'contrastive rhetorics'. This is a technique for denigrating certain curricular forms and securing collective decisions of their choice, whereby 'the boundaries of normal and acceptable practice are defined by institutionally and/or interactionally dominant individuals or groups through the introduction into discussion of alternative practices and social forms in stylized, trivialized and generally pejorative terms which connote their unacceptability' (A. Hargreaves 1981, p. 8). In Hargreaves's case, the 'contrast' was Countesthorpe College. As certain unusual features of life there were introduced into the discussion, laughter broke out – laughter which denigrated (albeit unconsciously perhaps) an opposing and threatening culture. Hargreaves found that in all cases, either the head or his deputy – the holders of formal power – introduced the contrasts; and that these contrasts depicted forms of extremism which were to be avoided at all costs. In this way 'they translate institutional power into interactional power and thus exercise control over the decision-making process' (ibid., p.15). Its effective use, however, depended on the rest of the staff recognizing the framework of the discussion and filling in many details for themselves.

Hunter (1980) noticed a similar phenomenon with respect to the exercise of power within a democratic rhetoric in the comprehensive school of his research. The rhetoric proclaimed the virtues of participation in decision-making by both pupils and staff. The reality, however, showed that the headmaster and head of school 'controlled the premises and assumptions upon which the discussion took place' (p. 220). Interestingly, the sanctions by which they secured this degree of control were not seen to be used – it was sufficient that the staff believed they could be used, together with the careful way in which they had been selected (i.e. to 'fit in with this type of arrangement'). In such ways can power and authority be used to define situations (see also Riseborough 1981, and chapter 7).

One way in which these factors of knowledge and power relate to external forces is suggested by Edwards (1979) in his examination of classroom talk. Like Hammersley, he analysed the means whereby teachers established their definitions of the situation. Some examples are: the 'pre-sequences' teachers employ to show that a question is coming, and what an appropriate answer would be; the interruption of pupil terms to 'dominate' what is being said, and the frequency and length of teachers' own expositions. Edwards goes further, however, and relates this context to social class cultures and differential knowledge among children. Middle-class children are more likely to have learned the ground rules for responding to authority in classroom settings. Edwards agrees with Bernstein, therefore, that classroom language uses are a 'microcosm of the macroscopic orderings of society', and that they 'both reflect and help to reproduce a particular form of social order'. Middle-class children are more likely to have the ground rules for generating appropriate performance in classroom situations because of greater experience of a 'tutorial' relationship with adults, involving orientation to the adult's frame of reference. They are thus better prepared in terms of situational competence, that is of knowing what to say and how to say it in this particular context. This squares with the work of Tough (1970) in which she found differences between 'advantaged' and 'disadvantaged' children in their readiness to reflect upon experience and seek explanations and predictions and so to project beyond the immediate context and take on the perspectives of others. However, this must not be interpreted as supporting a theory of cultural deprivation, and thus distract attention away from the educational context (Bernstein 1973, Keddie 1973).

The act of definition

How are definitions operationalized? This has been considered in a series of studies by Robert Stebbins (1975, 1977 and 1981). He distinguishes between cultural definitions, habitual personal definitions, and unique personal definitions. In the first, definitions are knowingly held in common by a group; in the second, definitions may be shared, but unknowingly, and the third refers to rare events where no cultural or habitual meaning exists, thus requiring improvisation. Most teacher definitions fall into the 'habitual' category (that is to say they are 'selected' rather than 'constructed').

Definitions are operationalized by a number of factors, which Stebbins groups into three main areas:

1 Perceptions of others. This includes identifying others present and their behaviour; perceptions of the evaluation others have made of the situation, of the action orientations of others while in the setting, and of their plans of action and justifications for them.
2 'In the looking glass'. This involves the definers' perceptions of how others in the situation view the definers in the same ways as in 1.
3 Reactions. This concerns the definers' evaluations of the situation established with reference to their identifications of themselves, their plans of action and justifications of those plans (Stebbins 1975, pp. 18–19).

Not all of these may be brought into action in any particular definition, indeed some of the knowledge may be unavailable or unnecessary.

Stebbins identifies two broad phases in cultural and habitual definitions. Phase I involves identifying events as belonging to a particular category of situation. Here, the first two sets of factors above are brought into operation. Phase II involves choosing a personal reaction guided by the factors in 3 above. This cannot be done until the setting has been identified, as in phase I.

Stebbins then examines how teachers in St John's, Newfoundland, and Kingston, Jamaica, define disorderly behaviour, academic performance and tardiness. The most compelling impression of the research is the complexity of teacher definitions. Consider, for example, *one* factor of those contained above in sets 1 – 3, that of teacher evaluations of disorderly behaviour. There were three 'justifications' given for teachers' defining a situation as disorderly, preparatory to taking action for its repair: its obstruction of teaching aims, its intrinsic de-merits ('order for order's sake'), and its contagious character. But these only legitimate a teacher's action, they do not necessarily bring it about. For action to be taken, five other factors were found to be relevant: (1) the reasons for not confronting disorderly behaviour; (2) the identification of the misbehaving students and their imputed evaluations, plans of action and justifications; (3) the personal knowledge about the students; (4) the identification of the type of disorderly behaviour; and (5) the teacher's principal action orientations (Stebbins 1975, p. 61).

Similar lists of sub-factors attend the other factors. Unsurprisingly, therefore, despite the cultural and habitual nature of most teacher definitions, there are great variations among them, both between teachers, and in a teacher's own definitions. In the last resort, also, the teacher has a choice.

> A teacher can pleasantly bid a tardy student good morning or angrily send him to the principal or select one or more of a variety of immediate alternatives. The choice is up to him; and it is guided predominantly by the information he has about the student and that particular instance of tardiness, rather than by the (mysterious) forces of culture and social structure. Social behaviour ... results largely from decisions and choices made on the spot with reference to oneself and one's activities and others and their activities (ibid., p. 119).

This, of course, may be true, but it is a 'recipe knowledge' (Schutz 1967) on which the teacher is workin~ in such instances, a rule of thumb that has been shown to yield results in those particular circumstances. For more theoretically informed definitions, which could well have implications for action, the teacher would have to take culture and social structure into account. This need not be 'mysterious', as Edwards has pointed out above, and as I shall discuss further in chapter 4.

Stebbins makes the point that classroom situations demand immediate action, and that one has little time for reflection. Apart from the restriction of resources that help to make this so, there is the complexity of factors. One way in which teachers rationalize is to ascribe simplified definitions to pupils, but as we shall see in later chapters, they are equally as complex as their own. Also, their behaviour through the 'looking glass' and their view of themselves is not as involved as other aspects. This may be simply because pupils' views of them as teachers is difficult to pick up in the conventional teaching situation, or because of the social distance some teachers cultivate between themselves and pupils.

Taken together with Pollard's 'rule-frames' and with considerations of resources, knowledge, power and accountability, Stebbins's theory gives an idea of the size of the task in defining a classroom situation. That the greater majority of teacher definitions are habitual is not surprising. But this is not to say that they are the best available to meet the teacher's aims.

Some pupil definitions

If power and knowledge are generally on the side of the teacher, not all pupils accept the teacher's definition of the situation, and some define it markedly differently. As I shall show in later chapters, some of these definitions owe much to social class, cultural and structural (for example, life-chances) factors. These outweigh any contextual variations the teacher might try, and, contrary to some teachers' assumptions, they are equally as complex as their own. Here, I shall merely give one or two examples of pupil definitions to make the point of their alternative nature.

One illustration of what one suspects is a fairly typical pupil definition of school is given by Birksted (1975). He studied a group of boys for whom school was an interruption in the course of the more important activity of meeting among themselves, playing cards, having a smoke, having a laugh, and so on. It does provide certain advantages: 'it fills in time, it is somewhere to be at. School is like a waiting-room' (Birksted 1975, p. 13). They see the importance of exams, in a purely utilitarian way, in connection with occupational futures. And if these are not relevant to them, school is largely a nothing.

If these pupils saw school as a 'waiting room', Paul Willis's group of 'lads' saw it as something distinctly oppositional. Here he describes how they use the official form of the lesson for their own ends, in a kind of mocking of the official definition of the situation.

> The lads specialize in a caged resentment which always stops just short of outright confrontation. Settled in class, as near a group as they can manage, there is a continuous scraping of chairs, a bad tempered 'tut-tutting' at the simplest request, and a continuous fidgeting about which explores every permutation of sitting or lying on a chair. During private study, some openly show disdain by apparently trying to go to sleep with their head sideways down on the desk, some have their backs to the desk gazing out of the window, or even vacantly at the wall. There is an aimless air of insubordination ready with spurious justification and impossible to nail down. If someone is sitting on the radiator it is because his trousers are wet from the rain, if someone is drifting across the classroom he is going to get some paper for written work, or if someone is leaving class he is going to empty the rubbish 'like he usually does'. Comics, newspapers and nudes under half-lifted desks melt into elusive textbooks. A continuous hum of talk flows around injunctions not to, like the inevitable tide over barely dried sand and everywhere there are rolled-back eyeballs and exaggerated mouthings of conspiratorial secrets (Willis 1977, pp. 12–13).

Paul Corrigan reinforces the point that there must be a mutual recognition of a context and the rules applying within it, for a common definition to prevail. The Sunderland boys that he studied carried on their normal behaviour in the classroom, characterized especially by talking and eating. These perfectly innocent activities were transformed by the classroom context into abnormal behaviour. They themselves, however, did not see it as wrong, and so it became a matter of tactics for them, and surveillance for the teacher (Corrigan 1979, p. 57). Sometimes, too, it became more than a continuance of normal activity – it became 'carrying on' – pointedly oppositional behaviour. In Corrigan's view, this is because of the prevailing power situation:

> 'Carrying on' represents *at one and the same time* taking no notice of the teacher, being aware of the teacher's power, and doing what the teacher doesn't want you to do. The only link

between these three is that the boy is asserting his right, in the given power situation of the classroom, to take part in whatever action he feels like. That action is not dominated by values of a pro- or anti-school nature; instead it is about the power situation perceived and experienced in that school (ibid., p. 58).

Willis reminds us of how arrangements of props and space can reinforce the teacher's power. As he puts it:

> Sitting in tight ranked desks in front of the larger teacher's desk; deprived of private space themselves but outside nervously knocking the forbidden staff room door or the headmaster's door with its foreign rolling country beyond; surrounded by locked up or out of bounds rooms, gyms and equipment cupboards; cleared out of school at break with no quarter given even in the unprivate toilets; told to walk at least two feet away from staff cars in the drive – all of these things help to determine a certain orientation to the physical environment and behind that to a certain kind of social organization. They speak to the whole *position* of the student (Willis 1977, pp. 67–8).

An example from my own research illustrating a different feature of the school, involved a boy drawing attention to what he saw as the growing depersonalized and bureaucratic character of the secondary school he was in as it grew in size, in contrast to the 'homely' character it used to have:

> 'I used to like it. There was an atmosphere of friendliness about the place – you could talk to most teachers, but now it's getting larger it's not ... and the teachers, I don't know some of the teachers, and ... there are some I've never even spoken to ... well perhaps there were one or two you didn't know when you first came in the 1st year, but that was all. Now, I don't even know, not even spoken to five or six of them. The friendliness of the place is gone ... and it's really gone, and it's really changed since the 1st or 2nd year. So I think I don't really like the school now ... it's more like a school than it really was when I was in the 1st year, and that's why I don't really like it.'
> I asked him what he meant by 'more like a school now'.
> 'Well, if you go into a house, there you feel some sort of security that you're in your own house, and when you came to this school, we didn't ... it seemed different from the house, but you sort of ... you was at home here, you could ... you know, you knew what you could do and what you couldn't do, but now everything seems to be a sort of a ... going away from pupils and

teachers ... and we don't seem to know them any more now than they know us better ... and that in the 1st year we knew each other quite well and we knew what we liked and what we didn't like.' (Woods 1979, p. 96).

This kind of feeling has led to some experiencing school as 'unreal' and teachers as not 'proper persons' (Blackie 1980).

Back regions

Indeed teachers may feel this themselves, and this increases the importance of 'back regions' (Goffman 1959). These are the areas where the stage actors take time off and relax from the part they are playing in the school's main function (see chapter 1, p. 6). For the pupils, these 'back regions' will be the playground, the school field, the toilets, the cycle sheds. In the official areas they disport themselves playing games, conversing, flirting, teasing, eating, doing nothing. In the 'unofficial' areas ('behind the cycle sheds', 'in the tennis court shrubbery'), they might engage in more activity that contravenes the rules of the school – smoking, fornication, plotting the overthrow of a detested member of staff, or some act of vandalism. Some of these unofficial areas may become tacitly recognized by staff, feeling that they are essential for the good order of the school (Reynolds 1976a). In these areas the pupils can be themselves, free from the rule-structures teachers generally try to impose on them or influence them into.

For the staff, the main 'back region' is the staffroom. I have written elsewhere:

Its privacy is well respected by headteachers and pupils alike. Pupils are often debarred from knocking on the door, or even approaching its vicinity, by 'out-of-bounds' corridors. Headteachers usually knock before entering, limit their visits to urgent matters of business, and conduct themselves discreetly while there. Its boundaries are usually clearly demarcated. One I know, regarded as ideal by its inmates, was a cellar in an outbuilding, protected from the rest of the school by ancient stone walls and two car-parks. It was the 'men's' staffroom, and the strength of its boundaries was well indicated by the women's confessed trepidation at entering it. 'Solidarity' was here expressed in distance, construction, site, and reinforced by others' recognition of it. The 'properties' of the staffroom often lend it a distinctive character – perhaps old battered armchairs which the teachers who 'belong' to them defend with great vigour, resisting charitable urges from the headteacher to buy 'brand new ones'; or stained tea mugs, which carry the evidence of many a happy break – both symbols of individuality; and frequently too, signs of vast disorder – masses of papers, books, journals strewn around flat areas – which contrasts strongly with the system and order outside. Above all the staffroom is characterized by a euphoric atmosphere, given off by the reactions of the people in it, whether they be smoking, doing crosswords, playing bridge, conversing or just relaxing.

This is indeed a haven in stormy seas, and recourse must be had to it at regular intervals. The 'collective' periods are again well indicated. The initial gathering at the beginning of the day is a leisurely and tension-free gathering, after which teachers register their forms, then go to assembly. This is followed by a short, transient but often highly significant episode in the staffroom, before lessons begin in earnest. There is then a mid-morning break of some twenty minutes, a lengthy dinner-hour and a mid-afternoon break. Some often stay behind after school for an 'unwinding session' (Woods 1979, pp. 211–12).

My observations in all the staffrooms with which I am familiar have certainly led me to conclude that they are 'relaxing', 'unwinding' areas, where teachers can, on occasions, leave their official role behind and, like the pupils in their 'back regions' be themselves. In the school of my research (1979) there was much laughter, which I saw largely as functioning to neutralize the stress and problems induced by the formal requirements of their jobs. Since the upper hierarchy were responsible for seeing those duties carried out and for the general organization in which they would be carried out, they were frequently the butts of staffroom jokes in the same way as pupils were with teachers. Since the pupils were responsible for some of their difficulties, they also were frequently the subject of humour.

Hammersley noted in the staffroom of his research a different strategy, but one that might have the same function as the laughter in other staffrooms, namely easing the task of their main role in the school. This took the form of building up, through conversations over time, a collective ideology about the pupils which accounted for the problems the teachers experienced. I shall discuss this in more detail in a later chapter, merely noting here the importance of the context in performing this essential work. D.H. Hargreaves (1972) has also commented on the 'norm of cynicism' in staffrooms, by which 'teachers are not expected by their colleagues to be enthralled by the job of teaching or rapturous about the pupils' (p. 405). This combines both humour and collective ideology.

If these represent two contexts for the teacher – the classroom context, where the demands of the job are pragmatically met, and the 'back region' which sustains and supports the teacher in meeting those demands and/or accounting for failure – there is yet a third area, which Keddie (1971) has called the 'educationist' context. This is distinguished by 'what ought to be' rather than 'what is', by theory rather than by practice. It may be the 'front' presented to the outside world, or it may represent the starting point for one's own action. I shall say more about these contexts, and the perspectives engendered by them in the following chapter.

Summary

In the construction of situations, people have considerable skills of improvisation and manipulation. This is as true of art, mathematics and science rooms as it is of abortion and gynaecological clinics. Some situations, however, impose themselves on definitions, and this is as true of teachers using the 'recitation' method in the classroom as it is of the police stretching the law on skid-row. Sometimes there are disjunctions between the material features of contexts and the purposes behind them, and the definitions of them. In such instances, teachers work to repair the breach, as when they attempt to 'close' open classrooms.

A prominent feature of situations is their prevailing rule-frames. Four of these were considered: (a) temporal, an example being how teachers typically phase a lesson; (b) ecological, an example being the lay-out of the traditional classroom; (c) curricular, an example being how teachers establish the form of lessons through talk; and (d) personal, of which 'showings-up' are a useful illustration. Other properties of teacher definitions are power, knowledge, resources and accountability.

How teachers construct definitions was considered. They employ cultural, habitual or personal definitions and draw on a range of factors in varying degrees covering their perception of others, their views of how others see them, their evaluations of the situation and plans of action. Given the nature of the task and the provision of resources, it is not surprising that teachers largely employ habitual definitions, and that some of the factors, such as pupil perceptions, are relatively simplified.

Pupils do not always define the classroom situation in accordance with a teacher's intentions. Some see it as a 'waiting-room', some as alien space to be resisted in all its features at every opportunity, some as depersonalized and unreal. This increases the importance of 'back regions', where pupils can be more themselves and are largely free to construct their own situations. Teachers, too, take advantage of the back region of the staffroom, using laughter to relax the more stressful elements of their formal role and constructing pupil ideologies to buttress their professionalism.

In this chapter, I have discussed how teachers (largely) and pupils (in part) define the situation. How they see their tasks and roles, and each other, I shall examine in the next chapter.

Chapter 3

Teacher and pupil perspectives

Teacher perspectives

On teacher perspectives, work has tended to concentrate on three main areas: (a) traditional/progressive views of teaching; (b) teacher typifications of pupils, and (c) teacher perspectives in relation to the production of school deviance. I shall examine each in turn.

(a) Teaching typologies

In seeking to understand teacher action, we need to examine its basic constitution in perspectives. This involves matters like how teachers define their task, how they view pupils, what constitutes good and bad pupils, and good and bad work, their views on how to teach, and subject content. Esland (1971) argues for the existence of two broad, contrasting paradigms, corresponding to traditional-progressive modes, which he labels 'psychometric' and 'phenomenological'. They involve different assumptions about knowledge and the world, and lead to completely different realities for teachers and pupils. The psychometric paradigm rests on the assumptions that knowledge is objective, to be discovered; that the child has a finite capacity, and therefore teaching consists of fitting knowledge into the child; that the child has a moral responsibility to seek to fill his capacity and the teacher to provide the means for him to do so; but that the child is innately socially irresponsible, and needs to be motivated to learn and to conform (see also Barnes and Shemilt 1974, Parlett and Hamilton 1972, and Lister 1974). Such beliefs lead to a strong concern for control and discipline, measurement and testing.

The 'phenomenological' paradigm, by contrast, sees learning as a growth process, knowledge as constructed, and the child as having an unlimited capacity. The teaching task is to discover children's frameworks, and how they interpret and learn, and to foster their development; the child is 'a candle to be lit, rather than a vessel to be filled'. Clearly, this would involve more 'child-centred' teaching (see also Postman and Weingartner 1969).

These are not just alternatives – they are directly oppositional, and can give rise to deep conflict between teachers and teachers, and between teachers and pupils. However, teachers do not take over one or other paradigm *in toto*. They are 'ideal types' – models towards which teachers approximate to some degree or other. We need to ask, therefore, how individual teachers relate to these paradigms, and how they work out in practice.

Once we get down to this level, teacher perspectives are seen to be very much more complex. They cannot be neatly categorized into compartments. An individual teacher might at the same time hold aspects of either view, and in varying strengths. Also he might vary these views over time and place. Hammersley (1977a) has tried to take this into account in a more detailed typology based on the dimensions listed below. Notice that they are conceived of as *dimensions*, along which a teacher may hold one of a large number of positions.

A summary of the dimensions

1 *Definition of the teacher's role*
 (a) authoritative role ↔ no distinct role
 (b) curriculum ↔ method
 (c) narrow ↔ wide
 (d) high degree of teacher control ↔ low control
 (e) universalistic ↔ particularistic
 (f) product ↔ process

2 *Conceptualization of pupil action*
 (a) licensed child ↔ apprentice adult ↔ adult
 (b) individualistic ↔ deterministic vocabulary of motives
 (c) pessimistic ↔ optimistic theory of human nature

3 *Conceptualization of knowledge*
 (a) distinct curriculum ↔ no distinct curriculum
 (b) knowledge objective and universally valid ↔ knowledge personal and/or tied to particular purposes of culture
 (c) hierarchical structure ↔ no hierarchy
 (d) discipline-bound ↔ general

4 *Conceptualization of learning*
   (a) collective ↔ individual
   (b) reproduction ↔ production
   (c) extrinsic ↔ intrinsic motivation
   (d) biological ↔ cultural learning path
   (e) diagnosis ↔ pupil intuition
   (f) learning by hearing about ↔ learning by doing

5 *Preferred or predominant techniques*
   (a) formal ↔ informal organization
   (b) supervision and intervention ↔ participation and non-intervention
   (c) imperative mode plus positional appeals ↔ personal appeals
   (d) class tests ↔ assessment compared to past performance ↔ no formal assessment
   (e) grouping ↔ no grouping
   (f) grouping by age and ability ↔ random, friendship or pupil-choice grouping

(Hammersley 1977a, p.37).

Hammersley went on to develop a tentative fourfold typology of teaching based on combinations derived from the dimensions. This has to be tentative, and by no means exhaustive, since we have few adequate studies of teachers. The types proposed were: (1) discipline-based teaching, roughly corresponding to Esland's 'psychometric' paradigm; (2) programmed teaching, involving an authoritative teacher role, but operating in terms of methods rather than a body of knowledge to be taught, and favouring one-to-one teaching relationships; (3) 'progressive' teaching, which involves an authoritative teacher role to be used in the interests of aiding spontaneous learning, a low degree of control, pupils seen as children, learning as resulting from doing rather than listening, and the curriculum as objective and universally valid; (4) 'radical non-interventionism', which has no distinct teacher role, acknowledges no method or curriculum as such, sees learning as the production rather than reproduction of knowledge and results from intrinsic motivation. This is the style of teachers in the 'free school' tradition.

These dimensions show the almost infinite variety of perspectives we might find amongst teachers if we go into sufficient detail. Further, as noted in the previous chapter, it has been suggested that teacher perspectives differ according to context. Thus Keddie (1971) from the study of a group of 'progressive' teachers in a

London comprehensive school, has argued that their views differ between 'educationist' and 'teacher' contexts. In the former relatively free and detached arena their views are more idealistically influenced by theory, in the latter by the practicalities of the classroom situation which often militate against some of the finer points of theory. Thus in the 'educationist' context, they saw achievement as a result of motivation rather than intelligence, and strongly influenced by social class; streaming by ability as an institutional reinforcement of class-determined inequalities, and a device fixed by inadequate and unfair criteria; and a divided curriculum being also a producer of divisions. In the 'teacher' context, however, Keddie holds that:

> What a teacher knows about pupils derives from the organizational device of banding or streaming, which in turn derives from the dominant organizing category of what counts as ability. The 'normal' characteristics ... of a pupil are those which are imputed to his band or stream as a whole. A pupil who is perceived as atypical is perceived in relation to the norm for the stream. 'She's bright for a B' (teacher H); or in relation to the norm for another group: 'They're as good as Bs' (teacher T of three hardworking pupils in his C stream group). This knowledge of what pupils are like is often at odds with the image of pupils the same teachers may hold as educationists since it derives from streaming, whose validity the educationist denies (Keddie 1971, p. 139).

Keddie's study has received support from other areas. Sharp and Green (1975), in the primary school of their research, found a strong contrast between the progressive doctrine of child-centredness of some of the teachers, and the reality of the classroom. Here, they argue, progressivism became a rhetoric to justify the same inequalities being perpetuated in the system. There was much talk of such things as 'needs', 'interests', 'children's readiness', without, however, any clear indications of how they would be operationalized. Teachers had to manufacture their own theory of instruction, and that inevitably was based on past and present procedures, and their colleagues. Another complication was the pressure on the school to teach literacy and numeracy, yet no guidance being given on how these could be developed from within the child as opposed to traditional methods.

Sharp and Green's argument is that the teacher is constrained by the circumstances in which he or she works, and, however good the intentions, forced to act in ways that often run counter to the 'educationist' claims. However, they take this further than the 'situation' arguing that the situation, including teacher perspectives and actions, are but a reflection and reproduction of the wider system of control and differential opportunities. For this, progressivism is a useful doctrine. The key concept of 'busyness', for example, satisfied the progressive outlook, while in practice allowing the teacher to spend more time with the more able children. Sharp and Green go well beyond interactionist concerns, finding those inadequate for an explanation of the inconsistencies they observed. In doing so, however, they attracted criticism from interactionists on methodological grounds, for example for not examining teacher constructions, meanings and definitions in sufficient depth (D. Hargreaves 1978, Hammersley 1977a).

The basic point of 'educationist' and 'teacher' contexts is well supported in other studies. American work pointing to a similar contrast is that by Gracey (1972 and 1976). The 'craftsmen teachers' felt a strong discrepancy between the goal of individualized instruction and the organizational necessities of group instruction and the required curriculum. The school system, parents, and the children, all appeared to define early childhood education as 'a formalized set of routine activities'. Above all, the craftsmen teachers felt the contradiction between relating personally to the individual child and organizing their classes into smoothly functioning and ordered groups. Gracey concluded that 'the organizational structure of the school negates the key craftsman goal of individualized instruction' (Gracey 1976, p. 84).

Chessum (1980) noticed a similar phenomenon with regard to teacher perspectives on disruptive incidents. Here, teachers can take a 'reflective' stance, when they will refer to wider sociological and institutional issues. However, when discussing particular pupils or crises, the emphasis shifted towards psychological and moral explanations. In the harsh reality of disruption, given the problems surrounding the teacher's job, there is not a totally free 'reflective' choice. Considerable stress is caused teachers by disruptive pupils (Dunham 1977). Moreover, teachers receive little training in the management of disruption, and their responses are almost inevitably intuitive and pragmatic (Parry-Jones and Gay 1980). Chessum found her teachers generally drawn to either a 'personal and family pathology of disaffection' or a 'hard core' theory of deviance (which attributed deviance to a 'hard core' of offenders within the school), both of which denied any rationality or legitimacy to pupil deviance. In the circumstances, these seemed the most helpful, being readily available, fairly uncontentious, reasonable, allowing room for both teacher influence and teacher failure, and personal and professional idealism. Teachers did not lack insight into other factors and other forms of explanation, but they leant towards these because 'in order to carry out their tasks and implement their teaching ideals, it was necessary for them to defend the organization and their professional role within it against attack' (Chessum 1980, p. 127). Grace (1978) has similarly shown how teachers in the late nineteenth century coped with a keen sense of their own civilizing role on the one hand, and over-identification with their pupils and the 'immorality' of their backgrounds on the other, which might bring that role into question. In short, teacher perspectives have to be contextualized. They are by no means free from the pressures of the job and the influence of the institutions and classrooms wherein they work.

Some of my own work supports this division of teacher perspectives (Woods 1979). In an analysis of school reports, I concluded that the teachers were operating in a professional context in their comments on pupils' achievements, characters, and futures, which contrasted strongly with their classroom practices, which, for the most part, had a 'survival' orientation (see chapter 6). As with Sharp and Green's teachers, therefore, those at Lowfield were forced to adopt certain perspectives towards their actual teaching practice, which varied from those represented in another context. Professionalism is marked by expertise, knowledge, the right to define and diagnose, a certain mysticism, and infallibility. Pupils were judged to be 'immature', 'lazy', 'to lack ability', 'initiative' or 'effort', 'confidence', 'concentration' or 'trustworthiness'. Subjects were difficult, pupils 'dim'. Parents were potential allies in recruiting their children to the Protestant Ethic. This is what is expected of professionals, not the admissions of perplexity, failure and resignation which were often expressed among themselves in the privacy and informality of the staffroom. This is well expressed in an American study by Lortie (1975, p. 144).

A seemingly simple question of problems of evaluating progress unleashed a torrent of feeling and frustration; one finds self-blame, a sense of inadequacy, the bitter taste of failure, anger at the students, despair and other dark emotions. The freedom to assess one's own work is no occasion for joy; the conscience remains unsatisfied as ambiguity, uncertainty, and little apparent change impede the flow of reassurance. Teaching demands, it seems, the capacity to work for protracted periods without sure knowledge that one is having any positive effect on students. Some find it difficult to maintain their self-esteem.

Such a gulf between aspirations and achievement might be expected to cause problems for the teacher. How do you resolve contrary perspectives? In some instances, it is a naturally occurring phenomenon – there is always something of a gap between what people say and what they do (Deutscher 1973). In others, like those of the teachers in Sharp and Green's study, and of my own, it is argued that rhetorics are invented to account for such discrepancies. In yet others, like Lortie's, there is no clear resolution – the teachers agonize.

All of these studies are posing contextual contrasts which are undoubtedly overdrawn to some extent. Berlak *et al.* (1976, 1981), viewing a number of English primary schools, observed that elements of different perspectives appeared to be brought into play in the *same* context. For example, 'letting one student decide how much maths to do while telling another exactly what was required' (p. 89). There were a number of such apparent contradictions, and this led to the authors formulating a number of 'dilemmas' which confronted the teacher, such as (1) teacher making learning decisions for children versus children making learning decisions; (2) intrinsic versus extrinsic motivation; (3) teacher setting and maintaining standards for children's learning and development versus children setting their own standards. How do teachers resolve these dilemmas? Berlak *et al.* found the teachers often drawn towards *both* poles of a dilemma. How they resolved them depended on fine judgments about differences between children and about their capabilities, about the task in hand, its capacity to motivate a child, about how important it is for a child to be intrinsically motivated in particular instances, whether a child can set standards for herself, and so on. A teacher makes hundreds of decisions in the course of a day, many of which may appear inconsistent judged against some raw external philosophy, but which are rationally based, according to some combination or permutation of these factors. This study illustrates the complexities of teacher decision-making and the inappropriateness of searching for pure, unadulterated 'progressive' practices, which can only lead to distortion. Berlak *et al.* maintain it is better to see how teachers handle the conflicting claims in the dilemmas they face; and then to see if there are any characteristic patterns in resolving them. Perspectives are not clocked in and out of teachers' heads like programmes in computers. They are generalized frameworks towards which a teacher may be drawn to some degree or other, and which always have to be reconciled with the practicalities of the situation. These may, on occasions, allow certain aspects of the idealized perspective to be maintained in some degree or other; at others, adjustments will have to be made.

(b) Teacher typifications of pupils

If one of the major means of resolving one of the teacher's dilemmas is knowledge of the pupil, how does the teacher go about assessing the pupil? Hargreaves *et al.* (1975), after detailed interviews with teachers, concluded that teachers developed very elaborate typifications of individual pupils over time, and that these formed part of their commonsense assumptions about them in the classroom. Hargreaves *et al.* proposed three broad stages in this process. The first is 'speculation', as a teacher tries to find out what sort of character a pupil has. The main constructs used are appearance, conformity to discipline role aspects, conformity to academic role aspects, likeability, and peer group relations. The teacher builds up a characterization over time from several constructs and many observed events and interactions. Apart from direct experience and observation of the pupil, a teacher may have the benefit of some existing knowledge of the pupil's background, brothers or sisters, records from the previous school, together with staffroom discussion. But it is provisional to start with, since much of the evidence is slender.

Eventually, however, as knowledge about a child accumulates, and behaviours and interactions are repeated, the typing process moves to 'elaboration'. There is 'verification' as the teacher tries to find out if some pupil is 'really like that', now he has settled down. He may be de-typed if early impressions are not confirmed, and the process must begin again. There may be 'type-extension' as more is learnt about a pupil, one particular facet perhaps being found to consist of many others. The further this develops, the more unique each child becomes, the teacher discovering both how and why a particular child commits certain typical acts.

The final phase is 'stabilization', at which point a teacher has a relatively clear and stable conception of the identity of the pupils. It may overlap with the 'elaboration' phase in some respects of the pupil's character, but not in others. Stabilization does not mean permanence. Facts may change, indeed pupils may 'change' as they grow older, some in line with previous typing, others along different paths, and one kind of stabilization might be transformed into another. The two basic features of this stage are 'type-fusion', where elements like previously elaborated typings, motives, and circumstances are brought together into a coherent whole; and 'type-centralization', where the various typings are ranked in order of priority for each individual. At this stage, the teacher feels he can claim to 'know' a pupil fairly well, and can predict behaviour reasonably accurately.

This research, like Berlak *et al.*'s, again gives us some idea of the complexity of the teacher's task. This is increased many times when we summon the other elements into play that bear on the situation, such as context, curriculum, task, the teacher's self, and colleagues. Unfortunately, owing to the mass nature of schooling, it is physically impossible for a teacher, and especially a secondary school teacher involved with hundreds of different children year by year, to proceed to the later stages of typing with many pupils. Their knowledge of some pupils, therefore, usually the broad band of 'average' and 'satisfactory' pupils, may be restricted to 'speculation', based on stereotypes and matching cues from pupils to those. This is exactly what the teachers appear to be doing in Keddie's (1971) research and in my own, at least in the compilation of school reports. There is, then, an alternative method of typing to that proposed by Hargreaves *et al.*, which we might term the static, stereotypical mode. This comes into operation when the teacher considers pupils *en masse* which means, for most teachers, for most of their time. The teacher-pupil ratio is such that 'although there are dyadic contrasts, a simple bit of arithmetic discloses that teachers can hardly spend more than a few minutes with each child in the course of a working day. Most of their teaching behaviour therefore must be addressed to groups of children' (Lortie 1975, p. 152). School reports appear to derive from a static, stereotypical model of typification which has been decontextualized to form 'master typifications' wherein the educationist context and ideal models are supreme, and the 'teacher' or classroom context put to one side (Woods 1979).

Against this, Grace (1978), in a study of teachers in ten London comprehensive schools found little evidence of teachers typifying pupils in terms of social categories as teachers were wont to do in nineteenth-century urban schools, with their 'pedagogy based upon large instructional units' (p.171). Instead, the vast majority showed concern for distinguishing 'individual differences' among their pupils and an unwillingness to classify them in broad 'catch-all' categories such as social class, race, or locality. However, Grace wonders how far this was a genuine celebration of the individual, or whether some other factor was responsible, such as 'a rhetoric of individualism absorbed as part of a modern socialization of teaching' (p. 172).

(c) Teacher perspectives on deviance

The implications of teacher perspectives for teacher action and pupil outcomes have been examined most in relation to the production of deviance. Here, also, two broad dichotomous categories have been suggested. Thus Hargreaves *et al.* (1975) distinguish between the 'deviance-insulative' and the 'deviance-provocative' teacher. In terms of Hammersley's (1977a) typology, this is nearly all based, according to Hargreaves *et al.*, on teachers' conceptualizations of pupils and pupil action. The deviance-provocative teacher, for example, believes that deviant pupils are work-avoiders, that it is impossible to cater for them unless they change; that they are anti-authority and deliberately rebellious, that they will behave badly, are not to be trusted, and are individually responsible for their actions. These views lead such teachers to take 'provocative' action, such as 'issuing ultimatums', causing confrontations, punishing inconsistently, 'showing them up', 'picking on them' and 'stirring'.

The deviance-insulative teacher believes that all pupils are basically good and want to work and that it is the conditions that produce the deviance and should therefore be changed – by the teacher. He is optimistic, and believes pupils will be cooperative. He considers it a privilege to teach and respects, trusts and cares about all pupils. Such a perspective enables this teacher to be fair and consistent to all, to treat pupils with respect at all times, indeed to take a delight in their company.

These, it should be noted, again are 'ideal-types', that is, few actual teachers correspond with them in every detail or on every occasion. But Hargreaves *et al.* did find clear manifestations of them to some degree. The deviance-provocative teacher oscillated between being highly moralistic about an issue and being highly pragmatic, that is avoiding making an issue of an act. The deviance-insulative teacher was more consistently pragmatic, but also a moralist in that 'serious misconduct is dealt with consistently but he avoids confrontations with pupils about his authority' (p. 262). The most significant difference between the two is that the former assigns a highly stable deviant typing to the pupil, whereas the latter does not. The latter focuses on 'acts rather than persons and makes an active search for signs of non-deviance to support his belief in their non-deviant identity'(p. 262).

These 'provocative' and 'insulative' types reappear in two

connected ·pieces of research by Reynolds and Sullivan (1979). They identified two broad strategies in the eight comprehensive schools in South Wales of their research which they call 'coercion' and 'incorporation'.

Again the emphasis is on the conceptualization of pupil action. In 'incorporative' schools, all pupils are encouraged to take an active and participative role in lessons, to work in groups, to take part in the maintenance of order in the school, and to engage in interpersonal rather than impersonal relationships with teachers. In consequence, there is a tolerant and supportive school ethos, into which parents are also drawn, and a therapeutic rather than primitive attitude towards any acts of deviance. In 'coercive' schools, there is no attempt to involve pupils and parents in the school in the same way, there are high levels of institutional control, low tolerance, and strict punishment of deviance.

Some teachers might respond that it is easy to be 'incorporative' or 'deviance-insulative' when you are allowed to be – when, for example, you have the right situation – the necessary resources, reasonable buildings and equipment, a favourable teacher-pupil ratio, cooperative parents and, of course, willing pupils. But Reynolds and Sullivan argue that many of these factors are not relevant. 'Incorporative' schools have better staffing ratios, but also worse buildings. Also the pupil intake is roughly similar in all the schools in terms of ability and social class background. They conclude that the most likely explanation lies in teacher perspectives. 'Coercive' schools consistently overestimated the proportion of their intakes that were 'socially deprived'. In one such school, teachers estimated 70 per cent of their pupils were deprived, as compared with 10 per cent in one of the 'incorporative' schools.

'Coercive' teachers regarded pupils as being in need of 'character training' and 'control', stemming from a deficiency in early socialization. Yet all these schools were held to be of the same social background. Certainly the authors found more children from council estates going to 'coercive' schools, but these children had performed just as well academically as other children at primary school.

One might think that 'coercive' strategies were in decline, if gradually. However, Reynolds believes the contrary is happening, and his work suggests how institutional change and reorganization might influence teacher perceptions. He thought the comprehensives in his research were directing their efforts to the top two-thirds of the ability range, whereas the previous system separated the top third from the bottom two-thirds. The present arrangement isolates the bottom third, and is likely to lead to more problems than formerly. This is because, it is argued, the new schools are moving towards increased coercion for all pupils except the most able, forced by the problems of coping with such numbers of pupils, declining instrumental rewards for pupils, and dealing with the least able who are excluded from the school's opportunity structure (Reynolds and Sullivan 1979, p. 55).

We should be cautious in interpreting these studies. All acknowledge that their categories are highly generalized ones which individual teachers shade in and out of. In relation to the association with deviance, also, it is difficult to disentangle cause and effect. Which comes first, the teacher perceptions or the pupil behaviour? Many teachers, I suspect, would argue the latter, and that their attitudes are adaptations to the circumstances that confront them. Reynolds claims to have demonstrated that teachers adopting different perspectives towards very similar children produce very different results. But it is extraordinarily difficult to establish that similarity and there must be doubts about whether the indices he uses – a particular social class scale, ability at primary school – are sufficiently sensitive to pick up aspects of background that might be influencing the pupils over and above school effects.

Further, the link between teacher perspectives – strategies – outcomes is by no means firmly established. Other research studies (e.g. Rutter *et al.* 1979) have found relatively weak associations between some 'coercive' or 'provocative' items such as corporal punishment on the one hand, and outcomes such as pupil behaviour on the other. Others (e.g. Bird 1980) have cast doubt on the degree to which any teacher labelling of pupils has deviant outcomes. Also as the authors themselves acknowledge, the comprehensives in question have not long been established. Any difficulties they might be exhibiting could be part of a settling down phase – a freak result in the transition period between two radically different structures.

All this is a reminder that teacher perspectives are a complicated matter, are difficult to categorize on a totally satisfactory basis, and do not exist in a vacuum. The influence of cultures and society will be discussed in later chapters, and, as we shall see, opinions differ as to where the point of inception must come for any significant alteration of outcomes.

Summary

In the study of teacher perspectives, there has been a tension between those who have perceived broad dichotomous categories and those who feel that more complexity is a more adequate reflection of reality. This can be seen by comparing Esland's typology with that of Hammersley. The work of Keddie, Sharp and Green, Gracey and Woods suggests that perspectives are not unitary, but compartmentalized according to, for one thing at least, context. Here again, however, it may be inappropriate to think in terms of the teacher making any sharp divisions, but rather, as the Berlaks suggest, advancing on a broad decision-making front, making gains where he can, adapting elsewhere, according to a wide range of factors. One of the most important of these is the teacher perception of the pupil, and work on this by Hargreaves *et al.* led to a comprehensive theory of teacher typing. This emphasized the teacher's knowledge of the individual pupil. An alternative model of teacher typing was proposed, based on teacher knowledge of groups, but of course both models might be employed variously by the same teacher. Grace felt that the teachers in his ten London comprehensive schools mainly saw their pupils as individualized, though other studies (Keddie, Woods, Lortie) have remarked on teachers, of necessity, having to view pupils as cohorts. The implications of different teacher perspectives have been examined in relation to the production of pupil deviance, and there is some support for different constellations of perspectives yielding different outcomes.

Pupil perspectives

Work on pupil perspectives can be classified into two broad areas: (a) pupil perspectives on teachers and on school which appear to be fairly common among several, though not all, groups of pupils, and (b) pupil perspectives that derive from social class and gender cultures, which yield particular outlooks on identity, school, achievement and career. As the second are better understood within the cultural context, I shall discuss them in chapter 5.

Pupil perspectives on teachers and school

Much pupil behaviour may appear to be aimless and meaningless, but it is, in fact, guided by clear rules and principles. The most important of these among the generality of pupils are that teachers should be 'human', should be able to 'teach' and make you 'work', and keep control. Some teachers are felt to be inhuman. They are too strait-laced, and interpret their role too literally. In pupils' terms, they are 'a load of rubbish' (Marsh, Rosser and Harré 1978). 'Mostly ... they're all straitlaced. Keep putting us down.... They go on as if they were never young and did the things we do' (ibid., p. 36). They are '9 to 4' teachers, not really caring about the job or the pupils. They might not even know who pupils are, thus depriving them of personal identities (ibid.).

School, similarly, can seem an inhuman place. In the school of my research (Woods 1979), in addition to particular instances of boredom and unease, there was generalized opposition among the pupils to the growing institutionalization of the school. Two fifth-year forms I studied, one examination, the other non-examination, differed, as one might expect, on an instrumental-expressive dimension. They were generally supportive of the curriculum, but for different reasons. The examination form emphasized the association with jobs and career. The non-examination form judged subjects by intrinsic interest or sheer physical pleasure. The two forms, however, agreed on a person-institution type basis. Thus, favourable comments about school took the form of: (a) institutional provision for relief from the usual constraints (a whole afternoon of games, activities, community service), and (b) institutional elasticity in interpretation of rules and constraints; while unfavourable comments condemned routine, regulation, and particularly restriction, direction and pervasiveness. Comments about teachers could also be interpreted as depending on their degree of institutionalization, dislike arising from ultra-rule consciousness, uneven and irrational use of power, formal and depersonalized relationships, superior attitudes, as well as certain aspects of pedagogy and personality. This person/institution dilemma, which is experienced by teachers also, is well expressed by the statement from a high achieving fifteen-year-old boy in the school, quoted on p. 37 in the previous chapter.

In view of this, it comes as something of a surprise to find that most pupils say that on the whole they 'like' school. Quine (1974) actually found most of the pupils in the two Midlands comprehensive schools he studied saying they liked school, and that this tendency actually increased towards the bottom sets or streams. However, this finding must be treated with some caution, especially as we are given no indication of *why* they liked school, and if this differed among the pupils. Some may have liked it, for example, not because of progress in work they felt they were making, but because of the opportunities for 'laughs' it presented. In my research, some liked it because it was where they 'met their mates'. Davies (1976, p. 3) discovered that one of her pupils liked a school because 'the tuckshop was better supplied with a certain variety of sweets than other schools' tuckshops'. Expressions of 'liking' for schools, therefore, have to be tracked down. It cannot be assumed that they are responding to the official programme.

They certainly like teachers to be human, and one of the criteria of humanity is whether they are able and prepared to 'have a laugh' with you. Jokes 'free things up', they are a way of making relationships more intimate (Walker and Goodson 1977). Sharing a joke means making an alliance, against, perhaps, threatening aspects of work or the school. Humour eases interaction when it has got into embarrassing or otherwise difficult situations. It is a great leveller, for though the teacher is in authority over them, it shows that basically he or she is one of them. Over time, teacher and pupils may develop a common framework of meanings characterized by humour, which may seem rather recondite to an outside observer. A good example of this is given by Walker and Adelman (1976):

> One lesson the teacher was listening to the boys read through short essays that they had written for homework on the subject of 'Prisons'. After one boy, Wilson, had finished reading out his rather obviously skimped piece of work the teacher sighed and said, rather crossly:
>
> Teacher: 'Wilson, we'll have to put you away if you don't change your ways, and do your homework. Is that all you've done?'
> Pupil: 'Strawberries, strawberries.' (Laughter.)

An outsider would be unable to understand this exchange. 'Strawberries' had become part of the commonly understood framework of meanings after the teacher had referred to the pupil's work being 'like strawberries' – good as far as it goes, but it doesn't last nearly long enough.'

What might happen to a teacher who won't have a laugh with pupils is indicated by the following conversation:

> Jane: 'Sometimes you can hear him shouting in the other room. He won't laugh you see, they try to get him to laugh, they do these stupid things and they just want … If he'd laugh they'd be all right, he won't you see.'
> Anne: 'Oh yeah, they'd do anything to try to make him laugh. He puts them in the report book and everything. They don't care.'

Deirdre: 'He put one girl in twice in one day. They do it on purpose. If he was to be more friendly with them like Mr. Lennox is, 'cos he'll have a laugh with you.'

Jane: 'You see, he won't smile and have a laugh with you like Mr. Lennox will.'

Deirdre: ''Cos we can have a joke with him, can't we?'

Jane: 'Yeah, and we do work as well, but in there they play about and don't do any work.'

(Woods 1979, p.114)

Of course, there can be no guarantee that if this teacher 'had a laugh' with them, that it would 'work'. If misused, it could worsen the situation. As Stebbins (1980, p. 84) says, 'Using humour is like driving on a poorly maintained road; one does so at one's own risk. A practical joke may be carried off with the hope of generating amiability, but be defined by the subject as an aggressive, irritating act. Funning may turn into teasing where banter becomes ridicule.'

Nor does this emphasis on humour and laughter mean that pupils simply have a 'good time' orientation toward school. For the laughter has to be seen for the most part within a context where they expect to 'work' and to 'learn'. In fact, most pupils of all types say they want to work, and that a good teacher is one who makes you work and teaches you something. In Delamont's girls' private school, a good teacher 'makes you learn very, very hard ... she really gets you to learn.... She's especially well organized ... keeps you working all the time ... doesn't let you stop for a minute' (Delamont 1976, p. 75). But the same was true for Furlong's low ability West Indian girls:

Q: 'Which are your best subjects?'

Carol: 'I think the two subjects I work hardest in are – '

Q: 'How much do you think it's the teacher or the subject – is it just 'cos you like the subject or what?'

Valerie: 'The teachers, you know, you can't talk in Mr. Marks' lessons, you just have to work.... So after a while you work and you enjoy it because you're learning a lot.'

(Furlong 1977, p.173)

In Davies's Australian junior school,

The constant concern of the children is that work should be done. The harassed [teacher] would probably have been

57

astonished if he had realized how anxious they were to be getting on with their work. Linda … hankers after a more structured work situation than currently exists. Given more structure, she claims, she can 'work more solidly' (Davies 1980c, p. 15).

These interactionist studies support the findings of an earlier survey covering 866 children in 17 junior and secondary schools by Musgrove and Taylor (1969), which concluded that, above all, pupils expected to be taught, and to learn.

In order for work and teaching to be possible the teacher must have 'control', and this also figures large in pupil perspectives. Rosser and Harré's pupils felt 'insulted by weakness on the part of those in authority who they expect to be strong, and this weakness, once established, provokes more playing up' (1976, p. 38). Furlong also found that the most important distinction pupils made among teachers was to do with their ability to keep order and to make 'trouble'. They were either 'strict' when they were taken seriously, or they were 'soft' when pupils played them up mercilessly. Gannaway's (1976) pupils were similar. They could make a 'non-starter' cry or 'a mad woodwork teacher' lose his temper. Though some might see such pupil actions as unfair and unfeeling, they are, as Gannaway points out, very moral actions since 'they are concerned with the basic quality necessary to establish a relationship with a teacher' (Gannaway 1976, p. 55). I shall discuss this pupil activity further in chapter 6.

There are degrees of control, and teachers may be 'too strict'. In this, they may be 'unfair', which was one of the biggest offences teachers could commit according to Rosser and Harré's pupils (1976). Some of the worst sins they noted were unfair comparison with a brother or sister, being 'put down' or 'picked on', and suffering penalties unrelated to particular rule-infractions. As well as personal victimization, the cultivation of favourites and 'pets' is equally despised.

Fairness also involves consistency and predictability. From her study of pupils in an Australian primary school, Davies concluded that:

Where punishment follows rule-breaking it is indeed critical for children to know precisely what each adult defines as right and wrong, and thus what they can expect will follow from 'wrong' behaviour. They felt angry if they made predictions concerning the normative pattern and these turned out to be wrong. If their predictions succeeded for some length of time and then failed, they felt the adult had betrayed their trust and was unworthy as a teacher: a highly favoured teacher could in these circumstances, become an object of derision (1980c, p.3).

This is an important point. It is the teacher's unpredictability in such instances, destroying their own sense of equilibrium, which leads to anger, not the fact that he may have punished them.

The consequences of this are explained with Davies's pupils' experiences with a new kind of teacher given to traditional style relationships after they had been used to more progressive techniques. He did not bother to explore their ground rules, and merely attempted to assert his own. But he was temporary, which undercut his authority somewhat, and the pupils stood by the framework developed by their previous teacher. Though not being able to express reasons for their opposition fully, they were able to assign responsibility to the teacher, for it was clear that the onus for teaching was on him, and this gave their opposition a certain rationality. One of the interesting features of this study is the way pupils 'orchestrated' a range of incidents to match their mood of opposition, when similar incidents in another situation with another teacher might have been harnessed to a supportive framework. It also shows the problems for pupils when faced by teachers of differing perspectives.

Teachers' rule, therefore, must be equable. They must allow a degree of freedom within an ordered framework, and, as we have noted, be capable of 'having a laugh', and remaining 'human'. They must control in a way that makes sense to pupils, not necessarily applying the heavy hand. For example, two particularly successful teachers of disruptive pupils made their authority personal.

'I won't be regarded as the stereotype 40-year-old teacher.... I don't keep the barriers up like some traditional teachers who say never be friendly with the kids ... if I'm feeling awful one morning and I'm taking the register, I'll say "Look, I'm feeling dreadful this morning, so for God's sake, shut up" – not just "Shut up!" I mean I'm human and they've got to know it. And in that they see me as different – but not anti-authority' (Grundsell 1980, p. 73).

Pupils said of the other teacher, 'You can talk to him like you want to talk to him. If you want to do something, he'll say you can do it or he'll say you can't.' Another said, 'Anytime you'd get mad, he'd get mad as well ... that's how he used to teach – if I picked up a chair to hit him, he'd pick up a chair to hit me' – though he had never once done this (ibid., p. 71).

The qualities of 'control', 'humour' and 'humanity' are also evident in Walker and Goodson's (1977) secondary modern school teacher, who is a 'joker', but a serious one. He uses a lot of self-deprecatory jokes, for it helps the self-images of his kids, which are fairly low. But he never starts with jokes, but always establishes the formal boundaries and relationships first. He himself draws the contrast with another teacher who had difficulty with pupils, not because he joked, but because 'he was weak and he couldn't make things stick, and he was using jokes as a way out of that' (p.207). Ron, on the other hand, is 'always' aware that 'I am the teacher ... and that my fundamental job there is to be a teacher. I think it would be patently false to say I was a mate, and that's all, because I'm not. I'm a mate, I'll joke, but in the end I'm trying to get them to do something, and one knows that' (ibid.). This appears to be the sort of approach that most pupils welcome, for it recognizes the distinction between teacher role and person and tries to meet the responsibilities of both.

However, even if a teacher successfully establishes all these conditions to the approval of pupils, it cannot be assumed that they make the same sort of sense of lessons as the teachers. It is not always realized how recondite the teacher's lessons sometimes are, or what pupils understand by 'work' and 'learning'.

Mercer (1981) reports a teacher who decided to test pupils' understanding of ordinary terms she used, and was astonished to find they thought 'evaporation' meant a process of thickening milk, and that a 'liquid' was thick and sticky like Fairy Liquid. They could use the words to get by in lessons, but had not understood the basic concepts. Mercer has found such misunderstandings quite common, either because teachers assumed the ground rules for class work were self-evident, or because pupils 'played the teachers' game' and gave them what they wanted, without having understood it. (For recondite teacher language, see Barnes 1969.)

The gulf between some pupils' and teachers' understandings is vividly illustrated by Grundsell (1978). Though his account derives from his work in a truancy centre, there is evidence that such perspectives are not uncommon among pupils generally (Furlong 1977, Woods 1978b, Barnes 1969). Some pupils do attach high currency to teachers who are capable of 'explaining' what they mean (Nash 1976, Woods 1979), and 'understanding' may represent the high point of learning. But for many it is a luxury they feel is not for them. Grundsell's pupils, for example, were not at all interested in 'understanding':

> What they demanded was 'chalk and talk', the more chalk the better: plenty of writing on the board, numbered points one, two and three to be copied into their books. Lessons got their value rating according to the number of pages filled. A.J. loved the copying down – it was real progress to him. Asked to explain what he had written, he felt outraged – it was a double-cross. He had achieved the aim of the lesson by writing everything down. To be told that the aim was something else, actually understanding, was a cruel deception (1978, p. 48).

Another pupil had almost a photographic memory. She learnt work, and whether she understood it or not was beside the point: 'I said it all right, didn't I? Well then, shut your face. What more do you want?' (ibid.). One boy learnt – and understood – a great deal of geography from accompanying his lorry-driver father on trips. But this was jealously guarded as part of his non-transferable private life. To some, learning was a mysterious code, the key to which was understood by teachers and some pupils; but for them, they had to cover up their failings (and possible humiliation) as best they could. To those pupils at the centre who could understand, lessons were a game, clever and irrelevant to their lives. What the pupils at the centre wanted, therefore, was:

> Structure and safety – neat self-contained packages of learning where we taught and they learnt. With the 'worst' kind of teaching method they felt secure: a fixed target, a fixed time-span, results they could see and measure. Copying maps from the board of places they neither knew nor cared about, the kids settled in peaceful silence. We could watch their faces relax as the anxiety died away. The anxiety was that they would be asked to give and think, when they supposed they had nothing to give or think with (ibid., pp. 49–50).

The curious thing about these habitual truants was that, although they had rejected conventional schooling, conventional schooling's rejection of them led them to seek security behind the strategies they had devised in 'proper lessons'.

These perspectives on teachers seem to be fairly widely distributed across the generality of pupils. They derive primarily from the experience of schooling. Of course pupils are not necessarily united in these views, and there are many different shades and nuances of outlook among them. In some respects, groups of pupils are markedly different in their views, especially where associated with structural sources external to the school. These will be considered in the following chapter.

Summary

Pupil perspectives on teachers appear to focus around three major guiding principles – whether they are human, can teach, and keep control. Many teachers, possibly because of the situation in which they work, appear inhuman to pupils. They appear to have low commitment to their job, do not know who the pupils are, find it difficult to 'have a laugh' with them. Many pupils also like to 'work' and to learn, though pupils' understanding of 'work' is a complicated issue (see also chapter 7). For the moment, we can say that the evidence suggests that the majority of pupils have a basic orientation towards school which is largely and potentially supportive of the official programme. This is further reflected in their respect for firm (though sympathetic and fair, and not authoritarian) control. Some brief illustrations were given of approaches which appeared to meet these specifications.

I have tried to show in this chapter the rule-based nature of teacher and pupil perspectives in the area of teacher-pupil interaction. But there are both wider (in the sense of being related to wider cultures, and to society) and narrower (in the sense of being related to sub-groups within the school and one's own personal identity and aspirations) perspectives, that are manifested in the various cultures of the school. Some of these are related to factors like social class and sex, some are connected with particular areas of activity within the school. These, I consider in the following two chapters, together with some typical kinds of groupings and associations among teachers and pupils.

Chapter 4

Cultures of the school – teachers

I shall consider teacher culture in the light of three prominent themes – ideology, power and role-management. One can approach the subject in a number of ways (for an alternative, see D. Hargreaves 1980), but I have chosen these not only because of the way they pervade teacher culture, but also for their potential in illustrating the interaction between self and system. The first two elements, incidentally, interactionists are often accused of ignoring. This rationale places the emphasis on beliefs and interests. The first concerns the formation of systematized beliefs among teacher groups, the second refers to the striving for position in order to secure the realization of interests, and the third is to do with how beliefs and interests are affected by the individual coming into contact with teacher groups. There is, of course, considerable overlap among these elements. They are used as foci rather than mutually exclusive categories.

Ideology

I use the term 'ideology' here to refer to a system of beliefs and values which are held by a group of people, support their interests and are taken for granted by them as the way things are in the world. The term is not without its difficulties, especially for interactionists. We cannot assume, for example, that such beliefs are necessarily a reflection of basic attitudes or that they form a platform for action. They may, rather, be a product of particular circumstances (Hammersley 1981).

Bearing this caution in mind, we can go on to look at ideologies that have been identified at various levels – representing the whole profession, segments of the profession against each other, teachers against parents, and teachers against pupils. The following are intended to be illustrative of ideologies operating at these levels and not an exhaustive set. The actual range and variety of beliefs among teachers is vast.

With regard to the profession as a whole, Grace (1978) has drawn attention to the development of two ideologies among teachers in urban schools in the nineteenth century, which show their political base, and which to some degree underwrite current teacher professionalism. One was the 'missionary ideology', which saw teachers tackling the problem of controlling the urban masses in the new industrial Britain by acting as 'social and cultural missionaries – a kind of secular priesthood dedicated to the work of "civilization"' (p. 11). This was an ideology initiated by the educational establishment, largely as a form of occupational control and therefore representing the interests of the ruling class. The other ideology was a 'professional' one, representing more specifically the concern of the teachers for respectability and advancement. At times, the two ideologies conflicted, at times they were complementary (see also Tropp 1957). Even today, the profession can be controlled by the prospect of advancement, though it has more autonomy than in the nineteenth century.

However, teachers today are not always clear and consistent in their views on professionalism. In fact, in a study of middle-school teachers, Ginsburg *et al.* (1980) found much variety and uncertainty. Their research, however, certainly emphasizes the ideological construction of teacher professionalism and trade unionism. The teachers were concerned to promote the projects of teacher exclusivity, status and autonomy, and elements were selected from each to those ends. The following major elements were identified:

Ideological elements of professionalism	Ideological elements of trade unionism
Performance of task or service	Solely for benefit of members
Mental (as opposed to manual) labour	Manual labour
Appeals to reason (rather than form)	
Sponsors the service ideal (orientation to clients)	In opposition to employers or clients
Individualism	Collective action

But Ginsburg *et al.* demonstrate that in practice these distinctions do not hold. For example, the claim that professionals 'appeal to reason' overlooks the fact that the negotiating position of many professionals rests on the strength of their market position. Similarly the belief that trade unions operate solely for the benefit of their members neglects both work that unions do which is not specific to their own members, and also professional groups working on their own behalf. Also, the distinction between pro- and anti-employers is a 'mystification', for professions are not necessarily on the side of their employers. In all, Ginsburg *et al.* reveal the wide range of views, even among a fairly homogeneous group of middle-school teachers, on professionalism and unionism and a large degree of uncertainty. The authors prefer to see teachers' views of professionalism and trade unionism as com- posed of various elements which include broad economic move- ments, and local and individual factors, which all come together in different ways to promote different perspectives and strategies.

Some of these may lead to political groupings within the professions. Grace (1978), for example, claims that there is currently an ideological struggle among various interest groups in inner-city areas. He identifies conservative, liberal and radical ideologies. Conservatives emphasize the rule of law and discipline, strong leadership and a reaffirmation of 'standards'. Liberals offer various alternative viewpoints: 'liberal pragmatism' sees the problem of inner-city schools as one of technical inefficiency, which can be repaired through better management and teaching; 'liberal romantics' look for a more progressive and relevant curriculum and teaching addressed more to the 'needs of the child'; 'liberal social democrats' believe that inequalities in society at large can be met by positive discrimination within schools. Radicals see the problem of the school as being that it acts in the interests of cultural domination which arouses resistance from the pupils. They feel the crisis will continue until schools employ a practice based on relativist and non-hierarchic view of knowledge, and become more 'free'. Marxists claim the schools are reproduc- ing the social relations of the capitalist order, agents themselves of ideological transmission. Some see teachers' espousal of the ideology of professionalism as 'false consciousness'. They feel that the crisis can only be resolved by teachers rejecting professional- ism, making common cause with pupils and workers, and working to raise political consciousness (Grace 1978, pp. 54–6, *et seq.*). Clearly the kinds of groupings of perspectives discussed in chapter 3 (p. 42) can be informed by ideologies (see also chapter 13 of Meighan 1981).

Teacher subcultures form on the basis of such ideologies, which are invariably constructed on different models of man and of society, and are inevitably in conflict. These ideologies of teaching illustrate one form of segmentation among teachers. Another lies in teachers in different parts of the system (Tropp 1957). Primary school teachers have a different set of concerns from secondary. But the attempt of teachers in a particular part of the system to establish a rationale for themselves is nowhere better illustrated currently than in middle schools. A. Hargreaves (1980a) argues that their emergence was due largely to administrative convenience, but Nias (1980) shows from a study of the documentation on middle schools that they have been justified on the grounds of their egalitarianism, democratic responsiveness to educational and social need, innovative tendencies, and pluralism. Further, their image is reinforced by great optimism, and an emphasis on integration rather than differences. Hargreaves, however, feels there is a big gulf between ideology and practice, and that far from managing to establish a separate identity, the old institutionalized dividing-line at eleven plus now appears *within* the middle school. Middle schools, like any other, have to be seen within the wider context of economic and political forces, and in the current contraction of the system, their future is uncertain (Lynch 1980).

This does not mean, of course, that teachers are engaging in intentional deceit. A case has to be made in order for them to do their job, and ideologies are a useful resource for coping with circumstances in which they find themselves. This is well illustrated in the professional front which teachers present to parents. The ideological nature of this can be seen from an analysis of school reports (Woods 1979), which, I argue, are not simply communications between teacher and parent about a child's rate of progress measured against agreed and absolute criteria, but a confirmation and furtherance of the teacher's status as expert. Most parents are not in a position to contest the judgments teachers make, judgments which admit of no shortcoming on their own part, but which serve as shorthand diagnoses of how pupils measure up to the teachers' conceptions of mental (and behavioural) health. They thus protect their own self-image and control access to information and criteria for evaluation, just as other professionals do (Friedson 1972). Reports are part of the professional defences of teachers against parents whom they attempt to convert from natural enemies (Waller 1932), to professional aides. Public occasions such as speech days, parents' evenings, and open days provide further examples of this side of teacher professionalism.

Teacher professionalism therefore contains much ideological construction designed to establish and reinforce their position *vis-à-vis* other groups. We have seen above illustrations of how they do this in relation to society in general, and to parents in particular. Hammersley (1981) has shown how an ideology about the pupils can be generated in the staffroom. In sharp contrast to the jealously guarded teacher autonomy in the classroom, it was the collective nature of the views that was distinctive, the teachers' mutual dependence in maintaining staff authority 'forcing the adoption of certain common ways of treating pupils' (p. 8). If one teacher adopted radically different tactics, it would threaten to undermine all teacher-pupil relationships. Thus the roles of the teacher and of the pupil were required to be seen in a standard way, primarily to defend the staff against the threat to their own sense of competence posed by the pupils.

The teachers at this particular school expressed three major concerns – a decline in the social status of pupils, change for the worse in pupils' response to teaching, and in teacher rewards and status. After reorganization of the school, they had got 'lots of coons' and 'yobos with empty heads'. The drive for equality was responsible, for it could only mean 'equal to the lowest level'. Teacher rewards and status in society had diminished, according to these teachers. At the same time, new demands were being made on them, especially with regard to the 'less able' pupils – another factor in the general worsening of standards. But they were unable to counter the worst results because of restrictions on their methods of control ('if you could cane him for that ... he would soon improve').

It is important to realize that this was a *staffroom* ideology, carrying no essential implications for beliefs and actions outside that particular situation. It gave the staff comfort in the face of severe difficulties. But like staffroom laughter, which can be highly sexist and racist, it ends at the staffroom door. Hammersley (1982) observed no evidence of racist attitudes in them elsewhere. Similarly, the front to parents is peculiar to that particular scenario. Lortie (1975) has shown how teachers can confess to perplexity, frustration and failure in certain situations. The political ideologies may be more pervasive, but possibly only among sections of teachers, while we have seen the mixed and divided views on professionalism. In short, the message of chapter 2 – the influence of the situation – must constantly be borne in mind.

Power

We have seen in chapter 2 how some try to influence others' definition of the situation. The quest for power is a common feature of teacher culture. Where there are opposing interests, there will be a struggle for power. Grace has illustrated the ideological conflict in urban London schools. The more numbers, the more senior personnel such groups have, and the more integrated they are in other ways, for example in subject area, especially if of high status, the more power they will wield. Grace quotes one teacher, typical of a number he interviewed:

> English departments are the most trendy and progressive. They seem to have almost a policy (or, at least, a unified approach) to these questions. There is more liaison between English departments and they have a very active professional group. I think it is true to say that there is *an alternative form of education* being espoused by English departments in London. They see themselves as the van of educational innovation. Invariably the largest department, they can exert a powerful influence (Grace 1978, p. 193).

Here, apparently, a strong teacher subculture is founded on two main keystones – ideology and subject. The latter, in fact, still probably represents the most common denominator in teacher subcultures, despite moves towards integration in the curriculum. Research suggests that these moves arise from interests of control, rather than from educational conviction (Grace 1978, Edwards and Furlong 1978, Denscombe 1980a, Ball 1981), and that the old organizing principles remain (see chapter 6). They continue to represent, arguably, the most common basis of conflict and power-struggles.

Subject identity is experienced early by teachers. Lacey (1977) found subject subcultures a pervasive phenomenon among student-teachers which had an effect on their whole orientation to teaching. For example, on methods of teaching, he found that 'French' students when taking the occasional 'English' lesson used the formal techniques they usually employed of comprehension exercises, question and answer and 'complete the sentence' exercises. 'English' teachers, however, were more concerned with developing powers of expression, and that entailed inducing a relaxed and informal atmosphere. Lacey also established that by far the greater majority of friends came from within the chooser's subject group. Moreover, this was not due to being organized in those groups since they met just as frequently in mixed subject groups. The subject, therefore, provides a point of unity, and confers identity.

It is also something to be fought for. Some have argued for the primacy of 'forms' and 'fields' of knowledge (Hirst and Peters

1970, Peters 1967). Others have pointed to the influence of broad socio-economic movements. But there is evidence that status has to be achieved from below, as it were. Goodson (1981), for example, has argued that geography progressed from a low status school subject in the nineteenth century, through the efforts of teachers and the Geographical Association, to ultimately a recognized academic discipline with a university base. Goodson insists it was a result of 'aspiration upward', in what was always a 'fiercely contested process', rather than 'percolation downward', and points out the close connection between status and resources. The higher the status of the subject, the higher the resources – and the better prospects for teachers, 'better staffing ratios, higher salaries, higher capitation allowances, more graded posts, better career prospects' (p. 177). The struggle for status, therefore, is 'above all a battle over the material resources and career prospects of each subject teacher or subject community' (p. 178).

However, such unity comes into play mainly as an initial drive for identity and position or as a defence against threatened inroads from other subjects. Within a subject area there may be bitter divisions, which themselves are the site of power struggles for intellectual control of the subject. Ball (1982), for example, shows how English teachers first established themselves as an epistemic community at the beginning of this century, breaking away from the dominance of classics. But soon English teachers themselves were divided between those who supported a traditional classics oriented approach focused on grammar, and those who preferred a focus on literature. This is an interesting illustration of segmentation, noted in other professions. The subsequent struggle for power is well conveyed by Bucher and Strauss (1976, pp. 24–5), in analysing similar events in the medical profession:

> The emergence of new segments takes on a new significance when viewed from the perspective of social movements within a profession. Pockets of resistance and embattled minorities may turn out to be the heirs of former generations, digging in along new battle lines. They may spearhead new movements which sweep back into power. What looks like backwash or just plain deviancy, may be the beginnings of a new segment which will acquire an institutional place and considerable prestige and power.

The 1960s saw the emergence of a new socio-linguistic approach, which some (e.g. Abbs 1980) saw as politically motivated, and others (e.g. Hoggart 1964) saw as threatening the integrity of the subject by submerging it within history, sociology and philosophy. The result is, Ball claims, that we have a situation in the teaching of English remarkably similar to that when the subject was first established as a separate curricular area – disputes within, involving struggles for intellectual sovereignty, curriculum content and approach, and assaults on the boundaries of the subject from associated discipline areas.

Despite such segmentation, which occurs at an epistemic level, and represents a struggle for intellectual control of a subject area (though not all subjects may follow such a career), subject groups still present a powerful common front against others at an organizational level. Ball and Lacey (1980, p. 150) argue that 'cohesion demands strategic compliance from actors on a whole number of issues that contain within them differences of importance when viewed from the perspective of the subject discipline. In other words, differentiation of the epistemic community is normally suppressed in favour of organizational and status gains.' Some of these are matters of resources, as noted by Goodson above. Others concern the defence of the integrity of the subject. Ball (1981), for example, shows how, at Beachside, the particular conceptual structure and curricular organization of the subject was appealed to as an argument against mixed ability groups by French, science and maths teachers. Once the innovation had been implemented, they were again presented as inevitable limitations on curricula and pedagogical possibilities. Interestingly, at Beachside, as Grace noted in his London schools, it was the English department who were the most radical and who spearheaded the change.

Among factors contributing to the strength of a department, other than a common approach to the subject, might be whether all members are specialists and have their major commitment to that department; how they are viewed by the headmaster, and are supported otherwise (e.g. by subject adviser); and by social bonds within the group. Ball and Lacey conclude that 'in some cases, in the context of a "strong" department, it may be possible for a group of teachers to influence school policy beyond the boundaries of their own subject' (Ball and Lacey 1980, p. 176).

However, the major component contributing towards strength is status – hence the struggles to achieve it. Generally, academic subjects enjoy higher status than practical ones, a difference which reflects the mental/manual distinction in society at large (Braverman 1974). Currently, science, maths and English are high status subjects, with major claims on resources. Others, such as languages and the humanities can maintain a reasonable credibility while they hold their position in the examination structure and channels to further education and occupations. In recent years, Latin has been unable to do this, and has been discarded altogether by many schools. Other subjects, such as the expressive ones of music, games and art, may have periodic high status within a particular school, for they have a key role in presenting the public image of the school. Some subjects, however (such as 'world around us', 'human studies' or 'modern applications of science'), are regarded as 'sink' subjects (Ball 1981), because they have little marketable currency, existing primarily as instruments of social control within the school. The manoeuvrings, struggles and jealousies between these groups can be considerable, as they seek to improve or maintain their status.

Subject and ideology are not the only rallying-points for teachers. There are also localized teacher subcultures that operate on a generational basis. Thus older members of staff may have progressed to the upper echelons of the hierarchy or been recruited to it on the basis of their general support for that establishment. And having been appointed, their support would be likely to increase. As Lacey (1970) notes: 'The more rewards the teacher accepts within the school system during his/her career the more difficult it becomes to see themselves apart from it.... Indeed ... teachers find it necessary to accept and present themselves in terms of the system in order to compete for these rewards, for example, scaled allowances, and head of department allowances.' Teachers thus may be drawn together in common cause through working in the inner councils with the headteacher, and inevitably, it may be characterized by a high degree of pragmatism. Whatever the faults and problems of education and schools, they have to be run, and the main responsibility for this falls on the headteacher and his senior staff.

Many junior staff by contrast, with fewer administrative responsibilities and comparatively fresh out of teacher training, may be nearer the idealistic, radical end of the spectrum. Apart from their positions in the hierarchy, there is another reason for this. They may, in terms of their whole generational cohort, be nearer the pupils than some of their senior colleagues. Their collective experience of the historical moment is entirely different from that of the older generation, who perceive with consciousness constructed on what *they* experienced in their youth (Mannheim 1952). There may be a profound difference in values involved.

Usually, younger staff enjoy less power within a school, and some of their aspirations may be curbed by powerful groups of their senior colleagues. But on occasions, particularly those involving radical reorganization, roles can be reversed. This happened in a school studied by Riseborough (1981), that changed from secondary modern to comprehensive. The 'old' staff in the former, practitioners of 'pedagogical expertise' (i.e. teaching children rather than subjects), found themselves displaced in the new school by subject-centred, examination oriented younger teachers. Two of the 'old' staff expressed themselves thus:

> 'I got angry about seeing these new people getting the plums we were considered not good enough for. All the teachers he appointed were youngish with bloody degrees' (Age 39).
> 'The head's idea of a good teacher is everything I'm not. Just look at the ones he's appointed. That's what he thinks a good teacher is. The rating really is on academic qualifications and examination record. This man has a tremendous fear he has to show results. From the beginning I realised the writing was on the wall. He'd looked up my record and saw someone who'd matriculated at sixteen, been emergency trained etc. He told me in an argument once that I was more a schoolteacher than master. He meant that I could cope with children much better than I teach, I suppose' (Age 56) (ibid., p. 21).

This is basically a clash of secondary modern and grammar school teacher cultures brought unhappily together in the new comprehensives, a phenomenon similarly noted by Reynolds and Sullivan (1979). Here, the problem is compounded by a generational factor.

For the 'old' staff, there was 'horizontal' as well as 'vertical' demotion. Like the pupils, they were streamed, very few having any examination classes. The loss of career prospects, the allocation of 'dirty work' (Hughes 1958) and the new philosophy caused an absolute split, and a polarization of the two cultures.

> They were caricatured by the new staff and the head as diehard, educational backwoodsmen because of their calls for returns to traditional standards of morality and order; their stress on didactic teaching; their support for selective schools, and the end of all 'trendiness' in educational ideas (p. 27).

These cultures seem to derive from the older 'secondary modern' and 'grammar' divisions. The staff of such schools worked out solutions to substantially different problems, arriving at different agendas, styles of teaching, aims and objectives, values and beliefs. Can comprehensivization bring about an amalgamation of these two radically different traditions? Riseborough's study, and that of Reynolds, shows the difficulties. What seems to be important in such circumstances, at least as far as Riseborough's study is concerned, is not common adhesion to an educational principle, but who holds the reins of power.

Role-management

The teacher role is the pattern of behaviour that others expect from teachers. The individual has to learn how to behave as a teacher, and in doing so, learn how to adapt personal aspirations and idiosyncrasies to a socially structured role. Role-management, therefore, is a critical task that a teacher faces all her career. Approaches to it become routinized and embedded within the teacher culture.

New teachers will experience considerable 'culture shock' when they first start teaching, and try to come to terms with the teacher role. This is because of the nature of the work, and the problems of handling large groups of frequently recalcitrant children. It might be a source of amazement how some manage to preserve order, to teach, and to achieve results. On all sides, it is a matter of adjusting or coming to terms with cultural forms and forces, if one is to establish the grounds by which one's competence will be judged. In one school of my acquaintance, the dominant symbol was 'the stick'. It ruled the school. Teachers were frightened to leave the staffroom without it, and in cases of emergency they could be bought from the headmaster for 50p. Pupils were caned on the hands, but not violently, all day long. It struck me as curious, since the teachers were not sadistic or violent in other ways, nor were pupils disruptive or resentful. In theory, the stick could have been easily dispensed with; in practice, it could not. It would have so undermined the teachers' confidence as to affect their whole performance; and pupils would have perceived teachers acting without canes as deviants, who warranted special treatment perhaps. Thus teachers beginning at this school would have to learn how and when to use the cane, and for what reasons. Deviations would invite penalty, so established had that particular way of life become in the school. This is perhaps an extreme example simply to illustrate the pressures operating on people to conform to strategical patterns designed to cope with the work, even though their underlying rationale may have been lost.

The young teacher might also find that colleagues judge competence not by pedagogical skills, but by more prosaic factors. Denscombe (1980a), for example, found that in two London comprehensive schools the basic criterion of classroom control had been displaced in importance by its indicator of quality and quantity of noise emanating from the classroom. Teachers may jealously guard their classroom autonomy in 'closed' classroom situations, but they cannot prevent some evidence of what they are, or are not, doing seeping through to the ears of colleagues. While some noises are acceptable, there is pressure on teachers generally to conduct quiet lessons, even though they may be pedagogically undesirable for the business in hand. Great kudos usually attaches to teachers who can keep difficult and rowdy forms quiet, irrespective of other qualities they may or may not possess.

If things go wrong, there is always the staffroom in which to relax, recover poise, draw strength, in short to help in managing the teacher role. One might subscribe to a staffroom ideology, as the teachers did in Hammersley's school. Whatever one thinks of the views expressed in this staffroom, there is enormous influence on individuals to conform to the collective view. There is reassurance, security, restored pride, personal dignity, power in belonging to a team, in a situation where individuals are working under conditions of poor reward and constant stress. To deviate from the general view is to throw one's competence or sanity into doubt. This comfort is extended to the new recruit. The fact that he may be experiencing difficulties is not surprising – they have all had difficulties:

> When a teacher [admits to problems], other colleagues [in the staffroom] will usually offer reassurance by providing stories of their own or explanations for why that pupil or class is like that, thus opening themselves up to similar potential discredit. What is involved is a ritual of self-exposure and repair and thus the expression of solidarity (Hammersley 1975, p. 48).

However, it is not simply a case of student or probationer teachers being naive and inexperienced. They constitute a threat. Just as a newly recruited factory hand, keen to get on, might attempt to do his particular job faster, and thus threaten the very carefully negotiated, though tacit, production speed of the whole line, student teachers pose a threat because, as one of Hammersley's teachers said, 'they're so damn idealistic'. With the impetus of their extra energies, willingness to put in extra work, failure to recognize pupils being as bad as the older teachers think they are, they can achieve what look like better results than normal. But the 'old hands' feel this is an unreal situation. Socialization into the teacher culture thus becomes essential to all concerned. Among the strategies employed by the seasoned teachers in the school of Hammersley's research to enforce conformity to the prevailing staffroom culture were: emphasizing the paramount need for control; denigrating the university training course; denigrating students' own 'idealistic' efforts and beliefs; confirming their own definition of the situation by constant assertion and mutual reassurance; threatening exclusion (often implicitly) from staff-room culture with all its supportive framework in difficult circumstances; and ridicule, by laughter, of contrary views.

Laughter, in fact, is a distinctive feature of staffrooms. At Lowfield, it was the most distinctive feature (Woods 1979). Lowfield was a beleaguered secondary modern school on the verge of comprehensivization, where the staff had many problems, which they coped with to a large extent by laughter. They did this in various ways. One was through ridicule or caricature, to strike a blow at their assailants, be they the upper members of the hierarchy, and especially the headmaster, or recalcitrant pupils. Pupils, of course, do the same about the teachers. If taken at face value, much of this humour seems rather wicked, especially as it capitalizes on personal idiosyncrasies. But if considered from the point of view of sociological function, it is an honest, and often ingenious, attempt to cope with a real and serious problem.

Another function of staffroom humour is to 'control' – that is to say, to enforce the norms of the staffroom. As noted above, one of the strategies in the induction of student-teachers in the school of Hammersley's research was to ridicule their more 'outrageous' ideas, or any such that ran counter to the mores of that school. In the telling and re-telling of certain tales that have become established in the staffroom folklore, key elements in the culture are confirmed and oppositional ones derided. In the secondary schools of my acquaintance, all heavily bureaucratized structures, I have noticed a prominent theme of person against institution, a personal distancing from the harsher aspects of the teacher role. Much of the laughter is directed against institutional elements, like rules (for example those surrounding school uniform), rituals (like hymn practice) or ceremonials (like Speech Day or Sports Day).

In such ways do teachers 'make' rather than 'take' or 'break' the teacher role (R.H. Turner 1962, Plummer 1975, Woods 1981b). In fact, we should be quite clear that though there are strong pressures acting on new recruits as they are socialized into the teacher role (Fuchs 1969, Keddie 1971), it is the individuals who adapt what is offered to their own personal requirements in particular situations. Lortie (1975), for example, found in the 'five American towns' of his research that degree and kind of involvement in the collectivity was entirely optional, and saw no indication of teachers trying to influence each other.

More usually, perhaps, there is a dialectical play between self and group. Bucher and Sterling (1977), for example, in a study of medical socialization, argued that a person's professionalism depended on a combination of structural and situational variables, which produced a 'programming effect', but that this was limited in circumstances where the individual already had a strong orientation towards the field, and was able to maintain it, and also when contacts with training staff could be minimized. Further, in constructing identities individuals selected from models those characteristics that impressed them most, making choices from a wide range and using their own judgment; and they got progressively better at actively evaluating themselves and others (p. 275). Bucher and Sterling's work is typically symbolic interactionist, in that it lays emphasis on the individual's capacity for self-interaction and thus the continual construction of meaning and interpretation, as opposed to mere response.

In constructing a professional identity, one may be aided by 'latent culture' (Becker *et al.* 1961, Lacey 1977). When a person leaves one group and joins another of different cultural form, the person might retain characteristics of the culture of the former group in a hidden way. Thus a teacher who has contributed to a certain subject subculture may find herself in a school where the predominant cultures are antipathetical. One can still retain such a subculture – it can still influence thought and action, but in a hidden way until the scenario changes or the opportunity arises to move on to more amenable pastures.

More generally, some have argued that our own individual past experiences form a latent culture for us all: 'The preparation of teachers does not begin in colleges, but in infant schools. Students entering college already *know* what teaching is' (Hanson and Herrington 1976, p. 12). Mardle and Walker (1980) also argue that the core of teacher socialization is in 'continued exposure to [the] curriculum, its practices and the commonsense assumptions by which it is rationalized' (p. 103; see also Ball 1982). This taken-for-granted framework is reinforced, they argue, in teacher training and practice, noticeably in the principles of domination (i.e. hierarchical divisions, subordination, etc.) and differentiation (division of labour). Very few students can reflect outside these parameters – hence the commonly perceived irrelevance of education theory (Mardle and Walker 1980, p. 110). Unless this was related to teachers' commonsense explanations, it was ignored by Mardle and Walker's students. These students, one feels, would have responded well to the general cultural orientation in Hammersley's research school, and to the power politics of teacher subcultures.

Summary

Three themes in teacher culture were selected for examination – ideology, power and role-management. A range of teacher ideologies was considered from the profession as a whole to local staffroom groups. Whereas nineteenth-century ideologies were around teaching those of today are largely within it. Ginsburg *et al.* showed current uncertainty and variety among teacher views, and how they oscillated between professionalism and trade unionism. More certainty may attach to the political ideologies that have been identified in certain inner-city areas. However, teachers in different parts of the system have different concerns, and it was noted how middle-school teachers have attempted to fashion their own distinctive educational rationale. Teachers have also been observed to construct ideologies in relation to parents and to pupils. Such ideologies frequently involve a struggle to gain, increase or consolidate teacher power. This was seen to be a major factor in the subcultures within teaching, for example, those based on subjects, as they vie for position, resources and privileges, and influence on school policy. Teachers of subject areas typically seek to establish themselves as distinctive epistemic communities, differentiating themselves from others, though subject areas themselves subdivide into opposing factions. Within these subcultures and the wider occupational culture, the individual has to come to terms with the teacher role. Management of role is particularly critical during early teacher socialization. The new recruit may learn that certain appearances count for more than realities, and that laughter in the staffroom is a useful aid.

However, individuals are not 'taken over' by cultures. They can both contribute towards, and be influenced by them in a dialectical process. In their contributions, latent cultures may be a hidden resource.

Chapter 5

Cultures of the school – pupils

Pupil cultures have been studied largely in relation to three factors: (1) the degree to which certain pupil cultures are aided and fostered by school organization; and the extent to which they derive from, (2) social class, and (3) gender. I shall want to add a fourth, personal interests, which is more typical of the interactionist attention to process and the fine-grained detail of school life. Together, these provide a fairly comprehensive view of pupil cultures. Again, there is considerable overlap between these in practice, but each provides a useful primary focus. I shall therefore examine each in turn, concluding with a consideration of some common themes widespread among a variety of pupil cultures.

School organization

D.H. Hargreaves (1967) and Lacey (1970) identified two polarized subcultures in the boys' secondary modern and grammar schools, respectively, of their research, which, they argued, owed a great deal to the rigid streaming of the day. There were four streams at Hargreaves's school ('Lumley'), and he noted the following values in each:

4A   *For* academic achievement, instrumentality, high attendance, punctuality, high standard of dress and hygiene.
Against misbehaviour, physical aggression, copying.

4B   *For* 'messing' and 'having fun'. Non-academic rather than anti-academic (achievement not completely rejected). 'Messing' a relief from hard work, not a replacement.

| 4C | Anti-academic (total abandonment of academic values). 'Messing' a replacement. |
| 4D | Active anti-academic. High rate of absenteeism. |

This shows a progressive dissociation from the official values of the school. The compartmentalization of views is not a device to categorize pupil views, but a product of the school's compartmentalization into streams, which ultimately, it was argued, fostered two subcultures, one pro-school and one anti-school. Those with positive orientations tended toward the top streams, those with negative, the lower. Over the years, schools with rigid streaming policies would further this process, weeding out the misplacements. The two subcultures became increasingly integrated within themselves (as the like-minded were herded together and reinforced their own outlooks) and differentiated from each other (each developing pride in their own group and dislike of the other). The two groups also pursued different paths and received different treatment, the anti-school group being deprived of status in the school's term, and being given the poorer teachers, poorer rooms, and so on. The differentiation may have something to do with initial like-mindedness, but as Lacey points out, the school's contribution is considerable, since the two groups are faced with fundamentally different problems posed by the school – the problems of success, and the problems of failure. Among the pro-school culture, there is continuous reinforcement, but the anti-schoolers solve their problem by rejecting 'the pupil role and replacing it with an autonomous and independent peer culture' (Hargreaves 1967, p. 172). This means a higher priority on *collective* behaviour and regard since the rewards of status can only come from the group, whereas in the pro-school culture, rewards come from *individual* effort in competition with others.

Both Hargreaves and Lacey regarded their analysis as an oversimplification, and recognized the potentially great influence of both locally derived working-class values and of teenage culture. Even so, these particular analyses have been much criticized by interactionists for laying too much emphasis on the influence of subcultural norms and not enough on the individual's constructions and definitions, which might have yielded much greater variety, both between and *within* pupils.

This is an important point, but there is some interactionist support for Hargreaves and Lacey. In my own research, I identified two similar groups at Lowfield, a mixed school, divided by those who took examinations and those who did not. They experienced different curricula, different teachers, teaching styles and aims which reinforced their differences in the fourth and fifth years. But I had identified two broad group perspectives towards subject choice in the third year, which owed something to social class background. This shows the two groups – boys and girls equally – employing different interpretative models, distinguished by instrumentalism on the one hand, and social and counter-institutional factors on the other. In making their choices of subject the conformist, pro-school pupils employed with some spirit the criteria of job-relatedness, their own ability at the subject, the learning situation, and interest. The 'counter-cultural' pupil, with some diffidence, had a mind to whether the subject was hard work, was examination governed, nasty and horrible, boring, allowed one to be with friends, and to have a certain amount of freedom (Woods 1979). A similar orientation toward subject choice processes has been found in studies of subject choice processes in comprehensive schools (Hurman 1978, Ball 1981), and raises the question whether options have now become the major selection device rather than more explicit organization by streaming. Streaming itself has by no means disappeared, operating in subtle ways within mixed-ability groups, and more obviously in 'banding', as Ball demonstrates.

His mixed comprehensive school practised 'banding', dividing intakes into three broad groups on the basis of ability. The third group, largely remedial and smaller than the others, was not considered a disciplinary problem by staff. The real divide came between bands 1 and 2, and they seem to reflect perfectly the pro- and anti-school cultures of the previous studies. In turn, the teachers construct stereotypes, thus helping to drive the wedge further between the two groups during the first two years at the school. Absenteeism grew in band 2 until it was double that of band 1 by the end of the second year. The band 1 pupils took much more part in school clubs and extra-curricular activities, and took more kindly to homework. Band 2 pupils had lost whatever enthusiasm they had had for school by the second year.

However, the school was also experimenting with mixed-ability classes, and in these, from teacher accounts at least, there seemed a weakening of the anti-school culture. This seems to be mainly because potential recruits were spread out over more forms, the groupings being 'neither large enough nor coherent enough to dominate the ethos of any form' (Ball 1981, p. 252). The teacher, also, has less of a problem to deal with, and more opportunities to deal with it. There were still anti-school pupils, of course, and mixed-ability groups still earned a similar number of detentions. Also, they came to an end in the third year. Most importantly, there were no changes in the teachers' 'organizing notions' of teaching, their support of mixed-ability being for its control implications, rather than any deeper educational significance. It would be reasonable to assume that, in these circumstances, the school counter-culture would reappear in the fourth and fifth years.

The teachers' stereotypical views are matched by pupils' own stereotypical views. Pro-school boys are 'weeds', not 'modern', not 'a laugh'. Other studies have also pointed to inter-pupil categorization as 'swots' or 'dossers' (G. Turner 1983), 'lads or 'ear 'oles' (Willis 1977), 'creeps' or 'thickies' and 'dibbos' (Woods 1979). Ball's pupils tended to keep to their own types, choosing friends within their own bands. As with the previous studies, Ball concludes that the development of the anti-school subculture is a reaction to the problem of school 'failure'. Its nature, also, is the same, showing much disruption of lessons, 'mucking around', disobedience, absconding. There are anti-school and anti-teacher sentiments, and, for the girls, a heavy investment in teenage culture which displaced much school time. Ball shows the personal difficulties a girl can have who wishes to do well at school and also is attracted toward the pop-media culture of fashion, pop music and boyfriends. She may be forced to choose, for a group with affinities for the latter may exclude her because of her orientation towards the former.

Both Ball and myself related our findings to social class, Ball concluding that 'working-class pupils tend to percolate downwards in the processes of academic and behavioural differentiation' (1981, p.108). Taking father's occupation as the indication of social class, Ball found that there was a higher proportion of middle-class pupils in band 1, and that friendship choices, and academic and behavioural attitudes correlated strongly with social class. In general, more of the middle-class pupils improved in academic achievement between second and third years than working-class pupils, while more of the latter deteriorated.

These studies are seeing the culture of a large number of pupils who appear basically opposed to school primarily as an anti- or counter-culture, that is, as a *reaction* to the official culture of the school. In this, they are following the deviance theory of A.K. Cohen (1955), wherein he identified a delinquent subculture, which he saw as a response to status problems associated primarily with the male working-class role. Upward mobility is governed, he argues, by middle-class criteria of status – ambition, self-reliance, deferred gratification, good manners, opposition to physical violence, respect for property. Working-class homes are less likely to produce young people with the ability to do well in terms of these criteria. So such kids come together, united by failure, repudiate these values, and develop their own criteria of status in reaction to the conventional system – a malice towards conformity, short-run hedonism, opposition to authority and so forth. Cohen emphasizes the importance of the group, whose members all experience the same problems and work out a joint solution. Hargreaves's, Lacey's and Ball's studies suggest how groups of pupils, initially predisposed to accept or reject school values by their home backgrounds, may be encouraged both in their rejection of middle-class criteria and in the formation of a counter-cultural response by the organization of the school.

If there is a polarization of pupil cultures fostered by school organization along broadly social class lines, there is another equally distinct polarization along gender lines. Girls and boys are socialized from a very early age and through a variety of agencies into the principles of gender differences, which are reflected in the subjects they study, the informal groups they play or associate with, and in their general interaction.

Complicating this picture of gender culture at the beginning of secondary school is the onset of puberty and the development of sexual differences. At about the age of twelve, it is quite common for there to be a sudden and complete segregation of the sexes, almost on an apartheid scale, in lessons, and in playground (Measor and Woods 1983; see also Ball 1981). Here too, therefore, we have a process of polarization and differentiation. Ball (1981), for example, found two forms typically dividing themselves into single-sex friendship cliques or pairs and one or two social isolates. So firm can the dividing-line become that crossing it constitutes one of the biggest offences with direct implications for one's identity. It also offers teachers one of their most keenly felt punishments – sending a boy 'to sit with one of the girls'. However, the gender divide is not always experienced as such a barrier as that between pro- and anti-school groups. In a detailed study of one form, for example, Ball observed 'a considerable amount of interaction between the [groups] of anti-school boys and anti-school girls ... but only essential and unavoidable contact between these groups and the other boys and girls in the form' (1981, p. 69). The girls approved of these boys. They were 'nice', 'funny', and 'modern'. The pro-school boys were not these things, they were 'weeds'. Also, as adolescence develops, interaction between the sexes ('boy friends' and 'girl friends') becomes an important criterion for status allocation within the informal culture.

Yet even though the informal divide might be repaired, there are serious divisions within the formal area fostered by the school, albeit unconsciously. Research has shown how girls can be discriminated against in the mixed classroom with male teachers, boys getting more of his attention, volunteering more answers, occupying more prime space; girls being largely ignored, and inhibited for fear of being 'laughed at' by the boys (Spender and Sarah 1980). Llewellyn (1980, p.48) also observed how the staff of a school encouraged certain views of femininity. A senior master tried to placate a rebellious pupil in this way:

> 'Just calm down, Sandy; with a temper like yours, my girl,
> you'll be lucky if you get a husband ... and if you do, you won't
> keep him if you treat him the way you do your teachers. Come
> on, calm down, do you really want to end up like your sister? ...
> back home no sooner out of it with two kids and bruises.'

The remonstration is put in the context judged to be most meaningful to the girl. If it does not succeed, the teachers will consider they have failed in one of their aims – to help shape a decent, respectable, home-loving person who will make a good wife and mother. It is not surprising that boys on the whole show higher rates of academic achievement, especially in the later stages of the pupil career.

Where girls do show prowess at schoolwork it tends to be in some subjects rather than others. Physics, chemistry, and technical subjects, for example, are something of a male preserve (HMSO 1977). Science (apart from biology, which has its own characteristics) is something girls do not do well at for two linked reasons. One is their alleged lack of analytical and problem-solving abilities, which these subjects require. It is argued that this stems from differential conditioning in early life. For example, in the home, girls and boys are given different toys to play with, encouraged in different interests and hobbies, and asked to perform different household tasks, all in accord with prevailing images of femininity and masculinity. This comes to be seen as natural, especially when it is reinforced in so many ways – through the media, for example and through the school. At primary school, it has been suggested, for example, that girls on the whole do better than boys because conformity is part of the feminine image, and in any event, it is a feminine world. If boys are more at risk of becoming alienated at this stage, they are actually being trained in independence, initiative and experiment which will serve them well later, especially in subjects like science (Maccoby 1966). Kelly (1976) lists eight main differences between boys and girls at the age of eleven relevant to attitudes to science: girls tend to be more verbal, less independent, more easily discouraged, more conscientious, more interested in people, less interested in science, less experienced in science-related activities and more restricted in their perception of possible future roles than boys. Not surprisingly perhaps, in view of this science is already being set up as a boys' subject from the pictures and pronouns used in primary school textbooks, which show that males predominate in the scientific scene (Leeds Literature Collective 1973; see also Kelly 1981). 'Girls' subjects' are traditionally the 'Arts' such as English, languages, and history; and the practical subjects of home economics, needlecraft, typing and commerce. Though more girls are now taking sciences than ten years ago, they are not doing so in relation to boys. The gap is still wide along the basic science/arts division and among vocational subjects and indeed in some areas, like languages, appears to be widening. Also, the higher achievement of boys the further along the educational career we go is still considerable (HMSO 1977).

Thus a school can foster two major polarizations in pupil culture, broadly along the lines of social class and gender. In the next section I consider how these two factors predispose pupils towards certain cultures, and how they relate together.

Social class and gender

We saw above how some studies of pro- and anti-school cultures drew on the 'reactive' theory of A.K. Cohen. The anti-school culture, it was argued, was reacting against the (middle-class) value system of the school. An alternative view celebrates the value system of the anti-school culture as a *product* of lower-class culture, and not as a reactive, delinquent subculture. Miller (1958) identified certain focal concerns of lower-class culture – trouble, toughness, being smart (quick-witted), excitement, fate and autonomy. Personal status would often be gauged, he argued, along these dimensions, toughness being highly valued, but also a certain amount of law-violating behaviour.

Support for this theory in relation to British schools comes from the study by Paul Willis (1977) of a group of 'lads' in a northern comprehensive school. Why, he wondered, do working-class kids choose working-class jobs? The answer, he argues, lies in their class culture. This not only operates as an external influence, through, say, families, but is actually re-created, produced and transformed by the lads in response to the school situation, which has similarities to the work situation. Willis argues:

> They exercise their abilities and seek enjoyment in activity, even where most controlled by others. Paradoxically, they thread through the dead experience of work a living culture which is far from a simple reflex of defeat. This is the same fundamental taking hold of an alienating situation that one finds in counter-school culture and its attempt to weave a tapestry of interest and diversion through the dry institutional text. These cultures are not simply layers of padding between human beings and unpleasantness. They are appropriations in their own right, exercises of skill, motions, activities applied towards particular ends (1977, p. 52).

The school counter-culture, therefore, has similarities to shop-floor culture – opposition to authority, rejection of the conformist, informality, a high degree of sexism and racism, a delight in being with one's mates, having a laugh, 'dossing' and 'blagging'. There is much violence and aggression – the means of expressing a number of important cultural values like 'masculine hubris, dramatic display, the solidarity of the group' (ibid., p. 33). But there are also many 'kiddings' and 'pisstakes'.The lads have great fun (in so doing presenting teachers and others in authority with great problems – which is all part of the fun) and far from feeling envious of the conformist 'ear 'oles', feel definitely superior to them. Their way is the only way to live. By this analysis, school organization, though it may be important, indeed decisive for some pupils, is a lesser factor for others. Moreover, the counter-culture is not simply a reaction to official policy to be defined in terms of negative, oppositional elements. It represents a way of life in its own right.

In rather similar vein, Corrigan (1979) points to the inevitable conflict induced by an unequal power situation:

> 'carrying on in class' represents the ability of the boys to continue their normal way of life despite the occupying army of the teachers and the power of the school, *as well as* their ability to attack the teachers on the boys' own terms (p. 58).

If the 'Smash Street Kids' reject the school, it is not in reaction to the school, but because of its irrelevance to them. In Corrigan's view their own class culture derives from completely different material conditions of existence, and the scenario is seen as one of 'struggle', with the repressive power of the state and its compulsory school attendance laws on one side, and the Smash Street Kids valiantly acting out the terms of their own class cultures on the other.

These working-class male groups are strongly sexist. Willis's 'lads' show the concern for machismo – toughness and hardness, traditionally associated in the working class with being male. They have superior attitudes to women. Girls are sex objects, the number of conquests a lad has had being one of the leading criteria in the informal status hierarchy. Yet sex, curiously, diminishes girls in the lads' eyes, and the 'easy lay', though sought after, is not respected. Not so the regular girlfriend, the 'missus', who is esteemed in the same way as mother. But she is still inferior, being a 'bit thick, like', and existing really to service the males, with cooking and housework.

This raises the question of whether pupil cultures are primarily male cultures, girls simply 'falling in' with the patterns of behaviour established and maintained by the boys, or whether the apparent comparative shortage of specifically female cultures in school is simply an artefact of the research that has been done, primarily by male researchers (McRobbie 1980). We know the attitude of Willis's lads towards girls, but we do not know the girls' attitudes toward them. The chances are that they will be subordinate, for girls are exposed to a general culture of femininity which fosters passivity and subservience. This stems from the sexual division of labour, which places the men in mainline occupations, and the women in 'servicing' and child-rearing roles in the home and casual support labour. This encourages girls to believe that marriage is the most important event in life for them, that they will need to 'find a man', and make themselves sexually attractive to them. They are also subject to highly idealized and romantic notions of love, marriage and parenthood. Competence for a girl, therefore, may consist in part of how well she projects this image. Hence the pre-occupation among teenage girls with make-up, jewellery, perfume and fashion (Sharpe 1976, Deem 1978).

These concerns are reflected in 'teenage' or 'pop' culture, to which girls in particular become very attached. McRobbie and Garber (1976) argue that the so-called Teeny Bopper culture of the 1970s was popular among ten to fifteen-year-old girls because it could be easily accommodated in the home (the 'female's preserve'); with record player and friends, was open to everybody and did not distinguish among them in the invidious ways that school did. There was no risk of humiliation, and the obsession with pop stars offered a 'defensive solidarity'. It enabled girls in a sense to 'negotiate a space of their own', but the culture is still replete with fantasy elements emanating from the romanticism of the traditional feminine role, which casts them in a subordinate position.

The pop culture spans pro- and anti-school orientations according to Ball's research (see also Meyenn 1980), where he found that the 'pop-media culture, especially in terms of clothes, hair-styles, shoes, pop-group allegiance, knowledge of dances, etc. was important for all the girls in [one form] irrespective of their attitude to school' (1981, p. 66). By the third year, the 'adolescent culture' was in full swing. Home-centredness decreased, and involvement in unsupervised activities with friends increased. There were concerts, discos, records, boyfriends, girlfriends. They went out to visit friends, to the cinema, cafés, pubs, parties, or just to hang about in the street. However, this outgoingness is partly sponsored by the search for males, and having found one, the 'home-centred' orientation will focus on him (McRobbie 1980).The values associated with this culture contrasted with those supported by the school. Whereas the school sponsors work/ production, preparing for the future, mind/intellect and self control, the pop-media culture purveys values of play/consumption, living in the present, body and emotion/feeling, and physical and emotional expression.

Quite apart from this general cultural clash, Vulliamy (1979) has noticed a clash of musical values: 'The classical tradition in music is a notated one, whilst the Afro-American tradition in music, the major influence on most brands of contemporary pop, is an oral-aural one' (p. 121). The prevailing tradition in schools, however, is that the sponsored forms of 'serious' music represent a higher form of culture (in the other sense) to which we should all aspire.

Ball found all kinds of pupils contributing to adolescent culture, but the anti-school pupils most, progressively so in the fourth and fifth years. Thus band 1 girls were certainly concerned with fashion and pop music, but none the less their appearance differed from bands 2 and 3 girls. The latter were more extreme – 'colours brighter, heels higher'. Many wore badges and favours for their favourite groups. Also personal investment differed, for school work occupied quite a large part of band 1 pupils' spare time in the form of homework and revision (Ball 1981, pp. 113–14). However, for all of them, it was an important criterion of status. Even the most conformist pupils looked to their peers, as well as to adults, for approval. If they did not, and just worked and conformed without question, they were not popular. But if they achieved highly *and* rated highly on the pop-media scale – with fashion, pop and boyfriends – they could be very popular.

The difference between anti- and pro-school girls was mainly that, for the former, teenage culture offered an entirely alternative value and status system to the school, with an emphasis on freedom and social sophistication. For the pro-school pupils, the fourth and fifth years brought closer relationships with the staff, more participation in extra-curricular activities, as well as continued identification with adolescent culture. Though judged highly by teachers, they were held in low esteem by the anti-school pupils, now of course applying the teenage values exclusively. Despite, therefore, a common identification with teenage culture, the two groups were driven progressively further apart.

Similarly, Llewellyn (1980) noticed a polarization of views on feminine propriety between top stream and non-examination stream girls in a secondary modern school. The top stream girls saw the non-examination ones as 'thick' and 'daft':

> 'You wouldn't catch us clomping round the place like them.'
> 'Ee – you hear the language on 'em.'
> 'Eh-up, the way they stick together it ain't natural, yelling at lads across park.'

To the non-examination girls, the top stream were 'snotty' and 'keenos':

> 'Exams won't get them nowhere, they'll be out with their prams next year – if anyone'll have 'em.'
> 'You seen the way they dress? – wouldn't be seen dead like that.'
> 'Taint never seen them with a lad.'
> (Llewellyn, 1980, p. 46.)

This is similar antipathy in some respects to that observed by D.H. Hargreaves (1967) between top and lower stream boys in a secondary modern school. But the girls are guided mostly by the code of femininity as they see it, the former emphasizing qualities of ladylike behaviour, the latter mocking the former's orientation to work (in the same way as Willis's lads did of the 'ear 'oles') and appearance.

The girls who do show devotion to school work may not do so for the same reason as boys. King (1971) suggested a class/sex model of pupil attitudes which distinguished between education's symbolic value (prestige, culture, knowledge) and its instrumental value (skills, qualifications, preparation for job). He argued that middle-class boys valued education for both reasons, middle-class girls only for its symbolic value, and working-class boys only for its instrumental value; while working-class girls valued it for neither. Where girls do show an instrumental approach, there is a distinct leaning toward those occupations that accord with the feminine image. Girls will aim to be nurses rather than doctors, air stewardesses rather than pilots, secretaries rather than business executives, college and polytechnic trained teachers, rather than university trained (Sharpe 1976, Byrne 1978).

Personal interests

To leave matters here would suggest a picture of cultural determinism. But individuals do not slavishly follow subcultural norms, nor imprint masculinity or femininity upon themselves without reflection. They do have choices. Some have more than others, certainly, but even the lowliest in terms of status and life-chances (black, working-class and female) has a degree of choice. Not all working-class boys by any means behave like the 'Smash Street Kids'. Not all girls aspire mainly toward mother-hood and the kitchen sink. How, then, can we accommodate personal interests, without losing sight of the influence of the other powerful factors?

A start on this was made with a refinement of the so-called adaptational model of pupil cultures. This derives from the work of Merton (1957), who proposed five major modes of adaptation to the social order based on combinations of acceptance and rejection of official goals and means. These ranged from conformity (acceptance of both), through innovation (acceptance of goals, rejection of means), ritualism (rejection of goals, acceptance of means), retreatism (rejection of both), to rebellion (rejection of both, but with replacement). Now there is nothing interactionist about this, for it is a formal typology constructed on functionalist principles. But it was given an interactionist twist by Wakeford (1969), when extending it as a result of his observations and work in a public boarding school. Working with a reformulation of the model by Harary (1966) which had introduced 'indifference' and 'ambivalence' as possible reactions as well as acceptance and rejection (with or without replacement), and using some insights of Goffman's (1961), he produced an extended version, which included the important mode of 'colonization' (indifferent to goals, ambivalent toward means). The colonizer 'accepts that the school is to provide his basic social environment during term-time for five years and attempts to establish a relatively contented existence within it by maximizing what he perceives as the available gratifications, whether they are officially permitted or proscribed' (Wakeford 1969, p. 139). In other words, he 'works the system', using both legitimate and illegitimate means to achieve his ends. He may make 'secondary adjustments' (Goffman 1961), that is standing apart from the role prescribed by the school and 'making out' or 'getting by'. There are indications that this is the most popular mode of adaptation among pupils in the state system, and indeed that it is encouraged by staff where intransigence or rebellion are, grimly, the only alternatives (Reynolds 1976a, Woods 1979). Figures 1 and 2 represent summaries of the adaptational model.

For the interactionist, the adaptation model is useful when linked to personal goals and means of both pupils and teachers. This allows for wide variation from situation to situation, teacher to teacher, time to time. Pupils may shade in and out of certain modes depending on such factors, but inasmuch as all schools show unified policies to some degree or other, pupils will show a major orientation over a particular period of time. This may change several times during a pupil's career. He may, for example, start out highly conformist, become ritualistic, turn to colonization and ultimately rebel.

There are also degrees of adaptation. We might say that a very positive identification with goals and means will yield an 'ingratiation' mode, well recognized among pupils as 'creeping'. There are different forms of conformity, depending on the pupil's intentions. For example, they can be based on an all-embracing but ill-defined optimism at one extreme, or a coldly rational instrumentalism at the other. The former might be more typical of early days in the school, the latter of more senior years especially if involved with examinations (Woods 1979).

The adaptation model, then, has considerable possibilities, if closely associated with pupils' real life-worlds. One thing it does enable us to do is to identify various modes of behaviour within the broad pro- and anti-school cultures of Hargreaves and Lacey. Not all working-class boys 'rebel' in the style of Willis's lads. No doubt some are intransigent, but equally many will be practising ritualism, colonizing and even conforming. This would have implications for Willis's theory about the connection between the lads' culture and social class. Equally, however, it is necessary to consider approaches such as those of Willis and Ball with the adaptational model to inform it with a wider perspective on matters such as school organization and social class.

However, some interactionists have criticized both these

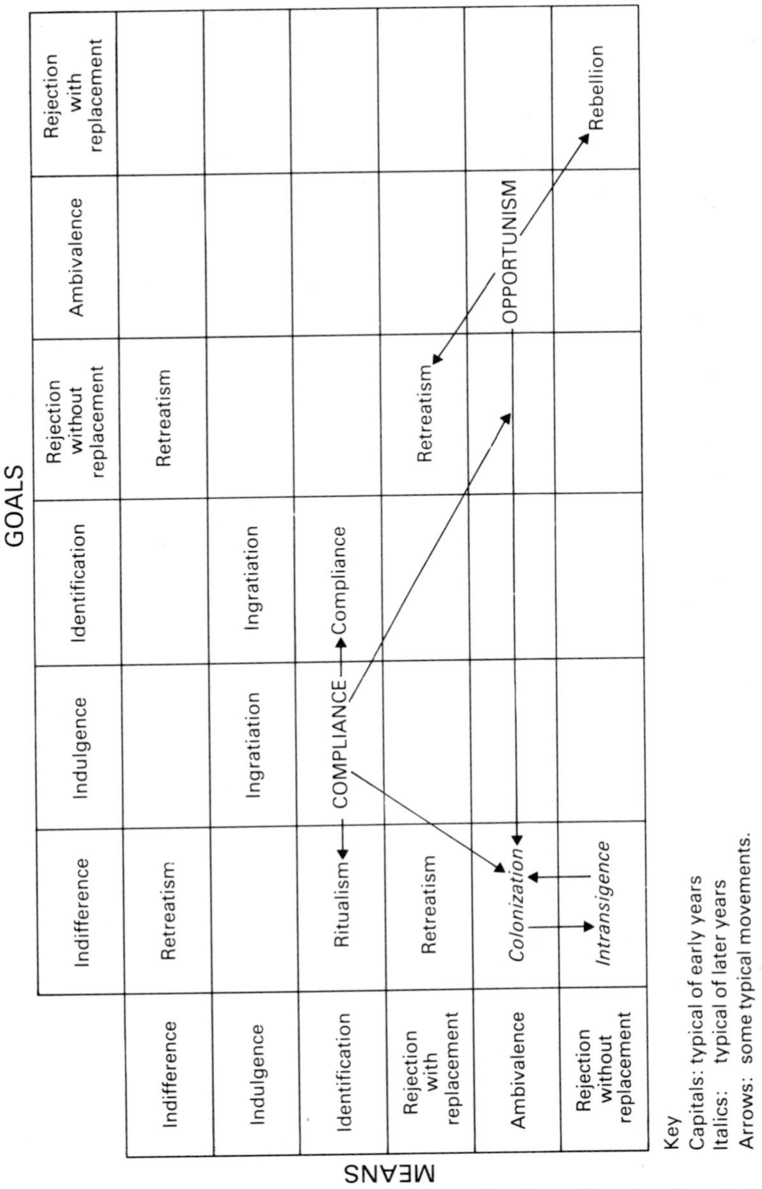

Figure 1   Revised typology of modes of adaptation in the state secondary system

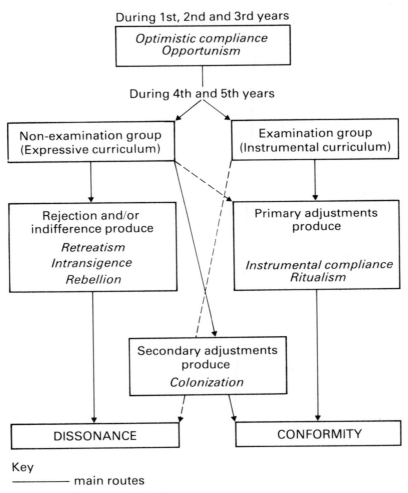

During 1st, 2nd and 3rd years

Optimistic compliance
Opportunism

During 4th and 5th years

Non-examination group
(Expressive curriculum)

Examination group
(Instrumental curriculum)

Rejection and/or
indifference produce

Retreatism
Intransigence
Rebellion

Primary adjustments
produce

Instrumental compliance
Ritualism

Secondary adjustments
produce
Colonization

DISSONANCE

CONFORMITY

Key
———— main routes
– – – – – lesser tendencies
Italics: modes of adaptation

Figure 2   Incidence of dominant modes of adaptation in a secondary modern school

92

approaches for making too many assumptions about pupils' experience. Furlong (1976), for example, saw no evidence in the London comprehensive school of his research of pro- and anti-school cultures or indeed of any consistent pupil grouping, and was more taken with transient arrangements which depended perhaps on time of day or who was present. Furlong has termed these 'interaction sets' and argues that they represent a more realistic portrayal of pupil life. For there is, he claims, no consistent pupil culture as such, and it is the individual who constructs his or her own action, not the group that dictates it. The key point is that it is the individual who defines the situation. When several agree on a definition and can communicate this agreement among them, we can talk meaningfully of a group or 'set', but 'the fact that different pupils take part in interaction sets at different times simply illustrates the point that they do not always agree about what they know. Teachers, subjects and methods of teaching mean different things to different pupils' (Furlong 1976, p. 169). Furlong illustrates by showing the great variety that exists within a single lesson as pupils move in and out of a number of interaction sets, defined not by cultural norms, but by common understandings.

Furlong in turn has been criticized for not tackling the reasons for a pupil's variable motives, and not relating pupils' perspectives either to their goals or values, or the structure of the school (Hammersley and Turner 1980). Their approach emphasizes the need, as Furlong did, to take into account pupil intentions and definitions. Once this is done, we can see that a pupil is faced with a range of options. Many factors govern the individual's choice, including possibly shifting goals and the impact of different contexts. The resultant picture is one not of consistent 'conformity' or 'deviance', but of variable behaviour. If we consider, for example, the range of factors involved in the definition of the situation, as discussed in chapter 2, and how an individual actively constructs a situation, we gain an idea of the complexities involved and the many nuances that might attach to an individual's outlook at any one time.

G. Turner (1983) illustrates some of the different and contradictory pressures operating on pupils. One pupil, for example, while conformity was his ideal in terms of his major expressed aim, did not feel that the school provided him with the appropriate resources (i.e. a good teacher) to achieve that aim. This affected his attitude and led to occasional non-conformity. In other words, his conformity was conditional on the school meeting his own instrumental aim. Another pressure also promotes this, that is the peer culture, which has certain norms for appropriate work-loads. The majority of pupils are unwilling to offend these norms for fear of being seen as a 'swot' or 'creep' or 'teacher's pet'. It is important for their identities that they be seen as one of the crowd, that is the group with which they are affiliated. Turner's pupil resolved the dilemma by exhibiting both forms of behaviour in the lesson – conformist, and non-conformist. But there are even more incidental pressures, such as which people are actually present (constituting which 'interaction sets'), which rule-frames are operating, time, mood and so forth, which call for ongoing decision-making. As Turner says: 'Pupils are constantly deciding whether to work, participate in disruption, chat to a friend and so on. Their assessment of their interests changes to some degree according to circumstance, just as the availability, or at least, ease with which different options can be taken up changes' (1983, p. 13).

The occasional triumph of personal interests against heavy odds is well illustrated by a group of aspiring black girls in a London comprehensive school (Fuller 1980). As blacks, and as females, they were doubly subordinate, but they themselves were very aware of this, and strongly refused to accept the academic and career implications. They were determined, by contrast, to do well in these spheres. They had a strong sense of their own worth, which they considered under-valued by others in comparison to boys. However, while strong academically, their behaviour in class was not a model of propriety. Fuller argues that their behaviour was linked to their positive identity with being black and female. They thus conformed to the behavioural norms of their peer group sufficient to retain their friendship without sacrificing their own academic aims. In charting this somewhat unusual course, they had come to rely on their own judgments and evaluations of themselves, rather than on those of others, including teachers. Lambart (1976) noticed a similar phenomenon among a group of white third-year pupils in a girls' grammar school. The 'Sisterhood' was characterized by above average attainment, but a great deal of mischievous behaviour. The group cut across the school's form structure and social class background, and seemed united by their common adaptation to the problems presented by being academically achieving females.

These studies, while demonstrating the power of the culture of femininity, are a useful corrective to any sense of 'cultural determinism' we may receive from some other sources. Some cultures are very influential, but in the last resort, individuals construct their own realities. In doing so, they often find considerable scope for manoeuvre. This active role is stressed by

Prendergast and Proust (1980), who interviewed some fifteen-year-old girls on their conceptions of motherhood. Their answers were much more detailed and less normative than anticipated. In fact, the girls held a great deal of what the authors term 'illegitimate' knowledge, since 'it calls into question the core definitions of female identity and female roles'. The existence of both this and the normative stereotype presented a problem for the girls, which they resolved by repressing their illegitimate knowledge and finding 'ways out' in which they constructed their own personal futures. The point is that the prevailing model is not just taken over, but adapted personally by the girls, who had a certain amount of 'illegitimate' knowledge as a private resource. The authors argue that this knowledge must be legitimated by educators if alternatives to the prevailing stereotype are to become socially available.

This focus on pupil interests is a necessary complement to the subcultural and adaptational models. For at their level of generality, they are in danger of neglecting the range of interests and options confronting pupils and the processual nature of their decision-making. On the other hand, the fact that for pupils as well as for teachers, many definitions are probably 'habitual' rather than 'uniquely personal' (Stebbins 1975, see chapter 2) means that there would be consistencies which permit the wider generalization. The interactionist concern is that these generalizations should be adequately underpinned by detailed consideration of pupil views, options and judgments.

All these models, therefore, are relevant. Class, gender and racial differences are general, and deep-seated, and will have broad effects. But these no doubt differ between regions, schools and individual pupils. In other words, their effects will be mediated differently through different regions, schools, teachers and pupils. It is these different effects the interactionist attempts to chart, but they should not be allowed to blur the wider forces. The institution's influence is seen in the rigid streaming of the 1950s and 1960s with the polarization that Hargreaves and Lacey discovered. Comprehensivization and mixed ability teaching has obscured some of it to some degree, though not entirely. The divisions are still there, but interwoven with the fabric of school life in more subtle ways – for example, through the options' system, banding and setting. This brings the variability of pupil cultures to the fore. One possible combination of these approaches is given in Ball's reworking of the Lacey-Hargreaves pro- and anti-school culture model. He proposes a fourfold classification, based on different forms of pupil commitment. On the pro-school side, he suggests there are those who are supportive of the formal system, and those who are manipulative, concerned to use the school for their own ends. The difference is between a moral and an instrumental form of commitment. John, the student quoted from Turner, is an example of the latter. They are instrumental conformists who colonize areas of the school in varying degrees. Among the anti-school group there are those who are 'rejecting' ('rebels' or 'intransigents'). But while these modes of adaptation may be applied to either groups or individuals, they will not account neatly for every pupil. Hence the need to establish a pupil's interest and intentions in their full range and variability, as a matter of priority.

Some common themes in pupil cultures

Despite the variability in pupil cultures and individuals' adaptations to them, it is possible to detect some common themes running through them which bear a remarkable resemblance to the themes Hargreaves (1980) detected in teacher culture – status, competence and relationships. It clearly says something about human association in society generally, for pupils also put a premium on these three elements.

We have seen in chapter 3 their insistence that teachers should be 'human', and we shall see in chapter 6 that 'work' is defined largely in terms of relationships. But there can be little doubt that what matters most to pupils here is friendships amongst themselves. Friendship groups form the structural basis of the child's extra-curricular life from a very early stage. Without friends, one is outside the pale of society. Friends help you get through some awkward moments and transitions (Measor and Woods 1983, Davies 1980b) and there are several of these in a pupil's career. The anxiety, for example, induced by a change of schools has been well documented (Bryan 1980, Galton and Delamont 1980, Measor and Woods 1983), as has the importance of friends in allaying it. Indeed, in several instances, the anxiety was induced by the threat to existing friendships, to be reduced when the threat was not realized, *or* when new friends were made. Friends are thus a prime consideration in decisions a pupil has to make, and to some, they are the very first priority throughout school and in choosing an occupation (Willis 1977). At Lowfield (Woods 1979), there were several expressions of 'being with your mates' as the best part of school. Among the girls in the middle school of Meyenn's (1980) research, the opportunity to meet and make friends was 'the best thing about school', and the 'group' was of vital importance. Pupil friendship therefore rests upon the functions it serves, rather than upon the adult notion of ties formed through love and affection. One may very well, in consequence, take the precaution of having 'contingency friends', in case the first team are unavailable (Davies 1980b).

Children develop rules of friendship just as they develop rules for assessing teachers. Davies, in her study of some Australian primary school pupils, showed that to them a friend was someone who was sensible and loyal, who knew how to cooperate and who would share their world with you. Non-friends would use you for self-elevation by putting you down. They would not cooperate with you over maintaining the world as a sensible place, and were not dependable. A friend is a helpmate who is nearly always with you, who accepts and fosters the relationship on an equal basis, who provides against a basic feeling of insecurity, who understands you and does not expect too much from you. Frowned-upon behaviours include showing-off ('posing'), since that aims to elevate the individual above the bonds of friendships; 'teasing' and so forth, which can aggravate any feeling of insecurity, and being 'stupid' which threatens the whole rule-based nature of pupil interaction.

To these rules, older pupils would want to add another – no 'splitting', 'grassing' or 'welching' on one's mates. Some teachers might encourage this and feel it morally sound in their desire to get at the truth, but if they do, they misunderstand the pupil code of honour. It is one of the very worst offences. So grievous is it, that a 'grass' is seen as having a fatal flaw in his personality (Willis 1977, pp. 24–5).

Fighting can be a form of posing or teasing among the boys. A boy can be seen as indulging in fisticuffs to win admirers. If you are weak in a fight, you will be teased. But all of these techniques – contingency friends, teasing, fighting – do not signal the end of friendships. They are, rather, strategic moves within friendship, checks and balances to restore the proper order. A group of Davies's boys had three or four fights among themselves every year, but always came back together. So did Meyenn's (1980) and Woods's (1979) girls. Much pupil attitude toward friendship, including their apparent fickleness, and occasional violence toward each other, can be explained by recognizing the functionality of friendship.

There are various indications of pupils' concern with status. Much school work from a very early age involves competition and comparison with others, and both teachers and pupils come to a sense of their worth *vis-à-vis* the rest of the group. Reputations are cultivated, made, confirmed, sometimes pre-ordained, and jealously guarded. To be 'top of the class', 'best at football', or to possess some other great skill at perhaps art, music or drama, will give kudos among pupils who conform to the school's value system. Some pupils will work hard, not for intrinsic satisfaction, but to improve their performance rating against their fellows – for position rather than performance. As one high-achieving thirteen-year-old boy told me, 'I would like to work for the fun of it, but they [his friends] won't let you. If they beat you, they tease you, they go "ha! ha! ha! I beat you!" and you do the same to them. I would rather get 49% and come top than we all get 90%.... You get a reputation which you have to try to keep up, and sometimes that's very hard.'

Examinations are still conducted on a competitive basis, and the sight of a pupil shielding work from a neighbour to prevent copying is still not unusual. The starker manifestations of this, such as lining pupils up in order of merit on prize days, may not be so evident now as formerly. But rivalry remains basic to our educational forms, despite so-called 'progressive' experiments purportedly involving more cooperation which seem to alter appearances rather than realities (Sharp and Green 1975, Denscombe 1980b, Ball 1981).

This sense of status applies within classes, or more particularly within friendship groups in a certain class. Individuals compare themselves with and rate themselves against other individuals. Groups also compare themselves with other groups – high achievers with low achievers within forms, higher with lower streams across year groups, boys against girls, 'O' level candidates with CSE candidates, and so on. But there will be different status systems in operation. Only academically-oriented pupils will value high achievement. In Hargreaves's secondary modern school, for example, the 4D boys considered the 4A boys 'a load of soft nigs ... a load of sisis ... bigheads they think they know everything' (Hargreaves 1967, p.70; see also Willis 1977). While the 4A boys felt 4D were '... thick, most of them ... the rough type, a bad type ... not willing to learn anything ... bullies and think they're tough' (Hargreaves 1967). Each judged the other in terms of their own norms, developed within their own stream. For the anti-school group, the chief element in the winning and attribution of status was not school work but ability at fighting. The group was dominated by Clint who, since he was the best fighter, was 'cock of the school'. At Lumley, the boys became conscious of a pecking order based on fighting ability in the fourth year. Clint's claims to eminence were based on a number of incidents, such as beating up a prefect, the lack of challenge from anyone else in his own year, and finally displaying himself quite systematically as hard and tough (D.H. Hargreaves 1967, pp.122–3).

Changes in the pecking order could occur if a fight was offered a higher by a lower light and refused, whereupon they changed places in the order, or if a fight took place, when the winner gained the higher rank. Second to Clint was Don, who might have beaten Clint according to some of his colleagues, but preferred to remain popular among them rather than risk losing that popularity by becoming 'cock' and thus building power over them. Clint had become unpopular – he was too big-headed, too much of a bully.

Though this was a particular group within one school, there are signs that fighting ability is a more general criterion of status among boys (Measor and Woods 1982). Another indicator is prowess among girls, judged by taking out either a large number of girls or a small number of very attractive girls, and from successful sexual expeditions (see also Willis 1977, Grundsell 1980). Teacher-baiting is also high on the list, as is the ability to withstand official punishment with fortitude. If one 'cries', or performs badly at such tests of endurance as cross-country running, one loses status. These last two examples illustrate how the informal culture of pupil interaction among themselves can interlink with the demands of the formal cultures, though the perceptions of aims and outcomes may be completely different.

For all pupils, however, status accrues to seniority. The higher status of older pupils is symbolized by their position at the back of the school bus, or the back of assembly, by the deference of younger pupils, and by the staff, who treat children in more adult fashion as they grow older and pass through a school. Especially in secondary schools, and particularly in sixth forms, senior pupils, in the eyes of junior, can occupy a similar status position to that of the teachers, or of other adults.

One indication of the importance of the seniority principle is the anxiety about losing status that they experience when transferring from junior or middle school to secondary or upper (Bryan 1980). Coupled with this is the fear of being 'picked on' and bullied in the jungle of secondary school. This is one of the main factors behind the telling and re-telling of the pupil myths that attend the transfer between middle and upper school. Pupils do not, in fact, get their heads flushed down the loo on their birthdays, nor hit by sports masters with corner flags. But such myths carry an underlying message of the qualities – in this case hardness and toughness – required in the new environment. If you survive to 'tell the tale', you relay the myths on to the new intake in celebration of your achievement. But part of the celebration is to do with 'codes of masculine hardness and age grade hierarchies'. It is the older, second- or third-year pupils who are identified by the myths as the threat, as the purveyors of hardness and toughness. This itself constitutes an excellent reason for the first-year boys to relay the myths to the incoming recruits, for it gives a substantial buttress to their *own* claims for toughness, and for an automatically elevated place up the ladder of the informal status hierarchy (Measor and Woods 1983).

As far as 'competence' goes, boys and girls are in the process of carving out acceptable identities for themselves. It is of prime importance that they themselves feel, and think that others also feel, that they are growing up as proper persons. Definitions of propriety will vary according to different value systems. We have already seen how crucially important gender identities are, and how among some groups, like Willis's lads, membership of the group is the highest accolade. At a very primary level, children seem to hold an ideal-type model of physical and mental normality, which allows for few blemishes.

The drive for recognition of competence is manifested in many ways, but in none more clearly than pupil humour. Several aspects of adolescent humour adults may find difficult to stomach – its arrant sexism and racism, the way fun is made of handicap and human misery, indeed any kind of abnormality. Through all of this, adolescents are establishing identities as male or female, white or black, and so on; and they are doing so at a time when their moral development is also undergoing change. In due course, their cognitive development and successful establishment of their own identities will bring a keener appreciation of other's realities and points of view. But for the moment, at age twelve, thirteen or fourteen, these things are not as important as 'old fogies' seem to think. Thus the young secondary schoolboy may be taunted if he shows signs of weakness, like wearing a big coat on cold days or crying when hit, with 'you're a woman!' Nothing more clearly demarcates the boundaries of the sex-role than the sharp edge of humour. The same is true of race. Racism is not a simple matter of consciousness. It is endemic in some cultures, and one of its expressions is to be found in pupil humour, which, for white English pupils, for example, makes fun of Irishmen, Jews, Scotsmen, West Indians and Asians. In some respects racist jokes are no different from 'deformity' jokes, and they arise from the great desire of the adolescent to be 'like everybody else'. Large noses, big teeth, bald heads, funny voices, mannerisms, stutters, and so on, are all mercilessly parodied and ridiculed. For the adolescent, perfection (judged by criteria evolved by one's chosen peer group) is the aim, and still seen to be within reach. Poking fun at others increases one's own self-esteem, one's own valuation, as well as sense, of one's self. 'Sick' humour, also, which at one extreme can delight in anyone, including one's own friends, suffering a misfortune, like getting hit or shown up by a teacher, and at the other can revel in the blood they witnessed in a car accident, is partly a release of their own aggressive instincts, and partly a celebration of new-forming selves. Moron jokes ('thickies' and 'dibbos' are popular targets for ridicule) are an expression also of problems caused by the expansion of knowledge horizons and the acquisition of new and more complex skills.

Summary

Hargreaves's and Lacey's pioneering work on pupil cultures in the 1960s led them to conclude that there were two broad groups, one pro-school and one anti-school, which developed through the processes of polarization and differentiation, aided by school organization. The groups showed a relationship with social class. Lest we think this division a product of an outmoded system, which, among other things, practised streaming, it has been generally supported by several recent studies. Ball, for example, found the very same process at work in a banded comprehensive school in the late 1970s. School organization and official attitudes also contribute to a gender division within the school. In mixed schools there are signs of, often unconscious, discrimination against girls, even though a school may be aware of the general problem of sexual inequalities. Early socialization into the principles of gender differences are reflected in different dispositions toward school, and the taking up of different subjects for study.

An alternative view to Hargreaves's and Lacey's 'reaction' theory about anti-school culture is that it is a product of lower class cultural forms. Paul Willis argues that the values, beliefs and behaviour of the 'lads' in his research were closely associated with cultural forms developed over the years by their forebears on the shop-floor. The gender division also has its roots in society. Boys and girls, subject to the enormous socializing influence of the home, the media and the school and the weight of tradition, come to assume the properties of masculinity and femininity. For the boys this consists of hardness, toughness, a superior and dominant attitude towards girls, and a work-centred orientation. For girls it involves passivity, subservience, romanticism, making themselves attractive sex objects, and adopting basically home-centred views. Girls in particular are drawn toward the 'teenage' or 'pop' culture which reinforces these values but which also stands in opposition to school ethos. This provides anti-school pupils with an alternative status channel, leading to increasing segregation from pro-school pupils. The latter are also drawn to teenage culture in some respects, though not to the same degree, and come increasingly to identify with school values as they proceed through the school. These gender perspectives are mediated through social class.

An alternative approach to concentrating on cultural norms, to which individuals might conform to some degree or other, is to examine behaviour in relation to pupils' reaction to school goals and means. Work here led to the formulation of a typology of pupil adaptations which ranged from ingratiating conformity to outright rebellion. As with the 'cultural reaction' approach, this was felt by some to attribute too much weight to external goals, and not enough to other elements in the definition of the situation, especially a pupil's own personal interests.

Furlong tried to accommodate this more adequately in his notion of 'interaction sets', though others have argued that for pupils in their research, the peer group was of prime importance. An individual pupil might vary his reaction to school in accordance with the personal aims and his estimation of the school's ability to meet them, and other studies have shown how some disadvantaged pupils draw on their personal resources to negotiate their school career lines.

Finally, I examined three common themes among pupil cultures, that also reflect concerns prominent in teacher culture – relationships, status and competence. Friendships are governed by clear rules. For some, 'being with your mates' is the main attraction of school, and the main criterion for evaluating work. Friends are essential for everyday life, but especially for negotiating difficult changes like a move between schools. Pupils construct informal status hierarchies. For pro-school pupils, status will be evaluated by academic and athletic achievement. For anti-school pupils, among boys, largely by fighting ability. Pupils are also greatly concerned to project a competent identity through their particular conceptions of normality. Gender identities are strongly to the fore, as are racial and personal characteristics, and others germane to one's background. A common expression of the search for personal competence and adequacy is through humour.

We have considered different, and sometimes opposing subcultures among teachers and pupils. What happens when teacher and pupil cultures meet? It will vary, of course, depending on which sub-varieties come together, and depending on level of understanding. Teachers can interpret non-conformity as conformity (Dumont and Wax 1971) and pupils' conformity to their own cultural problems as deliberate non-conformity to the school's (Woods 1979). Teacher groups of a 'radical' or 'Marxist' persuasion would probably get on famously with Willis's lads; 'conservatives' would not. The cultural ambience of some subjects (such as art) is more conducive to a spirit of togetherness among teacher and pupils than others (such as science). Younger teachers, in general, appreciate pupil culture, especially teenage culture, more than older ones. Yet the possibility remains that the greatest cultural divide in the school in general terms is not between top and bottom streams, nor middle and working classes, nor boys and girls, but between teachers and pupils. Waller (1932) argued that 'the greatest chasm is that which separates young persons and old' (p. 106). If this is the case, we must expect to find a multiplicity of conflicting aims within the school between teachers and pupils, and a great deal of strategical action as they go about trying to secure their different objectives. This is the subject of the following chapter.

Chapter 6

Teacher and pupil strategies

So far I have considered how teachers and pupils define the situation, what views they have of the task and each other, and the cultural groups that have been identified among them. What do teachers and pupils actually do? What is the product of these perspectives and influences? The interactionist sees it as a form of adaptation in which the individual weighs one prospect against another in the light of the situation and resources available, and makes a series of decisions to achieve a modicum of ends (Berlak *et al.* 1976). In the course of such activity, the ends themselves may be changed. Teachers and pupils therefore are constantly laying strategies, sub-strategies and counter-strategies.

Teacher strategies

Interesting facts have come from systematic observation of teachers. Thus Flanders (1970) discovered in American schools what came to be known as the 'two-thirds' rule – two-thirds of classroom time is spent in talking, and two-thirds of that is done by the teacher. Other studies, Delamont (1976) suggests, point to 50 per cent of the teacher's talk being 'spent in the narrowest sense: lecturing and questioning pupils about what she perceives as the academic content of the lesson' (p. 98) – the 'recitation' method. The other half is spent on establishing and maintaining the conditions for teaching, i.e. control.

But what is the nature of teacher talk? What intentions does it carry, and how does it react to circumstances? From an interactionist viewpoint, a great deal of teaching involves persuading the pupil to adopt the teacher's perspective: 'The pupil has to step into the teacher's system of meanings, which either confirms or extends or even replaces his own' (Edwards and Furlong 1978, p. 121). Edwards and Furlong (1978) show, from a close analysis of a number of transcripts of lessons, how teachers typically work for this. It is not sufficient that facts be known, but that they be understood; that is to say that pupils should be able to place them within the relevant framework of meanings. Teachers typically work for this by question and answer, guiding the pupils towards the appropriate context, rejecting wrong or inappropriate answers, or those that come in the wrong place in the framework. Pupil contributions are retained in their original form, though they may have undergone a transformation of meaning. The teacher outlines what he wants pupils to do, he selectively listens, evaluates and recapitulates.

Hammersley (1974, 1976 and 1977b) elaborates on the means by which teachers traditionally organize pupil participation in lessons in a way that has implications for the 'intelligence' they are required to show. They will seek first to establish and maintain proper attention. They will do this by a variety of means – establishing the boundaries and the compulsory nature of the lesson, arranging the classroom in a way conducive to their control, making clear the rules of conduct, persistently monitoring activity, even when not appearing to do so, careful stage-setting, and maintaining authority. Hammersley's (1976) teachers used three basic strategies in seeking to maintain their authority:

1 presenting authoritative appearances and assuming the normality of the arrangement wherein they decide the rules;
2 demonstrating their superiority, for example, by how they run the lesson and command the only acceptable definition of the situation, and
3 'easing the pains of pupilhood' (p.112), for example, by discreet relaxation of certain rules at certain times.

Having gained attention, teachers seek to encourage participation by asking questions. They might use 'question-prefaces' – guideline statements which channel pupils' minds into the appropriate framework (Maclure and French 1981). They will carefully control how pupils take turns in answering (Mehan 1978). But there are right and wrong ways of answering. Pupils must not shout out, they must 'put their hands up', observe due order in answering. Those who do not join in, will be 'shown up', for all will see their lack of knowledge. The teacher always starts the topic talk, and controls and develops it, the pupils being required to identify what 'the lesson is about' and to fill in the gaps in the teacher's framework. It is acknowledged that the teacher has a right to do this, and to judge answers to the questions posed. A peculiar feature of teachers' questions is that they already know the answers, and will work to get pupils to produce the 'right' ones (see also Barnes 1969 and 1976). This particular form of teaching – developing pupils to a particular definition of cultural competence – imposes conditions on what will be counted as 'intelligent'. It certainly involves accepting the teacher's lesson-organization framework. 'Knowledge' and 'ability' are thus firmly related to the school framework and are not qualities that are universally applicable.

Teacher control, in fact, is built into the very fabric of the language of the classroom. Stubbs (1976) calls such language 'metacommunication'

> communication about communication: messages which refer back to the communication system itself, checking whether it is functioning properly.... [Teachers] control the channels of communication by opening and closing them: 'O.K. now listen all of you.' They control the amount of talk by asking pupils to speak or keep quiet: 'Colin, what were you going to say?' They control the content of the talk and define the relevance of what is said: 'Now we don't want any silly remarks.' They control the language focus used: 'That's not English.' And they try to control understanding: 'Who knows what this means?' (p. 83).

It might be claimed that all of this might apply in 'traditional' but not 'progressive' situations. However, while there are differences between the two styles, notably in the kinds of pupil behaviour permitted, there are indications that the teacher remains the guardian of what is to be learned, and retains control. As discussed in chapter 2, this could be through enforcing a variety of rule-structures, or manipulation of the environment or generally setting the context within which decisions are made and action occurs. Kozol (1968), for example, noticed that in many free schools he visited, each one proud of the range of choice it allowed its pupils, none the less they all appeared to be offering the same kind of choice. This was because:

> *all* teachers and *all* adults in these kinds of situations do in fact dictate the options and preferences of the children in a number of important and inexorable ways: by the very familiar and predictable clothes they wear and life-styles they foster, by the very familiar and predictable tools, gadgets, gimmicks, and ornamentations they provide, by the physical location they have chosen, by the pupil-tuition they establish, by the race and social class of children they enrol.

Much of this may be inevitable, but Kozol argues for more recognition among teachers of the degree of control they have, and less delusion about freedom and 'spontaneity' in progressive classrooms.

Guided-discovery science, for example, was reputed to have some of these features, but Atkinson and Delamont (1977) revealed just how conditional it was upon prevailing knowledge and modes of learning. They identified some interesting parallels with bedside teaching of medicine at medical school. Nuffield science is based on the principle of pupil experimentation and discovery, as opposed to the kind of teacher filling-up with knowledge described above. The emphasis is to be on method, on ways of producing scientific knowledge, rather than on just the transmission of knowledge from teacher to pupil. The same principle underwrites bedside teaching – the student gains first-hand experience from real life situations. However, at the Edinburgh hospital where Atkinson (1975) did research, there are two kinds of the latter – bedside teaching, wherein a gang of students followed a clinician on a purely teaching round, and 'waiting nights'. These latter were occasions when emergency patients were admitted, and students were expected to attend. These were *real* and fresh hospital situations, where doctors and students began in a similar state of relative ignorance, where decisions had to be made on the spot, and students were a party to them, and perhaps joined in them. The students recognized these different situations and dubbed them 'cold' and 'hot' medicine. The teaching round was 'cold' because the students were in relative ignorance about the patients compared to the doctor conducting the round, who knows it all before he begins.

Guided-discovery science shares some of the features of 'cold' medical teaching. It obviously is intended to produce something akin to 'hot' reality, but it is more like 'cold' medicine. It is a 'mock-up' in the sense that it is not 'discovery' in a real-life 'hot' situation, but a carefully 'stage-managed recapitulation of already known "facts".... The teacher is in a position to organize and control the situation in such a way that the requisite answer will be forthcoming for the students' investigations' (ibid., pp. 141–2). Thus, in one biology lesson on photosynthesis, the biochemical processes were already known, and the pupils knew they were known although they did not know them themselves, and they were required to go through 'proper' procedures – stating hypotheses, designing experiments, and deducing conclusions. If it is to come off as a lesson, all must observe the stage-management.

But if the stage-management becomes too visible, the interaction can break down.

Clearly then, this is not an exercise purely in discovery and method, but one in which pupils are expected to produce the right answers, which are already part of the corpus of scientific knowledge. Sharp and Green (1975) would feel this has to be explained primarily in terms of the effects of a complex stratified society permeating through to the classroom. In the 'progressive' primary school of their research they found the teacher's major working concept was the emphasis to 'be busy' to 'get on on your own' or 'find something to do'. Does this offer pupils more initiative in and control over the teaching/learning process as progressive ideology would have it? Not according to Sharp and Green. They argue that 'normal pupils' for the most part settle down to routine activity and form a 'bedrock of busyness' (Sharp and Green 1975, p. 122). These are pupils who 'can be accounted for generally within the framework of the teacher's commonsense perceptual structures and rationales' (ibid., p. 122).

However, the ethos of progressivism allows the teacher to integrate the 'problem' children (i.e. the ones not in tune with the teacher's framework) within usual practice, for they can be encouraged to work on their own, and to pursue their own interests and needs. The management problem thrown up by the circumstances in which teachers have to work (such as teacher-pupil ratio, resources, demands that pupils be numerate and literate, compulsory education) is reduced, and ideologically justified by the doctrine of progressivism, as all pupils become part of the 'bedrock of busyness'. Sharp and Green claim, however, that, far from meeting the essential of child-centred philosophy that it should apply equally to *all* children, in practice it means the teacher is freed to spend even more time with the 'bright', teacher-directed children. In this way, the argument runs, social stratification is produced within the classroom without appearing to do so, since the onus of responsibility lies with the child. By their account, therefore, the method is not so much a conscious strategy on the part of the teachers, but part of a false consciousness in which they have taken over the rhetoric of progressivism.

Others, while noting the 'unprogressive' elements in purportedly progressive teaching, have come to different conclusions, which stress the strategical character of these methods and teacher improvisation of them. The Berlaks (1981), for example, who studied progressive teaching in a number of English primary schools, concluded that it was misleading to think in terms of 'progressive' and 'traditional' teaching as a dichotomy (see also Bell 1981). Certainly 'progressive' teachers seemed to do 'unprogressive' things, but this was not so much the working out of external forces as the resolution of certain dilemmas and making trade-off decisions between possible lines of action. These trade-offs varied both between teachers, and over time on different occasions with the same teacher. They were based on the teacher's choice and judgment of such things as the pupils involved, the activity in progress, time of day, and so forth – in other words, on the teacher's definition of the situation.

Similarly, Edwards and Furlong (1978), in a study of resource-based learning in a comprehensive school's Humanities Department, found that teachers recognized the limitations of the approach, and made no false claims. They were aware of basic contradictions, such as individual freedom and progress against the common need to master basic skills and knowledge, which requires teacher direction. Consequently, Edwards and Furlong argue that the resource-based teaching in this school was a coping strategy – 'a way of working developed to reconcile the difficult problems of maintaining order, communicating information, and providing at least some degree of pupil autonomy' (p. 149). By planning the curriculum, and providing some basic resources, the teachers both gave themselves time and space to concentrate on basic skills with slow learners and to deal with localized difficulties, and gave pupils a degree of control, at least, over the pacing of their work, though even this is limited since a pupil's progression through worksheets is usually carefully monitored (Ball 1981). However, it did make for more active learning, the expansion of the curriculum for some more teacher-individual (as opposed to teacher-class) relationships and typing, and a reduction in discipline problems. But Edwards and Furlong none the less felt that it constituted a change in the technology of teaching, rather than a real departure from the transmission of knowledge, which has been 'carefully packaged, structured and reinforced. They are still moving into the teacher's meaning system and leaving it relatively undisturbed' (Edwards and Furlong 1978, p. 142). Similarly, Barnes (1976) argues that most worksheets do no more than ask pupils to 'rehearse' information by reference to course textbooks, and in essentials are replicating recitation teaching (see also A. Hargreaves 1977, Ball 1981, Goodson 1975, Corbishley *et al.* 1981).

Given the situation teachers find themselves in, the lack of resources, and the clash of cultures, it is perhaps not surprising that several observers have, like Edwards and Furlong, preferred to conceive of them primarily as 'coping'. At one extreme this will consist of little more than a struggle for survival. At Lowfield Secondary Modern School, this is certainly what most teachers, caught between irremedial commitment on the one hand and intractable situation on the other, seemed to be engaged in (Woods 1979). The difficulties these teachers were operating under, I have mentioned before in chapter 2 – high teacher-pupil ratio, recalcitrant clientele, low morale, examination dominated curriculum, scarcity of resources and so forth. For most but the top examination stream, it was more a matter of 'survival' – getting through the lesson, day or term in one piece, with one's professional esteem reasonably intact, and, if lucky, some teaching done. These were grim circumstances, where the only relief for some, if professional esteem could not be salvaged, was to aim for a measure of 'role-distance', where the individual denies 'not the role but the virtual self that is implied in the role for all accepting performers' (Goffman 1961, p. 95). Teacher action may on occasions be simply a going through the motions not as routine but as bitter necessity, and on such occasions a teacher may detach and reserve his preferred 'self' for better times (see also Taylor and Cohen 1978).

The Lowfield staff worked hard at survival – it is a basic instinct – though not all succeeded. I identified eight survival strategies: socialization ('teach them right'); domination ('keep them down'); negotiation ('you play ball with me, and I'll play ball with you'); fraternization ('if you can't beat them, join them'); absence or removal ('teaching would be all right if it wasn't for the pupils'); ritual and routine ('you'll be all right once you get into the hang of things'); occupational therapy ('it passes the time'); and morale-boosting ('we have to believe'). The last allowed the teachers to account for all the others, often in terms of 'education'. For example, a form of potential trouble-makers had been separated from the other pupils, grouped together and given their own teacher, classroom and timetable. This is 'removal' from the main stream of school activity, followed by 'negotiation' and 'fraternization' within the group. But it was represented as an educational device in the best interests of the pupils, whose peculiar characteristics 'entitled' them to preferential treatment. The close relationship they developed with their teacher, which ensured the success of the survival manoeuvre, was then presented as evidence of the justification of the rhetoric.

If this all sounds rather grim, that is not necessarily how it is manifested within schools, for, as we have seen in chapter 4, humour is one of the teacher's main resources. The more difficult the circumstances, the more demands that are made on it. An increasing number of studies have remarked on the importance of humour and laughter in schools (Walker and Adelman 1976, Walker and Goodson 1977, Woods 1979, Stebbins 1980, Denscombe 1980a). Joking can ease the path into relationships with potentially difficult children; self-deprecatory jokes can elevate the status of pupils and equalize their standing with teachers; or teacher and pupil can join in common accord in conflict humour against a common enemy – the school, society, the headteacher, other teachers, other pupils or parents. But humour can also be used to control a situation, or to escape from embarrassing situations or confrontations. Walker and Goodson's teacher (see chapter 3, pp. 56–60, in fact, puts the control element first. Several pupils described to them teachers who appeared to be very informal, and were always joking, but were in fact using jokes to keep them within a tightly prescribed status. This is a form of 'fraternization', a strategy designed both to ease the teacher's position, and to win the pupils over to some recognition of official aims.

There is, too, a kind of in-between position some teachers adopt that distinguishes between role and person. While in the teacher role, it is teaching, with all its connotations and constraints that matters. But as a person, in 'off-moments' one can relax, and share a perspective with pupils that makes fun (and thus makes it easier to bear) of a common problem in what is basically a common, shared enterprise. Thus Stebbins (1980) argues that humour is a kind of sign-vehicle teachers may use to correct or supplement impressions of themselves previously communicated. This could be a distinction between role and person, or it could be 'comic-relief' – an easing of tensions in situations of long, sustained periods of deep concentration.

It will be seen that it is often difficult to disentangle 'survival' from 'teaching', a move designed for personal security or comfort from teaching method. Frequently the two meld together into a teaching, or rather 'coping' strategy (A. Hargreaves 1977, 1978, 1979). The value of 'coping' as a concept is that it acknowledges the force of constraints operating on the teacher while also allowing for creative individual input. Hargreaves gives the example of teachers in junior schools coping with the contradictory demands progressive education (which says to the child 'behave any way you like') makes on some working-class children (used to being given explicit cues) by evolving techniques of reverting to a more explicit, traditional model.

Elsewhere, Hargreaves discusses the related strategies of

'policing' and 'confrontation-avoidance' (1979). For the teachers of Hargreaves's research, the need for 'policing' arose from the teachers' definition of the situation, which included not only the material circumstances, but also their view of the children's needs. This was a working-class area where, in the teachers' judgment, the children expected and required to be 'policed'. Policing (a type of 'domination') involves crowd control – deciding who are legitimate members of the crowd, where and when it moves, what shape it takes; it also involves arranging the situation and activity. The most vivid example is perhaps to be found in Webb's 'Black School' (1962), where the typical teacher was a 'drill-sergeant'.

Hargreaves identifies three prominent elements of policing: (1) rigorous and systematic control over pupil talk and bodily movement; (2) an explicit articulation of the rule system and public display of the hierarchical relationship between teacher and pupil, and (3) moral features of classroom life taking priority over the cognitive. In this sense, 'forms of teaching ... and particular negotiative strategies ... which are organized primarily around principles of social control come to be, at the very least, indistinguishable from forms of teaching which are cognitively based' (1978, p. 144).

Confrontation-avoidance (a kind of 'removal') is 'either a refusal to act upon pupil challenges or a minimization of response to such challenges' (ibid., p. 147). This has been noted in many studies. Stebbins (1970), for example, neatly shows how the reasons depend on the teacher's definition of the situation. He may not react to a disorderly pupil, because he knows from past experience of that particular pupil that he will shortly desist, or because the correction is not worth the distraction to the whole lesson. As one teacher explained:

> Two children were writing. Several times I did stop and ask them to remove the things from their desks. However, I had discovered that since my class as a whole had been a discipline problem and since we were getting some place with the children, if one or two children were not paying attention, I would not make an issue, particularly at the time when I had the majority of the class listening to me. I found that before when I had done this that part of the class would lose interest (Stebbins 1970, p. 62).

Teachers may also wish to avoid provoking the pupil further, and causing greater disturbance. In some instances this may be through fear of the pupil (Webb 1962, Werthman 1963), in others to appear to maintain a certain sang-froid in the face of provocation. But there are other elements in the teacher's definition of the situation guiding the decision to act or not to act, chiefly:

1 the teacher's identification of the student in relation to the evaluation, aims and plan of action he imputes to him;
2 personal knowledge of the student;
3 identification of type of behaviour, and
4 the teacher's principal action orientation at the time (see chapter 2).

Avoidance of provocation by no means always works as a strategy. It may be perceived by the pupils as surrender on the part of the teacher in a conflict situation and lead them to greater deviance; or it can simply be misguided. Hargreaves (1979), for example, found that in one case at least, 'policing' and 'confrontation-avoidance' were mutually incompatible. Teachers who ignored a certain pupil's playing-up denied the identity he was trying to establish, thus inducing more deviant behaviour. This eventually incurred 'policing' which confirmed the deviant identity – and hence was self-fulfilling, and in the teacher's terms, counter-productive.

These, then, are some of the strategies that teachers have been observed using in schools. There are no doubt many more in the complexities of a teacher's professionalism, but these at least give the flavour of some of the interests involved, the problems they come up against, and how they are resolved.

A strategical model

How do teachers relate to different strategies? One teacher might practise domination, another avoidance of provocation, in relation to the same incident. Some teachers may make routine definitions all the time, others may seek to make innovations while practising fraternization and indulgence. Some may change their beliefs, amalgamate person and role and take the situation as they find it as the best possible one; others may be more detached, accept part of the situation, but seek to change the rest, as and when opportunity allows. Teachers differ in their general strategical orientations.

One attempt to conceptualize these differences in broad terms in relation to teacher socialization into school systems, has been made by Lacey (1977). This model has the advantage of allowing rather more scope for individual decision-making than the more customary one, which has teachers at the mercy of external determining forces. Lacey suggests three major orientations:

1 Strategic compliance, in which the individual complies with the authority figure's definition of the situation and the constraints of the situation but retains private reservations about them. He is merely seen to be good.
2 Internalized adjustment, in which the individual complies with the constraints and believes that the constraints of the situation are for the best. He really is good.
3 Strategic redefinition of the situation, which implies that change is brought about by individuals who do not possess the formal power to do so. They achieve change by causing or enabling those with formal power to change their interpretation of what is happening in the situation (Lacey 1977, pp. 72–3).

Within this conceptual framework, Lacey examines the early socialization into teaching of some student-teachers. He observed them using certain social strategies. One was, when they encountered difficulties, to displace blame away from oneself either upwards towards the 'system' or one's superiors ('radical displacement of blame') or downwards towards the pupils ('establishment displacement of blame' – rather like the teachers in the staffroom of Hammersley's research discussed in chapter 4). These perspectives emerged during early school work, and appropriate strategies followed upon them; for example, 'policing' would follow from an establishment displacement of blame, 'fraternization' from a radical displacement of blame.

Students also seemed either to 'collectivize' the problem they were experiencing, that is to share it with others, and legitimize the displacement of blame (again, Hammersley's teachers are a good example of more established personnel employing this strategy); or they would 'privatize' it, withdrawing into themselves and being unwilling to discuss their difficulties. A student might shift from one to the other of these strategies depending on the situation.

A certain combination of these strategies led to a classic 'risk syndrome', whereby the student-teacher was in danger of failing the course. This was the 'strategic redefinition' orientation of the teacher, the use of collectivizing strategies and the radical displacement of blame. In these circumstances, the survival of the teacher, Lacey argues, depends on his ability to redefine the situation, and to use compliance strategies where appropriate. Lacey describes this ability as 'sensitivity to the environment and to significant others within it' (1977, p.90), a similar quality to the 'cue-consciousness' identified by Miller and Parlett (1974), and the 'with-it-ness' noticed by Kounin (1970). However, there are other factors involved, such as the level and type of commitment and the identity concerns of the teacher involved. I shall discuss these in chapter 8. Suffice it to say here that they lead me to suggest a distinction within the strategic redefinition mode between para-digmatic and pragmatic strategies (Woods 1981b). The distinction comes from Hammersley's analysis of teacher perspectives:

> By paradigm I mean views about how teaching ought to be, how it would be in ideal circumstances…. The pragmatic component of teacher perspectives is concerned with what is or is not possible in given circumstances and with strategies and techniques for achieving goals (Hammersley 1977a, p. 38).

Hammersley draws attention to the difficulty of unravelling paradigmatically and pragmatically motivated elements of teacher perspectives. However, I discovered two teachers with similar views on teaching who seemed to embody the difference, one who allowed no compromise on his views of how teaching should be, the other who showed clearly a concern for 'what is or is not possible in given circumstances'. In the paradigmatic orientation of the one, ideals and principles were uppermost, there was little or no adapting to the situation, and any 'collectivizing' was done in the service of the ideals rather than in the more pragmatic teacher culture or subculture. Inasmuch as the norms, rules and values prevailing in the institution are at variance with those of the ideals, they will be subverted, not accommodated. Inasmuch as the power structure is tilted against the ideals, attempts will be made to swing the balance.

In the pragmatic orientation, there is situational adjustment (Becker 1977b), but also some strategic redefinition. The teacher concerned had come to prefer 'privatization' of his problems, near-conformity of career-structure, and acquisition of power within the prevailing framework. All this took place without the loss of vision of ideals, though inevitably there was compromise of principles in practice. The mode is characterized by opportunism, testing out chances on a limited front, and seizing whatever possibilities present themselves to further one's aims, which are not necessarily limited to the school.

This overall model of general teacher strategical orientation is at a very early stage of development. Further refinement awaits more studies of teacher socialization at all stages of their careers. It is important that we should have them, for within teacher strategies lies the key to what a teacher can and cannot achieve within schools.

Summary

The standard teacher instructional strategy is 'recitation' and 'chalk and talk'. Teacher talk, in fact, is by far the main component of most lessons. Analyses of teacher talk show how it is designed to marshal the pupil's thoughts into the teacher's framework of meanings, how pupils' attention is mobilized and their participation in the lesson organized, and how teachers keep 'conversational control' over topics. The same broad strategy, though in different guise, has been noted in so-called 'progressive' teaching situations. Teachers certainly retain control over learning in progressive situations in a variety of ways – for example by their life-style, appearances, equipment. Structures of knowledge and learning also are basically the same. 'Guided-discovery science', for example, was found to be guidance into the existing corpus of scientific knowledge while the 'busyness' of a progressive junior classroom was felt not to reflect child-centredness, but to legitimate the existing social order through a new ideology. However, it may be misleading to think in terms of the traditional/progressive dichotomy. One study found teachers making trade-off decisions in the face of certain dilemmas thrown up by the situation, decisions which might vary, as elements in the situation vary. Edwards and Furlong also prefer to see the resource-based learning they investigated as an attempt to secure a measure of control in certain areas, but also a measure of pupil freedom and independence. They refer to it as a 'coping strategy', which teachers devise when they come up against the burden of constraints and contradictions.

At one extreme, these coping strategies will take the form of survival, and teachers have been observed practising fraternization, absence, routine and ritual, therapy and so on. At their worst, all elements of teaching can disappear in the grim struggle to keep head above water. At their best, teaching becomes indistinguishable from coping strategies, which are devices to secure *educational* aims in straitened circumstances. In these, humour has a special role, to ease relationships, make light of difficult situations, facilitate control. Common forms of coping strategy are 'policing' and 'confrontation-avoidance'.

Finally, I outlined a strategical model devised by Lacey in which he suggested three major theoretical areas of strategical orientation – strategic compliance, internalized adjustment and strategic redefinition. I suggested, with regard to the last area, that it might be useful to conceive of paradigmatic and pragmatic strategies. Lacey also observed certain strategical tendencies among student-teachers – to displace blame either upwards or downwards, and to collectivize or privatize problems.

Pupil strategies

If teachers are forced into strategical action by the constraints of the job, the point holds even more strongly for pupils. John Holt was of this opinion:

> For children the central business of school is ... getting these daily tasks done, or at least out of the way, with a minimum of effort and unpleasantness. Each task is an end in itself. The children don't care how they dispose of it. If they can get it out of the way by doing it, they will do it; if experience has taught them that this does not work very well, they will turn to other means, illegitimate means, that wholly defeat whatever purpose the task-giver may have had in mind (Holt 1969, p.37).

This draws attention to the short-term nature of some pupil perceptions of school goals (as compared with teachers' longer-term perceptions), and a basic instrumentalism.

Conformist modes of adaptation will yield a strategical orientation of receptivity and response. D.H. Hargreaves (1972) draws attention to the desire among many pupils (especially from middle-class, or aspiring working-class backgrounds) to 'please the teacher'. This could be for a variety of motives, perhaps because they identify with teacher aims, or perhaps because they do not. It could simply be a form of colonization. They must learn, therefore, what the teacher wants, which itself is not always clear. Even more difficult, and calling for complex strategies, is responding to teacher demands without offending teacher, peers, or personal identity (e.g. being accused of 'being a creep' or a 'swot'). Hargreaves describes some typical colonist rules:

> In one school I know the pupils would write the date in pencil in their mathematics exercise books. If the teacher did not mark the work in that particular lesson, then on the next occasion the pupil could rub out the old date, substitute the new one, and spend the rest of the lesson on matters more important than mathematics, secure in the certainty that if called to account by the teacher he could produce incontrovertible evidence of

having worked that day. Sometimes even the common strategies pay off, not because the teacher is unfamiliar with them, but rather because the teacher is so engrossed in his own task that he forgets about the strategy. For example, the teacher wishes each pupil to answer one question from those set in the textbook. To make sure that no child is accidentally left out, he assigns the questions in a systematic way according to the pupil's seating position. However, this gives the pupil the opportunity to use the strategy of 'looking ahead'. He counts up the pupils who will have to respond before him, calculates which question – all being well – will be his, and then prepares his answer in advance. With such preparation his chances of giving a right answer are substantially improved. He succeeds in pleasing the teacher, but in so doing he defeats the teacher's wider purpose of giving him practice at a whole set of questions rather than at a single one. Ironically, the teacher, in approving the correct answer, reinforces the use of the strategy and sabotages his own goals (D.H. Hargreaves 1972, pp. 181–2).

One can cheat, or practise some other form of subterfuge. Holt (1969) mentions a whole range of these – making wild grabs at answers; waving one's hand in the air with all the others regardless of whether one knows the answer to the teacher's question or not; 'guess-and-look', that is make a guess at an answer and study the teacher's face for signs of whether you are close or not; go through the forms of working without necessarily understanding what you are doing; get other people to do the work for you (some pupils get the teacher to do the work by acting dumb); get the teacher to provide clues without knowing it; whispering answers so that the teacher might accept it if it 'sounds right'. Holt found the 'mumble strategy' particularly effective in language classes:

> In my French classes the student used to work it on me without my knowing what was going on. It is particularly effective with a teacher who is finicky about accents and proud of his own. To get such a teacher to answer his own questions is a cinch. Just make some mumbled, garbled, hideously un-French answer, and the teacher, with a shudder, will give the correct answer in elegant French. The student will have to repeat it after him, but by that time he is out of the worst danger (ibid., p. 28).

It might be thought that this kind of response requires a certain experience of the world, and reflects in part an accommodation to the accumulated pressures of schooling. But 'teacher-pleasing' without regard to learning has been noticed in an infant classroom among six and seven year olds (Tuckwell 1982). Here children were noticed not giving problems their serious attention, but searching for clues to the answers in the teacher's and their classmates' responses, faking attitudes and hedging their bets. Already, at the very beginning of their pupil career, they are conscious of the penalties of failure and the blows that can be inflicted to self-esteem and status among one's fellows (see chapter 5).

A similar strategical orientation was noticed by Delamont (1976) in a girls' private school in Scotland, though these older girls will play this game only so far as it suits their purposes. Delamont sums up the pupils' prime strategy as 'to find out what the teacher wants and give it to her – assuming that they can see a pay-off for themselves, in terms of grades, eventual jobs or peace and quiet. When there is no discernible benefit to be had by giving the teacher what she wants "disruptive behaviour" is likely to become the major strategy' (Delamont 1976, pp. 99–100; see also Hammersley and Turner 1980, and chapter 5, pp. 93–4).

So the girls' attention is not unconditional. And where it is given, there are a variety of short-cuts towards meeting the demands, like checking with others. One girl, in fact, 'ran remedial tutorials from the back of the lab' (Delamont 1976, p. 85). There was also continual bargaining, which I shall discuss at greater length shortly. There *was* some 'ingratiation', but it was recognized as a strategy. Above all, Delamont represents the situation, in a high status girls' public school, as one basically of conflict, and indeed represents the inmates as 'protagonists' and entitles one chapter 'Let battle commence: strategies for the classroom'.

The first salvos are fired by the pupils. In the examples given so far the pupils are very much on the defensive. The teachers exert their power, the pupils are motivated in the instances given by Holt at least by fear – fear of displeasing the teacher and earning rebuke or causing trouble, or of offending the norms of one's fellows and earning castigation from the peer group. But at times, the boot is on the other foot. We have seen some examples of where pupils might at least be said to be breaking even (e.g. Willis's 'lads') largely due to the strength of their cultural resources. Another such situation, where the power imbalance is redressed is when a new recruit first starts teaching, or when pupils meet a teacher or teachers for the first time. In these situations, pupils have been observed using 'sussing-out', strategies (Beynon 1979, Beynon and Delamont 1982). The purpose of these is to find out about the teacher concerned, what the teachers' perspectives are, their methods of teaching and of control, and what space, therefore, will be available for the development of their own pupil culture within the classroom.

Beynon identified six major 'sussing-out' strategies; (1) group formation and communication, (2) joking, (3) challenging actions (verbal), (4) challenges (non-verbal), (5) interventions, and (6) play. The group was an essential element of pupil organization and the basis of challenging the teacher – joint action is so much more powerful than that of an individual. The core group formed rapidly, and soon began to generate its own dynamics, egging each other on. The power of the core group rested in part on its ability to recruit allies, when, for example, they might do their best to ruin a lesson by over-reaction, orchestrating different responses, coughing and laughing. A popular gambit was to create 'diversions' to distract and confuse the teacher.

The boys used jokes – *risqué* jokes, lavatorial humour, repartee and wit, 'backchat' and 'lip', and private jokes among themselves, none the less used to create disorder. They challenged teacher actions by asking stupid questions, giving pseudo information, doing 'build-ons' (i.e. escalating an action or a joke), making requests for information specifically to 'needle' the teacher, 'third-partying' (i.e. treating the teacher as a third-party while conversing with friends, in direct contravention of the school code which gave control to the teacher), answering back and open cheek (voted by some pupils the major 'sussing-out' strategy), chattering and not listening, making challenging statements and actions, putting on a show, 'spattering and inking', making noises, shouting out, producing maniacal laughter or bellowed singing, making dramatic entrances, going 'walkabouts', fidgeting with pens, rulers, bags, blinds, books, playing desk football, etc., etc. Like Willis's lads (chapter 4) they had a great time.

It could be argued, again like Willis's lads, that much of this behaviour was related to background culture, and was a reaffirmation and re-creation of certain forms and aspects of that; and that it constituted 'a laugh' in its own right, unrelated to neophyte teachers or pupils. This is probably true in some respects and some of the 'getting at' teachers could be represented as exploration for cultural space, into which the teachers might get drawn in a status-inverted capacity. But this is not necessarily reproduction of social class culture. It could equally be a form of individual response to institutional processes, which are personified by teachers. The response may be flavoured by social class cultures or subcultures, but not determined by them. Ball (1980), for instance, argues that some sort of 'testing out' of the teacher is necessary for all pupils (though only a few may be involved, they act, in a sense, for all), in order for them to clarify how the teacher actually does define the situation, and to find out what 'tactical and managerial skills' they possess in establishing and maintaining it. It may not be so much a challenge, therefore, as a search for necessary information in order for them to be able to perform correctly within the teacher's framework. If the teacher under-reacts (by doing nothing) or over-reacts (by losing self-control), this shows 'the kind of lack of tactical skill that would be taken advantage of even by pupils in the most pro-school oriented classes' (Ball 1980, p. 150). Ball draws attention, therefore, to the basically conflictual situation where rules govern procedure, and teacher power and managerial skills count for a great deal in establishing them. Pupils' 'testing' or in their own terms 'sussing out' is directed towards discovering what they are.

On the basis of the discussion so far, we can make a threefold classification of pupil strategies – supportive, oppositional and detached. This accords with the schema of general orientations noted by D. Hargreaves (1972, pp. 192–3): 'pleasing teacher' (supportive), 'delinquescent' (oppositional) and 'indifferent' (detached).

In Figure 3, I have listed some typical pupil strategies that have been observed, and rated them according to this classification. The figure indicates that interpretation of pupil behaviour is not always a straightforward matter. The same strategy can have different pupil motives behind it.

'Doing work', for example, as implied in Holt's illustrations, is by no means as straightforward as it sounds. Certainly some pupils work because they want to, and in the form and spirit intended by the teacher, i.e. they *learn*. Others have formed different understandings of work and learning. Furlong's girls, for example, emphasized the importance of 'learning' and this was judged either by the receipt of some positive feedback or by simply carrying out the tasks specified by the teacher (1977). Their history teacher used a highly structured approach which enabled them to see exactly where they were. As Furlong notes, 'there is a striking similarity between what this teacher saw himself doing as a means of control and what the pupils appreciated in the classroom' (p. 181). Understanding something completely new was a rare occurrence. Learning was a matter of doing and producing tangible results, such as exercise books full of notes, with ticks and 'goods' (see also chapter 3, pp. 60–1).

In some respects, this seems the mirror image of 'occupational therapy', 'ritual and routine', or 'busyness'. This teacher's

121

	Oppositional	Supportive	Detached
Working		✓	✓
Bunking off	✓		✓
Having a laugh	✓	✓	✓
Mucking about	✓		✓
Doing nothing	✓	✓	✓
Flirting		✓	
Making a noise	✓		
Being friendly		✓	
Indulgence	✓	✓	
Having a chat	✓		✓
Threat /bribery	✓		
Sussing out	✓		

Figure 3   Some pupil strategies and intentions

approach provided something these girls could engage with, and they responded. At Lowfield, I came across another approach when I talked to a group of girls who spoke of 'doing work' in deprecatory fashion, as if it were a sanction the teacher could employ in the event of bad behaviour. If they had to do it, they would do it begrudgingly, hardly in a supportive fashion. School work, it should be noted, has special properties for pupils, quite unrelated to the 'real' world of work (Woods 1978b). Though they do speak of school 'work', it is better conceived of as a series of specific demands made upon them. I shall discuss 'work' further in chapter 7.

However, 'working' is in the main a supportive strategy, since it matches the teacher's intentions, even though pupils understand and relate to it in different ways. Other kinds of general supportive strategies, noted in chapter 5, are ingratiation ('creeping' in pupils' terms) and ritualism, a kind of aimless going through the motions. Denscombe (1980b) has drawn attention to others that reciprocate official aims, and which therefore are better conceived of as 'counter-strategies', i.e. responses to strategies initiated by teachers in accordance with their intentions, rather than created *de nouveau* to further the pupils' own aims and intentions. These include 'flirting' (an aspect of teachers' fraternization technique), 'being friendly' (which includes cultural identification and much humour), and 'indulgence'. This last arises from situations where pupils are allowed to go beyond the normal bounds of behaviour. In 'open classroom' situations this could at times be functional, as when one pupil circulated among the rest of the class, providing them with brief moments of relief, and avoiding work and confrontation with the teacher himself. In the two comprehensive schools of Denscombe's research, however, pupils used the new leeway incurred through the transition from 'closed' to 'open' classrooms to further the general strategical orientation of 'avoidance' (which clearly can work for both teacher and pupil!).

It is easy to see other mirror-images of teacher strategies, some of which are oppositional or indifferent. Truancy, or 'bunking off' in pupils' argot, is the 'removal' or 'absence' technique *par excellence*. Again, it is reactive – a counter-strategy. Furlong's girls would avoid unpopular lessons or teachers by hiding in the toilet, and occasionally took half days off. It was a response, primarily, not to weak teachers, but to boredom. If there is a growth of truancy rates generally, it may reflect the growing irrelevance for pupils of much school work (see also White 1980, Grundsell 1980).

'Bunking off' is also seen as a good laugh, and having fun. Of all pupil general strategies 'having a laugh' or 'mucking' or 'messing about' seems the most common (Denscombe 1980b, Woods 1979, Furlong 1977, Willis 1977, Davies 1980a). In Furlong's school, the ability for and predisposition towards mucking about was a defining characteristic of friendship. In Willis's school, too, it is a qualification of membership of the lads (Willis 1977, p. 29). But it is also a way out of fear and boredom, an antidote to almost anything.

Joey: 'I don't know why I want to laff, I dunno why it's so fuckin' important. It just is (...) I think it's just a good gift, that's all, because you can get out of any situation. If you can laff, if you can make yourself laff, I mean really convincingly, it can get you out of millions of things (...) You'd go fuckin' beserk if you didn't have a laff occasionally' (ibid., p. 29).

In my own research (1979), I distinguished between three types of pupil laughter: (1) 'natural laughter', which appeared to owe nothing to the institution, and was oriented to background culture, as with Willis's 'lads', but which, in fact, was sometimes misinterpreted by teachers as being aimed at them, and hence produced conflict; (2) 'mucking about', a kind of apparently aimless and 'silly' behaviour, which was a response, again, primarily to boredom; and (3) 'subversive laughter', which carried more deliberate intention of undermining the teacher's authority. This was done through practical jokes, 'subversive ironies' (Goffman 1961) such as name-calling, or confronting teachers with stark examples of their own cultures (such as, for example, the use of vulgar language), 'making a noise' when the teachers are doing their best to control noise levels to protect their image (Denscombe 1980a and 1980b), or what I have termed 'symbolic rebellion'. This might take the form of destruction of property, or anything associated with the school, such as school uniform or the school bus. It is all a 'good laugh'.

'Having a laugh' shades into another popular pupil activity – 'doing nothing' (Corrigan 1976 and 1979). This was observed in the street-corner world of working-class kids in Sunderland. It could, of course, be anywhere. There is certainly 'carry over' into school. Doing nothing is talking, joking, exchanging stories, carrying on, being together, having 'weird ideas', fighting. It's twanging rulers, shining mirrors, playing conkers, 'playing' with school equipment and furniture, having a scrap, teasing teachers, taking the mickey, rejoicing in others' misfortunes, lazing around, daydreaming, talking, flirting. Those associated with feelings of boredom are usually individual activities. Others, which produce fun, laughter or satisfaction of another kind, are group activities, penetrated by strong feelings of comradeship. There is a strong strain of hedonism and immediate gratification. Sometimes laughs just happen, sometimes they are ingeniously contrived. Some devote all their talents to them. Combined with the quest for fun and amusement and the sheer enjoyment of the social experience of being together is a search for a meaningful and valued identity and dignity in what, to them, are hostile surroundings, where the highly-rated qualities belong to others. Dominant teachers can obstruct the development of fun and identity, others, wittingly or unwittingly, might help promote it. Often, clearly defined cultural groups form, with their own norms of behaviour, as discussed in chapter 5.

Summary

Pupils have to go to school. There demands are made on them in response to which they develop strategies in order to handle them in line with their own interests. One general line of response, especially, we might argue, for those from middle and aspiring working-class backgrounds and for younger pupils is to aim to 'please the teacher', giving her what she wants, even if it is only barely understood. Some pupils, especially older ones, will only do this if there is a pay-off for them. If there is not, they might take to disruptive behaviour.

In other circumstances, such as meeting a new teacher, some pupils will engage in disruptive acts in an attempt to 'suss out' the teacher and discover the boundaries of tolerance, the area of cultural space they will be allowed to develop, the rules and framework within which future interaction will occur, and the teacher's managerial skills in establishing them. Pupil strategies can clearly be supportive of or oppositional to the teacher's aims, or they can be indifferent. In this they are in line with the modes of adaptation discussed in chapter 5.

Some have suggested social class connections with these, and this would certainly be supported by some of the studies reported in chapter 5. But the connection is by no means clear cut. Also, a strategy can have both external cultural connotations and be reactive to teacher or institutional processes.

While some strategies are clearly products of a particular general orientation, others could be products of more than one. 'Doing work', for example, could be supportive, or indifferent, being simply a 'going through the motions'. Pupils, like teachers, practise absence, and on occasions reciprocate teacher fraternization techniques, like 'flirting', 'being friendly', and 'avoiding confrontation'.

Of all pupil strategies, 'having a laugh' appears the most popular. With some pupil groups, willingness and ability to promote 'laughter' is a condition of membership – it is the group's main activity, a way of life. Having a laugh takes many forms – mucking about, snapping round the edges of institutional rules and teacher tolerance levels, subversive ironies, symbolic rebellion. Some pupils for the most part are 'doing nothing', talking amongst themselves, hanging around, being together.

One question that arises is – what happens when oppositional strategies are brought to bear by pupils or when they are threatened? How, for example, do teachers react to 'sussing-out' strategies or other forms of disruptive behaviour? There are three logical possibilities. The teacher can respond with a counter-counter-strategy, like 'policing' or some other form of domination in an attempt to retain or regain control; or the teacher can give way, thus 'avoiding provocation' but also possibly surrendering a degree of power. Both of these, we suggested in chapter 3, were normally likely to be deviance-productive (see also Ball 1980). The third alternative is to make a deal with the pupils, to come to an agreement in a shared understanding of the rules in force, so that strategies employed are complementary and relatively harmless. This 'negotiation' is probably the most important strategy engaged in by teachers and pupils since upon it depends the democratic social order of the school. I have therefore selected it out for special study in the following chapter.

Chapter 7

Negotiation

Negotiation is arguably the main strategy employed by teachers and pupils in interaction with each other. Indeed, as discussed in chapter 1, it is the essential mode of interaction. Negotiation implies a search for agreement. Before 'teaching' and 'learning' can ensue, certain rules of procedure have to be established and maintained. Gone are the days when teachers used to imperialistically prescribe such rules, and pupils dutifully followed them, though even this, as we shall see, involves some form of negotiation. They are now more likely to 'suss out', and teachers have to come to terms with them, openly or otherwise. This applies not only to general rules of conduct, but also to attitudes to and standards of work. For pupils, 'work', especially school work, is a problematic area. Even for those who practise 'hard work', it is not a natural activity, which healthy people do almost by instinct, as the Protestant or 'work' ethic would have us believe (Weber 1930). I shall examine also, therefore, forms of negotiation over school work, noting also that this form of teacher-pupil interaction puts a premium on relationships. For where external norms and rules prescribe roles and behaviour, personalities and relationships are less important. Where the norms and rules are constructed in interaction, they are of the essence.

Negotiating order

A great deal of negotiation is implicit in what has been said earlier. It is not simply a matter of pupils responding to teachers. For pupils have their own interests, which are often at variance with the teachers (even 'conformists' as we have seen in chapter 5).

They are also, as we have seen, not without power. Classroom activity then becomes a contest, at its worst a battle, at its best a game, for the maximization of those interests. It is an ongoing and changing process as both sides shift their interests, seek out strengths and weaknesses, win a point here, lose one there, devise new strategies and so on.

Negotiations need a base upon which to start. This means an agreed rule structure. Quite often the bargaining that goes on is about the establishing or maintaining of those rules. Rosser and Harré (discussed in chapter 3) give one example of rules that pupils held implicitly about teacher conduct, upon which their cooperative behaviour depended. If teachers broke these rules, pupils employed a number of principles of retribution, which fall into two broad categories: 'reciprocity' and 'equilibration'. Under the former, one pays back in kind, insult for insult, slap for slap: 'And if they turn nasty, well, we can turn nasty too' (Marsh, Rosser and Harré 1978, p. 44). Equilibration involves tactics to neutralize the possible loss of dignity and self-esteem as a result of the offence. Most commonly this involves the pupil withdrawing or 'switching off': 'I just go quiet, and that annoys them even more.'

Werthman (1963) shows how gang members in an American school add another dimension to the usual pupil expectations of fairness, humanity, and treating them with respect and dignity; that is, how they award grades, and upon what basis. This was critical, for pupils' evaluations could be used as a potent weapon against them. If gang members decided a teacher's claims to authority were illegitimate – if, for example, a teacher disciplined unreasonably and in a belittling fashion, or if they assigned grades on any basis other than fairness – they would employ sanctions like arriving late, leaving early, not responding to the teacher's overtures, and above all, 'looking cool', a demeanour obviously, yet subtly (for it is hard for teachers to find something specific to attack) oppositional. 'Looking cool' consists of a 'walking pace that is a little too slow for the occasion, a straight back, shoulders slightly stooped, hands in pockets, and eyes that carefully avert any party to the interaction. There are also clothing aids which enhance the effect such as boot or shoe taps and a hat if the scene takes place indoors' (p. 42). It proved very infuriating to teachers, and thus highly effective as a negotiating counter.

As Werthman points out, much of this could be represented as a by-product of lower class culture. But be that as it may, as with Rosser and Harré's pupils, he shows the behaviour to have a rational basis in response to situational exigencies and to be consistent in those terms. It is variable depending on the teacher's recognition and acceptance of the agreed criteria on which the negotiation rests. Werthman thus shows why this group of pupils was difficult for some teachers – those who failed to recognize or accept these terms – and not others.

Werthman was concerned with pupil perceptions of the teacher's legitimate authority. What does the teacher judge to be legitimate behaviour on the part of the pupil? Upon these definitions, equally, peace and harmony depends. A number of studies have investigated this area, and come to similar conclusions: classroom interaction rests on a negotiated treaty. This has been variously represented as 'aided colonization', 'a truce', 'working consensus', or 'negotiation'. The distinguishing feature of these is the construction of order in which both sides participate. Avoidance techniques, such as those discussed in chapter 6 – avoidance of 'provocation', or 'confrontation' – are more associated with 'control' programmes, and invariably seem to lead to the attempted imposition or re-imposition of control. In a sense they are the opposite to negotiative techniques, for a 'prop' is responded to by a 'copping out', for better or worse. There is no agreement, no reaching out of minds, simply decisions made on either side in what carries on being a confrontational situation. Negotiation, however, involves agreements, implicit or explicit, through which each side's interests may be maximized. At Lowfield (Woods 1979), I found the predominant mode of pupil adaptation was colonization. Many of the teachers there had accepted that that was the best that could be achieved under the circumstances and actually 'aided colonization'. They helped pupils, who might otherwise have been very difficult, to 'work the system' (Goffman 1961). Reynolds (1976a) discovered a similar phenomenon in the nine secondary modern schools of his research. He found less deviance in schools where the teachers and pupils made a 'truce'. They had a mutual agreement to 'go easy on each other'. Teachers did not press 'character moulding' goals, since in their judgment that would only produce rebellion; nor did they seek to extend their authority, as some teachers do, beyond the school gates. For most of the pupils, school was an irrelevance. Both their aspirations for and expectations of their future occupations were low, and perceived as independent of anything the school had to offer. Teachers could be a great nuisance in trying to force them along paths they had not the slightest desire to venture upon. So for them, also, there were advantages in striking a bargain – less written work, and more football, perhaps, concessions about dress and appearance, and not too vigorous application of some rules, for example, smoking. One of these

129

schools also had a 'smoking game', which consisted of a group of smokers moving round the school from point to point always just ahead of a 'smoking patrol' of teachers who knew very well the smokers were there, but made no real effort to catch them.

For the teachers, the advantages are fairly obvious. Many of them, according to Reynolds, are out of sympathy in any case with many of the old-fashioned rules and attitudes that still obtain in schools and the 'character-moulding' task. But even if they supported them, to attempt to prosecute them would probably produce rebellion, and hence be counter-productive. A 'truce' is more comfortable all round, allows for some work to be done, diminishes noise and disorder, and hence is good for one's professional identity (Denscombe 1980a). Interestingly, each side may employ its own sanctions on fellow members to keep the understood terms of the truce, teachers warning an authoritarian colleague to 'ease up a bit', and pupils quashing any of their number who might 'cause trouble' (Reynolds 1976a, p. 134). Lessons thus ceased to be occasions for conflict, and more agreeable interaction took place. Traditionalists may feel this smacks of 'surrender', and the teachers in Hammersley's school (chapter 4) would certainly not approve, but it is in the nature of 'truces' for them to be made after a period of warfare which has driven both sides to the point of exhaustion. They are also temporary, and not altogether satisfactory agreements which hold 'for the time being', until somebody devises something better. They are certainly in line with the 'deviance-insulative' behaviour discussed in chapter 3.

Lest 'truces' might be thought appropriate only to secondary schools, since there is generally acknowledged to be more conflict there, a similar phenomenon has been noticed in primary schools. Pollard (1979) distinguished two types of censure, one based on unilateral use of teacher power universally disliked by pupils, and liable to promote deviance (i.e. 'deviance-provocative'), the other a 'working consensus' between teachers and pupils. There were three broad groups of pupils distinguished by their attitude to teacher censure – 'good' groups, 'joker' groups and 'gangs'. 'Good', broadly speaking, show a certain deference to perceived teacher authority (though all pupils felt that unilateral teacher censures were unfair), while 'gangs' do not. 'Jokers' like to have a laugh, but within acceptable limits. The latter were by far the largest group, and in Pollard's opinion, the working consensus – 'that body of tacit understandings by which the social order of the classroom is defined' (Pollard 1979, p. 89) – is a product of negotiations between the pupils and the teachers. They thus 'survive by negotiating a tacit set of understandings with the teacher which allows them room to develop viable adaptive strategies for themselves. In the right context they can have a laugh, talk, tease, run and play without incurring "serious" penalties' (ibid., p. 91).

Studies on the pupil perspective which have been discussed in earlier chapters generally support this argument. For example, those on pupil groups (chapter 5) have illustrated the degree of 'negotiation' that is required with each group to achieve order. We might recall, also, from chapter 3, the studies of pupil perspectives of the 'ideal teacher', and their views about being able to teach, keeping order, but also having warm and friendly relations with pupils, or, in other words, negotiating qualities.

The negotiated character of school work

So far, I have talked about the negotiation of general rules regulating the conduct of teachers and pupils. But the kind and amount of work that pupils do, and the methods that teachers employ are also negotiated. I have said that pupils seem to view school work as a series of short-term tasks rather than as an entity with a long-term rationale. But the interpretation of those tasks depends very much on the teacher and the relationships she has with her pupils, and the kinds of definitions of the situation she can persuade them to accept. In this sense, work is relationships – it is a negotiated activity. Thus, pupils' attitudes to work are by no means clear cut, to be taken for granted. For many, school work is not 'real'. They are not paid for doing it, and to many of them, that is the crucial criterion of real work. It is often difficult for pupils to see any point in it. It has to be taken on trust for a long time, in the form of marks, grades and reports. This conception of work is reinforced by artificial stimulants which dominate the atmosphere of the school – on the one hand motivators, such as competition and inducement, appeals to vanity, pride, and one-upmanship, and on the other, penalties – reports, detentions, reporting to parents. How a teacher uses these is very much a matter of personal judgment. It is not uncommon therefore to find pupils who feel that work can be both odious and burdensome, *and* pleasant and enjoyable and that what makes the difference is not so much the content of the work as the relations with the teachers concerned. In other words, teachers can actually transform the experience. It is not surprising, therefore, that we find views on work reflecting some of the pupils' perceptions of teachers discussed in chapter 3:

> I think if you were made to work in a different sort of way, in a sort of friendly atmosphere ...
>   If you've got the right kind of teacher. With some teachers, like if you like working in the lesson you do work hard, but other teachers, when you can muck about like, you enjoy it, but really at the back of your mind is really you should be working, and if teachers don't seem to take no notice of you and they're not interested in you so you don't feel like working. But with other teachers like Mr. Kingley and Mrs. Coles, you know they make you work and you enjoy it in a way. They make the lessons interesting, and they're interested in you, you're interested in them (Woods 1978a, p. 172).

These pupils recognize a need to work and their own recalcitrance. That means an acknowledgment of a need for discipline, but that in itself is not enough:

> Kathleen: 'Some teachers can make the lesson interesting but that don't mean you're going to work. They've got to sort of treat you like human beings – you know, listen to what you want to say, not treat you like kids' (ibid., p. 173).

Work can be a weapon, bribe or reward in pupils' dealings with teachers:

> 'He's always so happy, isn't he? ... friendly. He comes down ... like most teachers expect us to come up to their level, he's prepared to come down to ours. He's more like a friend isn't he? Because you like working for him, you don't mind. A lot of teachers you don't want to work for to spite them' (ibid.).

It is possible to see in such instances how negotiation is not just about making concessions, where the two sides economize on some conflictual aims in order to achieve others, a kind of reduction of level of intent. Through certain dispositions they can rise to new achievements, which may either maximize the original aims of both sides in ways not envisaged before, or bring about a re-casting of aims.

However relationships between teacher and pupils are not always ideal, and the negotiation of school work can take several forms. One model containing very broad categories linked to pupil adaptations is given in Figure 4 (see also Martin 1976, G. Turner 1982).

'Hard work' implies full commitment, and is practised mostly, but not always, and not only by conformists. 'Work avoidance' at its extreme implies total lack of commitment. 'Bunking off' is its most obvious manifestation. However, the majority of pupils, most of the time, are found somewhere in between, indulging in 'open' or 'closed' negotiation. Both arise from partial commitment and hence a mismatch between teacher and pupil aims, requiring some form of contract. Open negotiation is where parties are aware of the contract, move some way to meet each other of their own

Type of work

	Hard work	Open negotiation	Closed negotiation	Work avoidance
Pupil adaptation	Conformists		Retreatists, rebels, intransigents	
		Colonizers/ritualists		

Figure 4   Pupils and work

volition, and subsequently arrive at a consensus. Closed negotiation is where the parties independently attempt to maximize their own reality in opposition to and conflict against the other, and each makes concessions begrudgingly, and only if forced. However, they do make concessions, unlike the 'work avoiders' and rebels, who wish to push opposition to its limits and give no quarter. The difference then between open and closed negotiation is one of intent. Both involve mutual agreement, but the former is made willingly, the latter unwillingly. For this reason, the latter has sometimes been seen as 'utilization of power' (Turner 1982) or 'enforcement strategies' (Hammersley 1980a). I shall discuss each of these, using illustrations again from Lowfield Secondary Modern School (Woods 1978b). I shall also discuss the pupils' constructions of 'hard work', since, as we shall see, the implied full commitment still has to be worked for. I should emphasize that I am using these examples to illustrate the model, and not the views and attitudes of the pupil population as a whole.

Open negotiation

Command of the process of negotiation is at the heart of the craft of teaching. Quite often, if the teacher overdoes his concessions, as we have seen, the pupils will see it as weakness and demand more. If not enough concessions are made, pupils might become resentful, and potential colonizers or even instrumental conformists are turned into intransigents or rebels. What the standard lesson consists of then, is a number of checks and balances, prompts and concessions, motivations, punishments, jollyings, breaks and so forth, as the teacher displays his professional expertise in getting the most out of his pupils. While the pupils, seeking basically the comfort of their own perspective and reality, will tend to react according to how the teacher's techniques mesh with that reality.

One of the most common gambits the teacher makes is to offer to do a great deal of the necessary burdensome work, 'carrying' the pupil along. For the pupil this is what I would term 'distanced work', because the pupil himself is a long way from its point of origin. In the standard teacher talking pupil listening mode, pupils are constantly reminded of the terms of the contract:

Example 1 Teacher:
'I'll do the algebra for you now. There are six methods of factorization, give me one.' (No hands go up, a certain lethargy.) 'I'll make you do the lot if you start yawning!' (Several hands go up.)

Example 2 Teacher:
(During experiment on expansion of liquids) 'I'm going to record the results now' (noise increases in class). 'I gather some of you would rather *write* the whole double period!'

Example 3 Pupils – Ricky and Lawrence:
(To me, after teacher experiment in science lesson): 'We've got to work now.' (They came back automatically after the last reading, armed with a piece of paper from the front.)

Example 4 Teacher:
'I've talked enough, now I think it's time you did some work. I'm going to give you four essay titles, choose one and make a start in these last 20 minutes. You can get half your homework done if you get your minds on it.'

In this last example, there is a double bargain. The teacher has 'worked' for 20 minutes of the scheduled 40-minute period, while the pupils took things easy. Now it is their turn. Furthermore, extremely valuable leisure time in the evening is offered as an extra inducement. This teaching and learning is far from being an intrinsically cooperative enterprise. There is never a pure state of 'open negotiation' because of the disparity in position between teacher and pupil. Pupils have to be continually set up for it and reminded of the fairness of it, the necessity for it and what they immediately stand to gain from it. This has immediate impact, quite often the teacher appealing to their sense of fair play and relying on the bond between them to assume that they would feel it appropriately applied to them.

> Teacher: (After a few admonitions at beginning of lesson, and one pupil getting moved up to the front) 'I'm going to start with a promise, or two. In the second period we'll have a film – if you're good, and work well this first one! Then I thought next week we'd go out and do the nature trail in the forest.' (Pupils talking.) 'I think you're adopting a very anti-social attitude, and that became apparent the moment you walked through the gate this morning.' (Quiet, but a ripple of noise again.) 'Now don't let me have to nag.'

Here, then, is another element of the contract – not only do pupils stand to gain pleasurable experiences if they comply; if they do not, they will earn the teacher's wrath and precipitate what Furlong's pupils called 'trouble' or invoke a 'domination' strategy. Individuals might get 'shown up' or verbally (even physically) assaulted:

> Teacher: 'If I hear another burble from your stupid little mouth, I shall push your head through the top of that desk!' (With nose an inch from pupil's and eyes wide and unblinking. Ghostly quiet in room, and they go on writing.)

Thus, negotiating tactics of the teacher are not always pleasant ones, and shade into domination.

> Sandra: 'I think some of the teachers are frightening. They frighten you into working. I don't think it should be like that really. I'm frightened to walk into some lessons.'

The extreme bargain derives from situations where children do hardly any 'work' at all, and teachers have long since given up trying. But because teachers can cause 'trouble' and kids can be extremely awkward, both trade appearances for tolerance. Some 'work' in the school day therefore can be counterfeit, performed semi- or unconsciously. No productivity rates are required, there is no factory line, no next stage in the process waiting, and for non-examination forms, no examinations. The only kind of productivity rate demanded by 'supervisors' is a semblance of work and a semblance of good order. Interestingly this is maintained when the teacher is absent. The semblance of work and good order will be preserved by the semblance of a teacher in the form of notes mediated through a proxy stand-in teacher. Notice how the bargaining is built into these notes:

Classwork 2B/2H Thursday, 7th February

Read the notes carefully and then copy them into your books. On Tuesday I shall collect 2B's exercise books in and on the Thursday of next week 2H's.

Read and copy these notes
(Two pages of notes, and a diagram follow.)
If you do not finish this in class it is your homework to finish it off. I will collect your books next lesson to make sure you are doing your work. Those of you who have taken notes on paper during lessons get those copied in as well.

There is a negotiated ambience in established classrooms which all implicitly recognize, and teachers and pupils are continually reminding each other of the terms, if one or the other steps over the boundaries:

Teacher: 'Hey! Now look! We know there has to be a certain amount of noise – as long as it's a working noise!'
Teacher: 'How many have not brought pencils? Now look! This is not on! You've been told before!'

In stating the terms of the negotiation, some teachers keep constantly in mind the ideal product they would like to see, while many pupils' ideal at Lowfield was 'doing as little work as possible'. Again, the 'mass' nature of the work, causes the teacher to take action on the basis of how the majority behaves. One or two pupils might aspire to the teacher's ideal. They serve to reinforce the point for the majority.

There is a great deal of 'play' in pupil work. Teachers, who are interested in pupils *learning* by whatever means, or if that is completely impossible, keeping them occupied in as pleasant a way as possible, often devise games as part of their teaching strategy. This again parallels management's efforts in industry to counteract the effects of job design. Teachers thus provide curriculum forms to compensate for the basic curriculum, which, for many pupils, has little meaning. This is one of the paths to 'good relationships'. Those teachers high on the pupils' list in this respect were adept at humanizing the basic drudgery with departures from routine, attention to individuals, skilful use of laughter, converting 'work' to 'play' and so on.

They might sell such activity to the pupils as 'play' both as a learning enterprise in itself and as a balance to more grisly business. Thus, artwork, pottery, craftwork, needlework, domestic science, science experiments in the labs – such activities could often more appropriately be classified as play. Pupils might seek to transform any dull activity into play. For example, in one physics lesson observed, pupils were set four problems of balance to work out. The class proceeded with these in a mood of happy and casual industry, chattering in groups, sorting through the problems, but with frequent and cheerful digression to the state of the football league or the current pop scene.

'You can't expect much from these' the teacher told me. 'If you wield the big stick, they rebel. At least like this we stay friends, and they do learn something.' Some pupils thus are perceived as having 'limits' in their capacity to do school work. Some need extending, others need indulging. And for the latter there is much play, games and laughter. If the teacher can incorporate some of these elements into his programme, rather than allowing them a subterranean, illicit existence, he might achieve some learning via the back door, as it were. At worst, he will achieve a *modus vivendi*, and a spirit of sociability, which some might argue is more important than work, a view which would certainly accord with the 'relationships' preoccupation of these pupils.

Some teachers thus deliberately construct the learning process as a game. After all, it is not self-evident to pupils *why* one should have to learn about Roman villas, upland sheep, the area of an annulus, the Citizen's Advice Bureau, how to make a canoe, the principle of levers, similes, and so forth. Thus a social studies lesson on 'educational expenditure' was relieved by sending pupils all over the school to get essential information from the caretaker, the cook, the secretaries, and so on. A history lesson on strip farming was lightened by allocating the class character parts in the mediaeval village. A project on housing was spiced by sending pupils around householders with a questionnaire. The point of the Citizen's Advice Bureau was incorporated into a strip cartoon and the pupils invited to supply the words. The pupils entered all these activities in a friendly and lighthearted manner. They were all games with various winning points. They were certainly not 'work'.

Hard work

We have seen some examples of the techniques teachers and pupils use in negotiating over work in the ordinary course of events. But on occasions pupils speak of doing '*hard* work'. It might be thought this is not a negotiated activity but an illustration of complete agreement, with full preservation of both teacher and pupil goals. So it may be in some cases, and it is in that sense that it occupies a space in the model. But in pupils' own terms, it is not, and it provides an instructive example of how commitment has to be worked for and traded over.

What, therefore, is the pupil's understanding of 'hard work'? It varies, of course, among pupils. 'Copying notes from the board' seems a fairly easy task, but can be extremely 'hard work' for some pupils. The difficulty, as Gannaway's pupils found (chapter 3), lies in the extreme mental effort required in concentrating on reading, and in the act of writing. What has become easy and second nature to some, almost a natural extension of the self, to others poses the greatest problems:

'He gives us loads and loads of writing.'
'What I don't like is when they get on about your writing.'
''E makes us do a load of writin'.... I don't mind the drawin', but writin' – huh.'

This might not be perceived as hard work for the pupils by the teacher, since she has devised the notes and written them on the board or dictated them. She is more likely to put into this category work that more obviously requires some intellectual initiative on the pupil's part, and that releases the teacher from the effort of production. Thus, working from work cards, doing exercises – this kind of set work which involves some form of problem solving on their own initiative is the ultimate in pupil hard work to many teachers. So it is, of course, for many pupils. I joined in one group activity with some 'deviant' fourth-year boys based on a comparison of two housing estates. We had to find answers to a list of questions from the evidence presented in the form of photographs, statistics, tenants' comments, etc. I taped this discussion, and playing it back to them several days later, one remarked:

'Cor! We was workin' 'ard then! That's the 'ardest I've worked all term!'

What made this 'hard work' for these pupils was the extent of application of mind needed to grasp the series of problems, the *creative* task of producing ideas in interaction with the elements presented to produce solutions, all of which made it an individualistic effort. Contrast this with the routine procedures of 'distanced' work which can either be a drudge in calling on one's powers of attention, but nothing else (e.g. interest), or euphoric in permitting its sublimation in some other activity. To get pupils to do hard work requires special skill and techniques. In any event, pupils ration it out, employing it as a useful negotiating counter themselves. If they work hard this lesson, or fraction of a lesson, they might expect an easy time next.

Curiously, perhaps, this did not seem to apply to the hardest work that pupils did from an observer's point of view. The greatest physical effort I witnessed at Lowfield was in the gym, especially circuit-training, which involved press-ups, shuttle-running, sit-ups, bench jumping, and rope climbing, all performed against the clock. The staff certainly perceived this as the hardest sort of work. It involved application, determination and the utmost investment of one's physical resources:

'Old Gary Sampson, he works, but he never seems to be on his beam ends' (PE Teacher).

The games' teacher's approach was framed in a 'workish' rhetoric. Thus, in games, pupils were often urged to 'work'. 'You must work for it' was often impressed on them. The techniques were ground out to them in forceful terms: 'Serve, dig, catch! Serve, dig, catch!' Games involved skill, which requires practice, but other gym activity tests the limits of human endurance. Some pupils have an instinctive fascination for this especially after the boredom and distance of classwork, and will rally group support to push an individual on, as when they all shouted Gregory Beech up the rope for a third, very painful, time within 60 seconds at the end of his circuit-training.

However, this does not constitute work for the games-inclined pupils (though it might be slavery for those who detest games!). For them it is a respite from the usual school chore, an opportunity to release energy in a direction that they can comprehend. For some pupils, therefore, it comes under a different and opposing category. It is perceived as a peripheral activity within the school's official programme, but in some pupils' school lives, it is central – 'the best part of the week' – but as 'play', 'sport', 'leisure', uncontaminated by the alienating characteristics of 'work'. For such pupils, games' teachers require little negotiative skill.

Most 'work' at Lowfield was done by the examination classes. The rest of the school appeared to do very little 'work' in proportion to their other activities over the week. There were frequent references to this divide. Exams meant 'work' for both teacher and pupil. Perhaps the small demands during the non-examination period are evidence of the teachers 'going easy' on the pupils in the spirit of the kind of truce spoken of by Reynolds. But it can make the later task of motivating for work more difficult for both teacher and pupil, though the final comments indicate that self-motivation is not entirely absent.

> Dianne: 'They should push you now and then, 'cos up till the third year or fourth year really if you didn't want to do a thing, they just let you get on with what you wanted to do. They didn't tick you off much, they used to occasionally moan at you an' that, but I don't think they did enough about it really.'
>
> Vera: 'I thought that was the only time we really worked hard, for exams. The rest of the time we was just told to do some work and that was it. Then when it come to the exam and they mentioned that, we was all working very hard and I found it difficult really.'
>
> Dianne: 'As you get nearer the end of the school, you more aim for something than during your first years an' that. So you do work harder.'

Much of this work, as noted, is seen through the medium of relationships with the teacher concerned. But what of the activity itself? Often I got the impression that pupils felt they were 'shovelling away at a giant slagheap' (Taylor and Cohen 1978). This applied even to the supposedly 'creative' work of CSE projects and English essays. This is illustrated in one way by the quantification applied:

> 'I got a bit bored when I was doing the geography project and I couldn't decide what to do and had to do about forty sides, and after about ten I was fed up with it.'

The same applied to the English 'folder':

> Andrew: 'In English, homework was one or two essays a week, and that was purely for the folder, wasn't it?'

John: 'That was about the 'ardest, building up a folder.'

But mostly, for examination pupils, work consisted of attempts to commit to memory slabs of knowledge by various means of varying tedium:

Dave: 'The metalwork homework was to copy 10 pages out
          of a book, and that took 3–4 hours.'
P. Woods: 'Was that usual?'
Dave: 'Every week, for a year.'
Ken: 'It seemed pointless, because we kept the book
          anyway.'
Des: 'The idea was to make us learn it, I think, but he said
          "copy it down and learn it," but I just copied it down
          word for word and didn't achieve anything from it
          anyway.'
Daphne: 'I would have been happier taking fewer exam
          subjects, because there's so much forcing you to do
          what you don't want. Then they try to cram more in
          at the end, and that was too much. Especially
          physics, I found that very hard, and chemistry.'

I found few expressions of 'enjoyment' of work amongst these pupils. This answer was typical:

P. Woods: 'Was there anything you really enjoyed?'
Julie: 'No. Nothing I really enjoyed.'
Elaine: 'I didn't mind English, but I wouldn't say I enjoyed
          it.'
Julie: 'It's just something you had to do. You had to do it,
          you couldn't get out of it.'
Elaine: 'There's security at school. Other people are
          bothering about you. Other people are doing the
          planning. When you leave you have to do it all for
          yourself.'

Elaine seems to be suggesting that in return for board and lodging she will contribute something toward the upkeep of the house. But it is not her house, and reality begins when you leave it and set out on your own.

Kate: 'I don't think it's been really hard work. I mean
          when people go out to work, I bet they find it a lot
          harder than at school.'

The demand of examinations appears to militate against the personal relationships so highly regarded by pupils. What seems fairly clear is that there is a misfit between demands and resources.

Suddenly and dramatically between the comparatively easily negotiated calm of pre-exam work and the rather exciting prospect of remunerated, independent, responsible and meaningful employment, comes this period of peculiar pressure, for which it was difficult to find a consistent rationale. The main negotiative technique is to appeal to a higher legitimacy, external to the situation, which all should recognize. But pupils cannot easily forget the personal bases on which previous interactions occurred:

Shirley: 'I thought the normal homework during the year was quite interesting – maths and English I didn't mind doing them, but at the end when it gets towards exams, it gets you down a bit. They say you've *got* to learn this, you've *got* to learn that, or you won't pass your exams, and things like that.'

Some of the work has a mechanistic quality:

Debbie: 'I don't like geography because it's all on the blackboard all the while, and I can't stand the teacher ...'

Angela: 'He doesn't speak to you as ... well, I dunno ... 'e kind of treats you as machines really (yeah!). It's "come in" he'll say, probably talk about something, not very often, it's usually straight out of a book or atlases, or off the board.'

Also it seems to squeeze out those other (non-work) areas of school life that make it a humane institution. So that, for some, it is the total impact of the exam programme that impinges. Asked what they would remember most about school, many of these fifth formers referred to 'hard work' in some form or other.

Barbara: 'It starts the first day of the fourth year. We have homework sheets every month. If we miss one lot of homework or two lots of homework we get "unsatisfactory" and if you get two "unsatisfactorys" you have to see the year tutor and get told off by him, get put on report and everything. Really gets us down. That's why half of us don't do it really, to rebel against them, I think' (laughs).

Not all my conversations with pupils were so dominated by a tone of complaint. Many did express an enjoyment of the work here and there, though that was invariably defined through relationships with the teachers rather than intrinsic quality of the activity. What these examples do is illustrate some pupil perceptions of what constitutes 'hard work', the inadequacy of relying on external pressures to legitimate the work in pupils' eyes, or of sanctions to persuade them to do it, and the need for rather more subtle negotiative skills on the part of the teacher. Though teachers may distinguish sharply between examination and non-examination work and change gear easily themselves, pupils continue relying on, and expecting, the same interactional formulae.

Negotiating techniques

At this point we might review some of the techniques employed by teachers and pupils in negotiating with each other over both order and work. The following list is largely based on one constructed by G. Turner (1982) arising from his work in a comprehensive school. You will recognize several of them in the examples already given in this chapter (see also Martin 1975, 1976).

(a) *Persistence*: this could involve not making concessions until absolutely forced to, or persisting with a demand until concessions are made. This kind of brinkmanship can be very successful in achieving more of one's ends than otherwise would have been the case, or disastrous, if one goes over the edge – a teacher fomenting outright rebellion, or pupils forcing teachers into taking punitive measures, signalling the move from consensus to conflict.

(b) *Comparisons*: used to advantage by both pupils and teachers – 'Mr. Smith lets us eat sweets in his lessons'; 'Miss Jones lets us go five minutes early'; 'Call yourself the "A" form ... what sort of standard is this?'

(c) *Justifications*: teachers continually emphasize the importance of working and behaving well, and the implications if one does not. Pupils are quite adept, too, at accounting for the poverty of their work by the teacher's own failings, impossibility of the exercise, their other, very necessary, commitments, and so on.

(d) *Reminders*: previous agreements are called to mind, and parties asked to honour them.

(e) *Promises and threats*: frequently used to get round an apparent impasse, but as in (d) above, neither promises nor threats should be empty ones, or the negotiation will not be taken up. One might also add 'bribes' and 'rewards', team points, money, early departure, etc. Among the threats the fear of shame and embarrassment, of being shown up before one's peers is a potent one. While for teachers the pupils might do the same by, amongst other things, 'making a noise', which we have seen constitutes one of the biggest threats to a teacher's professional self-esteem (Denscombe 1980a).

(f) *Vehemence*: Turner refers here to an apparent 'loss of temper', a feigning of the situation to lend teacher (usually) more power than he actually has. We might, on the pupils' side, cite 'looking cool' as practised by Werthman's gang members as a comparable attempt to deceive by appearances.

(g) *Appeal to tradition or a higher authority*: 'This is the way it has to be done' borrows the weight of legitimacy from history and from the institution – massive forces against the individual. But if 'my mum' or 'my dad' says the pupil hasn't to do it, that too, can create problems. All kinds of appeals can, in fact, be used, for example, to 'fair play'.'It's not fair, Sir' is a common pupil ploy, possibly geared into implicit rules of conduct (Werthman 1963, Rosser and Harré 1976), while teachers commonly appeal to 'reason' and 'good sense', honesty and self-esteem (Waller 1932).

(h) *Adopting an 'extreme' position*: i.e. deliberately playing for more than one hopes to get, thus allowing room for compromise, whereby one achieves the real aim.

(i) *Offering a choice*: this can have the effect of removing undesired possibilities out of court.

(j) *Offering a party 'what it wants'*: this involves discovering the aims or interests of the other party, and wrapping up one's own aims within them. This is a form of fraternization (which, in fact, can be either an instructional, or survival or negotiative strategy, or a combination of all three, depending on teacher intentions).

(k) *Stalling*: teachers and pupils play for time in meeting the other's demands or in fulfilling promises until their own resources are disposed to meet them, or perhaps in the hope that they will be forgotten.

(l) *Mobilizing support from another party*: we have had a good illustration of this with pupils' 'sussing-out' strategies, whereby they mobilize support from other groups. Teachers also can enlist aid from colleagues (usually headteacher or deputy headteacher), or from groups of pupils against others. Hence the advice often proffered teachers of making sure to win over the 'leader of the gang'. This is also the rationale for group punishments, and the argument against individuals of 'spoiling it for others'.

(m) *Pretence*: as discussed earlier.

(n) *Cajolery and flattery*: praising a pupil's work or abilities, or humouring them to get them into a receptive mood. This also can work both ways. Pupils have their ways of getting round teachers by, for example, appealing to their personal vanity.

(o) *Friendship or collaboration*: the central 'relationships' theme. A charismatic teacher can blur the distinction between separate teacher and pupil aims. They come to have a common aim and agree on the means. The need for negotiation is removed as long as that teacher remains. Personality has been the bargaining counter and has transformed the situation to a plane where negotiation is no longer relevant.

(p) *Laughter and play*.

(q) *Moderation*: i.e. making work easier, lighter, more bearable.

This is by no means an exhaustive list, but it gives the flavour of the kind of interaction that goes on in schools between teachers and pupils in the quest for achievement of their respective aims. It also illustrates the range, accommodating different teacher styles, from threats and subterfuge to softer blandishments, from techniques involving domination to those relying more on fraternization and collaboration.

Closed negotiation

'Open negotiation' is based on a certain amount of good will toward each other, recognition of the value of cooperation, and belief in the possibility of consensus. But sometimes teachers and pupils take action independently of the other either in a spirit of less than good will or resignation, or in adapting to the circumstances that have been negotiated, thus engaging in the activity that I have called 'closed negotiation'. For pupils this includes skipping homework, pooling knowledge and resources, cribbing, skiving, tricking the teacher into doing it for them, or simply 'mucking about'. It is the most popular replacement of routine 'distanced' work, which can sometimes be a drudge, but on the other hand can often be euphoric in that it permits its sublimation in some other activity. This experience, again, is remarkably like that of some factory-line workers (Beynon 1975).

If teachers do not collude with them, and connive at the 'working game', pupils will sometimes transform the activity of work into an activity of play themselves, and, in a sense, do the teacher's negotiating for her. Thus there is a great deal of playing at working, and playing at listening. Intricate class and individual games, which the teacher might ultimately detect as 'a lot of fiddling with pen and rulers', abound. There is a great deal of pretending to work while doing something else, time-filling, going through the motions for appearances to avoid 'trouble'. If they slip up, through sheer negligence or forgetfulness, they might incur the teacher's wrath:

Teacher: 'Oh! I wish you people would come prepared for lessons!'

However, since the chances of winning at this particular game of forcing pupils to work are remote, the teacher more often falls back on the old collusion, in exchange for some, if only a little, work:

Teacher: 'Paul! What have you done with the pencils? Who have you sold them to? Who can put him out of his misery and lend him a pencil? ... That looks suspiciously like one of mine! Mr Lawton's is it? ... Anyway, when you've finished about from whom you nicked it, will you please get on.'

There is a great deal of time passing and time-fillings, not as an adjunct to a large purpose, but as an overall end in itself. This is earmarked by endless performances and rituals around the distribution, collection and finding of rulers, pencils, paper. The term, day, period is there, inevitably, and it is more necessary that it be 'got through' than is the syllabus, especially with regard to non-examination forms. There is a great deal of what we might call 'condoned colonization' allowed in a spirit of resignation, rather than as a considered strategy (like 'aided colonization'). The critical nature of time, as ruler of content, is often conveyed by teacher comment to pupils, perhaps filling a space in one lesson by talking about the next subject which 'will take up to half term'. Or, by talking about the compartmentalization of knowledge and how it is geared to time: 'That's got "maturity" done. Now we'll go on to "availability". We've only got "curiosity" after that, then we'll call it a day.'

In these examples teachers and pupils are similarly affected. The 'closure' is not all that great, and the negotiation in the condoned colonization works, at least in the sense of keeping order. In the following example different constructions of reality are more obviously in play.

Fourth year, set 5, maths observation: Excerpts from lesson. Noisy lot. First few arrivals are quite jocular with Len. David asks, 'What are we doing today Sir?'
Len: 'Decimal division this afternoon, page 46.'
Harry: 'Oh these aren't too bad, Sir.'

Len:	'Right now, pay attention everybody, just like you did yesterday.' (Len explains how to divide decimals.) 'Tell me what you do, Jane.' (General commotion while Len tries to explain division of decimals.) 'Just shut up talking when I'm talking, will you, you have the chance of talking when you're working. Listen to me now! Now pack up this chatting and turning round, will you!!'
Fiona:	'What do you do with the decimal point, Sir?'
Amanda:	'Which side goes which, Sir?'
Derek:	'What page are we on, Sir?'
Len:	'The idea of this introduction is to tell you how to do it, so stop asking questions!... Now, when dividing, you move the decimal point two places to the left.'
Amanda:	'Right, Sir?'
Len:	'No, *left!*'
Amanda:	'That's what I mean Sir, right left, Sir.'
Len:	'You said *right!*'
Amanda:	'I meant you were right, Sir.'
Sheena:	'I said left Sir, I *did!*'
(Later)	
Sheena:	'Oh Sir, do we have to do these?'
Len:	'Yes, you do, it's very important.' (He explains some more.)
Sheena:	'You haven't moved the point.'
Len:	'You don't have to with this one.'
Sheena:	'Oh, it isn't 'alf 'ard, Sir!' (Len explains some more.)
Sheena:	'Can I have another piece of paper then?'
Len:	'Well, you shouldn't have started yet!'
Sheena:	'I did, I thought we 'ad to!'
Len:	'I've been here explaining, how do you know what to do before I've explained it?'
Sheena:	'That was before I knew!'
(Later)	
Amanda:	'Sir, is that right?'
Len:	'No, that's not right! Look, you're all working, and half of you don't know what you're doing! Why don't you put your hands up and ask?'
Sheena:	'Init 'ard?'
Len:	'No, it's not hard, it's ever so easy, it should've been done in the second year!'
Christine:	'Who invented the decimal point, Sir?'

> Len: (To me) 'I thought I'd give them something easy to
>   do so I could get on and mark their books – blimey!'
> (The lesson continued in this vein.)

Clearly, there is not much consensus in this lesson. It is a good example of 'closed negotiation'. Teacher and pupils attribute different meanings to the lesson. The teacher keeps trying to impose a formal structure in the traditional mould, and keeps resolutely to it despite its apparent failure. The pupils play with the teacher, pretending at the game of learning, contriving fun and jokes out of it where they can, and devising their own amusement where not. Whereas in open negotiation, the teachers might provide a game or some form of play in an attempt to induce pupils to work, here pupils provide their own, and it is the condition for their working, the only terms by which they will go along with the lesson as organized by the teacher. The teacher's complete immersion in his own paradigm was shown at the end when he confided to me that: 'that wasn't too bad. They worked quite well that lesson.' Most of the pupils, however, had played their way through the two periods.

In 'open negotiation' teacher and pupils manage to arrive at a 'core' universe of meaning which has properties recognized by all parties to it. Perspectives, to some degree at least, lock into each other at certain points. In other areas of school life, as in the example above, teacher and pupils remain firmly within their own 'sub-universe' of meaning. The physical points of contact are mentally transformed into matter appropriate to the sub-universe (Berger and Luckman 1966), but also matter that obviates open conflict and allows a semblance of work to take place. It is this that qualifies it as a form of negotiation, as opposed to a form of oppositional behaviour promoting conflict as an end in itself.

Summary

Much of school life consists of negotiation of one kind or another as teachers and pupils each try to maximize their interests in opposition to the other. It has been observed how largely implicit but clear rules concerning the conditions under which pupils will accept the legitimate authority of the teacher pertain in some classrooms. In some schools the phenomenon of teachers actually 'aiding colonization' has been observed, and in others, teachers and pupils have been seen making a 'truce'. Even in primary schools, a 'working consensus' has to be established.

School work, as well as conduct, is a negotiated activity. This focuses attention on the teacher's skill as a negotiator. From the pupils' point of view it accounts for why their attitudes to school work are invariably interpreted through their relationships with the teacher. A model of general ways of accommodating to school work was proposed, consisting of the categories of hard work, open and closed negotiation, and work avoidance. The first three of these were examined. 'Hard work' is a pupil construction, and has different meanings for different pupils. It can imply total agreement between teacher and pupil. More often, at Lowfield, at least, it was either a negotiating counter used by the pupils, or a problem connected with examinations that was largely felt by the pupils here to have been unsuccessfully negotiated.

'Open negotiation' finds teachers and pupils engaged in attempts to find the terms of a contract that will best suit their purposes, and that each will accept. A number of techniques that teachers and pupils have been observed using were noted involving various forms of persuasion, appeals, pretence, justifications, concessions and collaboration. In 'closed negotiation' each party acts independently of the other and comes to terms with themselves on the conditions under which they will meet the other's expectations. A contract is made, though its terms may or may not be recognized.

We have now discussed what kind of place the school is from the teachers' and the pupils' point of view, what kind of perspectives they have on each other, on themselves, and on the task, the groups and cultures that they contribute to, and what they do in the school in interaction with each other. It remains to consider the longer-term perspective – teacher and pupil careers.

Chapter 8

Teacher and pupil careers

Strategical interaction is not limited to concerns that lie between teachers and pupils. We have seen in chapter 5 how there is similar activity in the pupils' informal culture with regard, for example, to friends and status, and in the teachers', in inter-relationships among subject departments. We have also seen some of the values that are important to teachers and pupils in terms of their careers. In Lacey's model, too, in chapter 6, we have noted a strategical orientation to career. But we have not yet examined how individuals relate to these values, orientations and activities over time, the nature and strength of that relationship, how it changes, and how they themselves are changed. This is the subject of this chapter.

Teacher careers

In chapter 4 we noted some mixed and some rather ambivalent teacher views on professionalism and trades unionism. Teachers aspire to the former, but the conditions of the job do not match those of other professions. Purvis (1973), for example, has noted certain key features of the professional career – a strong measure of autonomy, subscription to a distinct code of ethics, certain criteria for promotion, like expertise qualifications, length of service, increased remuneration and status as the career advances, the internalization of the work or Protestant ethic so that work and career become the main focus of life.

However, as Purvis notes, the teaching career is like this only in part, even at its most structured. At Lacey's Hightown Grammar (1970), for example, there were two career structures: academic and house organization, the former much higher in status, judged by allowances awarded. Heads of department controlled resources and the allocation of teaching. They themselves spent more time teaching sixth forms and express streams, while others in the department spent more with the lower school and bottom streams. Thus career advancement meant not only more money in terms of allowances, but more desirable and prestigious teaching.

Lacey noticed a 'seniority principle' at work, often corresponding with age (see also D.H. Hargreaves 1967, Riseborough 1981). It was not only connected with one's main position as, perhaps, head of department, but with the accumulation of other chores and responsibilities – running the bazaar, liaising with the PTA, doing the timetable, supervising the issue of stationery – all of which, while complained of, were jealously guarded. Even these activities were graded, so that the school magazine 'counted' for more than the 'savings bank'.

Thus careers in this typical grammar school were all status hierarchies, even in the informal non-teaching area. There was keen competition here among the staff, and Lacey felt this was due to both desire to establish a personal reputation, and as an aid to promotion prospects. The informal elements, in fact, often counted for more than formal teaching in terms of promotion, as long as the latter was satisfactory. In comprehensive schools today, apparently 'familiarity with new ideas on education' is felt to be top of the list (Lyons 1981).

Qualifications are also important. Graduates advance further and faster than non-graduates, as do men (Delamont 1980), and those who teach certain subjects, such as science and mathematics (Warwick 1974, Hilsum and Start 1974, and see chapter 4). However, as well as these qualifications, for a headteacher post at Hightown in the 1960s, it was necessary to show 'active participation in organizations such as the church, scouting, local choirs, local government, local societies (e.g. history, drama), the Workers Educational Association, the YMCA and other youth clubs; attending a wide variety of courses, having interests of a liberal and cultural nature' (Lacey 1977, p. 148). It would appear that academic, social and political qualifications all have a bearing on the teacher career.

At Hightown in the 1950s a new house system was introduced to replace the form teacher system, and gave rise to an alternative career structure. Its demarcation from the more traditional 'academic' career was emphasized by the opposition to it of senior staff, firmly entrenched within their subjects. Later the school's reorganization into a comprehensive brought new career opportunities and problems, and some of these will be discussed shortly.

However these kinds of career structures are not available to the majority of teachers. On the contrary, most are faced, rather, by 'flat, dead-end opportunities' and consequently 'horizontal rather than vertical career patterns' (Purvis 1973). There might be some fairly rapid ascent in the early stages, but for most it soon levels out (Lyons 1981). As Lortie (1975, p. 84) notes, with regard to the USA, teaching is relatively 'career-less' compared with most other kinds of middle-class work, and with reorganizations and contraction in Britain, the career structure pyramid acquires an even wider base. Scales of remuneration are also low, with fewer and less increments, compared with other professions.

However these are all 'objective' careers – the ordered stages in hierarchical patterns that are presented to people. The interactionist is more interested in *subjective* careers where the emphasis is on the individual's construction of meaning and the career as a continuous process in which the individual changes in accordance with his own choices, aims and intentions (Hughes 1937). These are limited by objective circumstances and possibly influenced by objective career structures, but they are none the less the individual's own construction. Once we take this view we find many careers within teaching. Lyons (1981, p. 11) uses the analogy of a tree: 'The trunk represents the large number of those who enter teaching as the start of a career in education; with each career stage, as they progress along the main branches, greater and greater specialization is displayed; there is correspondingly less and less opportunity to retrace steps or transfer between branches, certainly at the extremity of the branches, as the career advances.' Thus one might branch, for example, into administration, advising, counselling, the upper hierarchy, increased specialisms, or, simply, more satisfying class teaching. There is no inevitable or automatic career advance in any direction. The individual is indeed limited by the objective structures with their typical 'flatness', but the particular route taken depends to some extent on our perceptions, abilities and attitudes, and, if progress is desired, a degree of flexibility, and a willingness to change oneself.

Few teachers appear to have a perception of their ultimate goal when they first enter teaching. Rather, they negotiate and re-negotiate in their own minds as their careers proceed, and they continually 'set and reset the goals themselves in that process' (Dale 1976, p. 76). They pick up gradually the outlines of a possible career chiefly through observation of their colleagues, and they continually re-adjust. Lyons (1981) argues that this facilitates the making of a 'career-map'. On such a map will be 'bench-marks'

– dividing points along the career serving as signposts (such as posts of progressively higher responsibility), controlled by 'gatekeepers' (such as headteachers, and others who have an influence on promotions). Attached to these stages is a 'timetable' by which one can measure progress through the chart of the intervening blocks of time between the benchmarks against the prevailing norm. Lyons argues that:

> A 'good' map takes note of the need to be built in sequential compartments, it will have a 'fast' timetable, and it will enable the teacher to acquire the relevant experience, qualifications and attitudes for each successive stage before the consideration of any move between stages. It will recognize the need for the teacher to seek sponsors, it will orientate him towards holding fulfillable goals, thus lessening the chances of his becoming blocked at any one career stage, and it will therefore become capable of revision as new timetables and gatekeeping devices emerge. It will limit fortuity (Lyons 1981, p. 134).

However, as Lyons notes, not all teachers choose 'fast' timetables, which is perhaps as well, given the general shortage of opportunities beyond the initial stages. Some do not perceive career maps at all clearly, especially beyond the immediate future. For some, movement from one benchmark to another is felt to be a huge step, involving a much longer time-span. Some are unsuccessful and disappointed, and have to re-align. Others reject altogether the values associated with 'successful' maps, and go in their own directions. Some indeed may have other careers, outside teaching, which may be more important to them.

Teachers, therefore, make their own careers. For most, this will invariably take a horizontal rather than vertical direction. In fact, to some individuals, different positions in the same rank may hold out greater attractions than those in the next rank. Teaching being comparatively 'career-less', most teachers have to assess their careers by other criteria – additional increments, 'better' classes, increased security, acquisition of more skill, and so on. Becker (1976) found this to be so for the Chicago public school teacher. These teachers identified three major problems in their work – teaching, discipline, moral acceptability; and three distinct strata of children, who varied on these criteria. Positions in teaching could be satisfactory or unsatisfactory depending on having the 'right' stratum. Teacher careers in such circumstances consisted of movement between schools to optimize their working conditions. However some careers were spent entirely in slum schools. But this does not mean that the person does not change or progress. On the contrary:

> During this stay changes take place in the teacher and in the character of her relations with other members of the school's social structure which makes this unsatisfactory school an easier place in which to work and which change the teacher's view of the benefits to be gained by transferring elsewhere (Becker 1976, p. 77).

These changes consist of new skills and attitudes, new teaching and disciplinary techniques, new expectations of the teaching possibilities, and new explanations which aid her understanding of pupils she formerly perceived as extremely difficult. She may gain a position with prestige and authority in the school and community which is hard earned and given up with reluctance. The career of the teacher with this outlook is one of progressive consolidation of her position.

Some teachers may progress downwards in relation to formally structured careers. This may sometimes be regarded as 'opting out'. It is less commonly regarded as 'opting in' to a different kind of career pattern. Thus it is not unknown for teachers who have progressed up the career ladder, perhaps to headteacher, to revert to classroom teaching, though it is a comparatively rare occurrence. We might speculate that, where it does occur, one reason might be that, along the way, the nature of the job changes (in this example, from teaching to administration), and the person judges his interests better served in the former state. This has been called 'planned demotion'.

There are, therefore, a number of opportunities before most people, even in unstaged career structures. Even where there has been a close association between career and self, there is an alternative. One such example, which highlights certain features of the teacher role and career, is given by an ex-head of English in a comprehensive school, who actually resigned his position because his local authority would not allow him unpaid leave for a year (Bethell 1980). What he needed was a 'break from the pressures', a chance to rediscover 'whole areas of his life which his job, while giving him much else, had denied him' (ibid., p. 23). He had become a slave to the 'constant pressure of immediate demands', which he had 'internalized', so that attendance day after day was 'not just a routine, it was a deep-seated imperative'. So ingrained were these routines within him that he had to force himself to construct similar ones during his year off. At school he had a strong sense of moral obligation – his 'every action' as a teacher 'was tainted by guilt'. However much he did there was more to do, and a strong feeling that he should do it. He had reached the stage where he felt his job was stunting his growth rather than promoting it. The educational possibilities lay in the greater latitude in finding out what he was best at, the personal control of his time and activities, the flexibility, and ultimately the rediscovery of forgotten or unsuspected parts of the self. It was, therefore, a quest for 'personal enrichment' and not simply 'professional improvement'.

This raises the question of commitment. As a 'career' teacher, Bethell had become tied to his job, as Merton (1957) suggests happens within bureaucracies. But instead of adapting to it, his self had rebelled against it. For most teachers, however, it is not such an all-or-nothing concern. Most, indeed, have a limited commitment. Among Lortie's (1975) American teachers, for example, the main hope for major advancement among men was to leave teaching for administration. Consequently few looked forward to long careers in teaching. For most women it was contingent on their main family concerns – marriage, childbirth, husband's change of job. Most women, therefore, saw it as an 'in-and-out' engagement (Lortie 1975, p. 87), and the unstructured nature of the career facilitated this sort of involvement. Lortie concludes that such a system favours 'recruitment rather than retention and low rather than high involvement' (ibid., p. 99). There are similar indications of restricted commitment in Britain (Purvis 1973).

This suggests, therefore, that there is a range of degree of commitment, from near total through partial, to almost complete lack. Career-bound teachers tend toward the first, misplaced teachers the last, but most show partial commitment. It says nothing, of course, about kind of commitment. Here three main types have been identified which we might label vocational, professional, and career. In practice there is overlap among these analytical forms, and teachers may vary from time to time, though a teacher may show an affinity for one particular type. Lacey identified two of these types among students on PGCE courses. One common form of vocational commitment was to education in its broadest sense. Such teachers 'acquire jobs in the schools which they feel will give them the freedom to teach in the ways they wish [comprehensive schools], and already see their careers taking them outside the classroom and outside the school' (Lacey 1977, p. 126). They are committed to a set of ideals about education and society, not to teaching as such, and if blocked from achieving their ideals through teaching will explore other means of bringing them about. Nias (1980) found other examples of vocational commitment among the hundred primary school teachers of her inquiry. It involved a 'calling to teach', the examples including a missionary sense deriving from religion, or the promotion of other ideals, or 'caring' for children.

The other form Lacey noted was a professional commitment to teach, to a career in the school, and to subject-based teaching. The students rated their teaching abilities very highly, and were dedicated to their advancement. Nias also found this prominent among her primary school teachers.

The different ways in which teachers with different forms of commitment perceive their careers is illustrated by this young male teacher of 'radical' (vocational) inclinations in Lacey's study:

> My views on education have not changed very much since leaving Sussex. I feel like the proverbial small cog and realise that education, like some other professions, is a rat-race for promotion. At the moment, being unmarried, I feel that I am free of some of the pressure that can be brought to bear on some of the staff [i.e. by heads of departments] (Lacey 1977, p. 137).

As Lacey points out, a 'professionally' committed teacher would probably not interpret the teacher career as a 'rat race', and would see the 'pressure' from senior colleagues as helpful advice rather than as something to hold out against.

It is not surprising that Nias, among primary teachers, and Lacey, among student teachers, should find a preponderance of vocational and professional commitment, while in the hard-pressed secondary modern of my research, the prevailing mode appeared to be 'career-continuance'. A teacher with such a commitment finds that 'what is profitable to him is bound up with his position in the organization', is contingent on his participating in the system (Kanter 1974, p. 132). In one form, the teacher opts to become Merton's prototype bureaucrat as he identifies more and more with the role, making sacrifices in other areas, as he comes to invest increasingly in the organization. A particular career within teaching may be the main attraction, advancement and status the spur. In another form, career-continuance is forced. It may be that higher ideals have been destroyed by difficult circumstances, only other involvements and responsibilities, like family, house, community, pensions, keeping them going.

As well as degree and type of commitment, range may be an important factor. This was suggested to me in a study of two teachers of great vocational commitment working in adverse circumstances (Woods 1981b). One of them was near retirement, the other, a young teacher of some two years' previous experience, in two different schools. As with them, he survived at his third school for just one year. He saw himself, I felt, as a reformer, and one way of managing this identity was to move from school to school fairly rapidly. This allowed him to test the elasticity in the norms and rules of each institution, and to act out his professional career in that area of temporary tolerance.

The other, however, was a teacher of long-standing, more committed to the principles and practice of teaching, and over a wider range of application. For example, he was the director of the evening school classes which took place in the same school; and he lived in the community, fraternizing with pupils and parents in out-of-school settings. This *range* of commitments enabled him to juggle his interests (Pollard 1980) depending on circumstances, as now he achieved satisfactions in one and disappointments in another, while on another occasion, these feelings might be reversed. Thus he was able to maintain an admittedly precarious teaching experience, but none the less retain his ideals (Woods 1981b). This 'juggling' of interests has similarities with the 'trade-off' decisions teachers make when confronted with situational dilemmas (Berlak *et al.* 1976, Berlak, A. and H. 1981).

The nature of one's commitment may change over time thus bringing a change in one's 'moral career'. Goffman (1961, p. 119) has described this as 'the regular sequence of changes that career entails in the person's self and in his framework of imagery for judging himself and others'. There are a number of such changes in a teacher's career. Perhaps the most significant is beginning teaching. We have seen in chapter 4 how the occupational culture bears on new recruits. As it does so, the self and consequently the view of career undergoes transformation. But change has already begun. As Lacey (1977) noted with student-teachers from two universities, 'after only one year of training, the new teachers are seeing themselves more definitely as members of the profession and less convinced by the idealistic stances of yesterday' (p. 130). There are numerous studies which point to the 'disillusionment and disenchantment of the first year of teaching' (Hannam *et al.* 1971, Hanson and Herrington 1976). As a teacher goes through this 'trial by ordeal', either her whole perspective changes or she acquires a new one. The teacher culture helps to pull her through with a strong sense of corporate identity in the face of adversity (Hammersley 1980a). In my own experience, there were jokes about 'losing one's sense of mission' (a commentary on a change from vocational to career-continuance commitment), a strong and

157

general feeling of the inevitability of compromise, and growth of a great mystique about skills and aptitudes for such compromise. It was on this basis that teachers evaluated themselves. Their moral career underwent a transformation in adapting to circumstances.

This applies to almost any job. In a study of bread salesmen, for example, Ditton (1977) shows how, faced by similar pressures (harsh employment conditions, personal responsibility for profit, methods of calculating, the 'inevitability' of shortages, relief at finding a solution, etc.), the naive recruit is turned into a fully fledged fiddler. He might go on to use these newly acquired techniques for his own benefit, as well as the organization's: 'If the learner wishes to stay with the firm, he must emerge as a fully fledged fiddler' (p. 34). This is the nub of the identity crisis. People often face dilemmas wherein they are more or less forced to act in certain ways not in line with their original intentions, because of greater need. Such acts are then rationalized as 'not too bad' or as things that 'everybody does'. The probity of self-identity is thus sustained, but the individual and his sense of potential for the future are changed as a consequence.

Further developments in the moral career wait along the way if and when one reaches the position of head of department, deputy head, and headteacher. It is important to realize that 'moral career' does not necessarily imply a change of standards – simply that the bases for one's judgments differ as one acquires more and new responsibilities. A good illustration of people at different stages of such a career was provided in the 1960s by a dispute over supervision of school meals. In the school I was teaching in at the time, 'professionally' committed teachers in the interests of what they saw as advancing the cause of teachers generally, stood out for ending voluntary supervision; 'vocationally' oriented teachers thought they should do it, because of a felt responsibility towards the children; the headmaster, under pressure from the LEA and reminded of his total responsibility for the school, tried ordering his staff to do it on the grounds that they were part of that responsibility. He was supported generally by the older heads of department, but totally opposed by the younger professionally oriented staff (mainly men), with a large number of staff (mainly women) non-committed.

This illustrates three different kinds of subjective career. The women appear to conform to the cultural norm which limits their aspirations and conditions their attitudes, e.g. as 'secondary breadwinners' and 'marriage and family oriented' (Purvis 1973, Lortie 1975); the group of obdurate 'professionals' are acting in the interests of what they see as the professional role and career and in this, it is teaching that counts, not 'nose-wiping and overseeing', while the headmaster is concerned with covering all functions of the school in the most efficient manner, and that means dinner supervision by teachers.

Careers thus have longitudinal, horizontal and sectional features, and there are elements of choice within and between them for the individual. But it is a choice that consistently has to be made in the light of circumstances. This is what Becker has termed 'situational adjustment':

> The person, as he moves in and out of a variety of social situations, learns the requirements of continuing in each situation and of success in it. If he has a strong desire to continue, the ability to assess accurately what is required, and can deliver the required performance, the individual turns himself into the kind of person the situation demands (Becker 1977b, p.131).

We might recall the strong influence of teachers' occupational culture here, which is a reminder that 'situational adjustment' is a collective experience. Where one does not actually physically experience a situation with many others, such as beginning teaching, many will have gone before, and the main lines of the adjustment will have been laid down. You only have to recall the teacher adaptation to noise (Denscombe 1980a) and the staffroom (Hammersley 1975) to appreciate this.

However, as Lacey (1977) points out, Becker has rescued the adult in his development from personality fixation only to rivet him to the situation. As discussed in chapter 6, Lacey proposes a threefold classification consisting of two kinds of situational adjustment – strategic compliance and internalized adjustment; and one which allows more scope for the individual influencing the situation, and his own career, strategic redefinition. This provides an overall more satisfactory model of teacher development, though it is largely hypothetical and their character and the actual distribution of numbers among the categories and indeed how an individual varies among them over time and in different contexts awaits empirical clarification. If an individual, far from adjusting to the situation, actually offends some basic principle of it, without accomplishing some redefinition of it, he will experience difficulty, even leading perhaps to a 'spoiled career' (Goffman 1961).

There are some fairly obvious examples, as when a teacher is sacked, made redundant, forced into early retirement, or downgraded. In these instances, it is others who perceive the need for making the disjuncture, and it invariably comes as a shock. Career structures cannot be re-formulated in one's head overnight. In other cases, the teacher himself perceives a disjuncture between his aspirations and the situation, and may leave to find something more suitable. This may be something in line with his broad educational ideals, perhaps in further or higher education, or some related field, like social work, in which case it simply shows an alternative career (Lacey 1977); or it may be something completely different, opting out of teaching altogether – a 'spoiled' career (Woods 1981b). Or he may, because of outside responsibilities, be unable to do this, and simply try to accommodate it, by perhaps lowering commitment to that part of his life, and increasing it in others. With recent reorganization and with cut-backs, spoiled careers are becoming more common. Lacey (1977) points to a typical example, where the 'seniority principle' that prevailed at Hightown Grammar was subverted by the appointment of junior more highly qualified men to deputy head of department. This offended one of the most sacred principles of the career structure as they knew it.

This, in fact, must be fairly common in reorganized comprehensive schools, and has been well documented in one such case by Riseborough (1981). This involved seventeen teachers in a secondary modern, which was reorganized to comprehensive, with a large influx of new staff. The ex-secondary modern staff were all non-graduates except one, most were two-year trained, and all were long-serving. All had a strong sense of the 'seniority principle', and in the secondary modern had a stable and satisfying view of themselves, with status, posts of responsibility, good relations, and recognition by the headmaster that they were 'good' teachers. They had mixed views about comprehensivization. On the one hand it might damage their career rewards and prospects. On the other, it might lead to an extension of career opportunities. This it undoubtedly has done in some comprehensives, particularly in the field of counselling, but also in subject departments in some instances. However, the new head, who himself felt under great pressure to produce 'results' quickly, soon made it clear to the 'old' staff that they did not fit into his scheme of things, as they had done under the secondary modern regime. They lost out, therefore, when the posts of responsibility were re-distributed. Though their salaries were protected, they were demoted in the status hierarchy. This was bad enough. As one said, 'You know, if you take this [status] away, not all the money in the world will make him feel content with his job, and this is what teaching is all about. You've got to feel right' (Riseborough 1981, p. 15).

But there was worse to follow when those appointed to the new posts turned out to be younger, less experienced teachers, who had good honours degrees and a record of examination success. The contrast was made, and at a stroke the careers of the 'old' staff were both brought to an abrupt halt in themselves, and subsumed within a larger career framework at a comparatively low level. Moreover, the new regime was soon publicly acclaimed, as the examination results began to come.

Even this was not all, for the old staff had no consolation in any horizontal projection of career, being allocated lower stream pupils (see also Hargreaves 1967). The 'comprehensive' principle was operated only in so far as it was felt not to endanger the drive for 'results'. Hence both pupils and teachers were streamed, but more invidiously than before. They were now doing the 'dirty work' (Hughes 1958). Since they were held in such low esteem, they reacted in kind, forming an isolated and diametrically opposing clique to the head and his new teachers. This massive disillusionment carried into the classroom. One of them admitted: 'The amount of help I give pupils is minimal really. I mark out time. Just give the kids some work. The drive has gone out of my teaching. It's hard to teach a class now ... I've actually stopped teaching if I'm honest' (Riseborough 1981, p. 23).

This teacher's career, he feels, has come to an end. He maintains a physical presence, just for the money. It is as joyless, and much less productive than any factory line. Yet out of this misery, they strive to recreate some self-respect. They will not accept the new headmaster's line, and are something of a thorn in his side. They maintain the old values and beliefs, the old ways of doing things, the old career structure. Yet the reality of the situation now weighs so heavily against them, that some are broken men. As a colleague remarked, 'They'd worked hard. The whole basis of their life had been stopped. They scratched their way up some sort of ladder and then quite suddenly their professional lives were over. These men are tragic.... There is no way out for them' (ibid., p. 27).Riseborough concludes that his study:

> shows ... the importance of intra-school, as well as inter-school, vertical and horizontal aspects of career; the interrelationship of vertical aspects with horizontal aspects ...; the importance of associated moral careers with implications for teacher ideologies and pedagogical styles; and the role of the head, qua 'critical reality definer' pursuing desired organizational goals, as the teacher career gatekeeper who in the making of strategic

choices constructs and sustains through interaction the professional identities of teaching staff (ibid., p. 30).

Summary

Teacher careers have only some of the features of a professional career. Typical teacher careers revolve round the academic line through subject departments, or round the counselling line through 'house' and year organization. Money and status are involved, but also a 'seniority principle' which relates to extra-curricular responsibilities, also organized as a status hierarchy. Teachers make career maps for themselves with 'timetables' and 'benchmarks'. But for many teachers, their careers do not involve vertical mobility. Yet they make their own careers, possibly moving horizontally to another school, to improve their working conditions and accomplishing personal change in the process; or even moving downwards in 'planned demotion'. We examined the case of a teacher involved on a similar sort of exercise, who had a successful teaching career yet felt he needed 'personal enrichment' and so resigned his post. The case highlights certain subjective features of careers, particularly the pressures on the person of the teacher role. It also illustrates certain features of bureaucracy, of which the graded career is a symptom, and the limitations and possibilities for the self.

Bureaucracy, because it allows for separation of role and self, also permits different forms and levels of commitment. Three main types have been identified – 'vocational', 'professional', and 'career-continuance' – being major modes of teacher attachment to their jobs. But one can also have a range of commitment which allows for a certain 'juggling' of interests between career sections. One's identity concerns will also influence kind of career.

One also undergoes changes in moral career – the criteria by which we judge ourselves and others. The biggest adaptation teachers make is when they first meet the teaching situation, and they have to redefine some of their own outlooks in order to cope. A similar process occurs in other occupations, for example, in that of bread salesmen. This is an example of 'situational adjustment', the process by which the individual changes to meet the demands of a new situation. However, we must not assume a 'situational determinism', any more than a 'personality determinism', and Lacey's model of strategical orientations shows the range of adaptations that can be made, from total immersion to 'redefinition'.

We concluded with a consideration of spoiled careers, careers that have been untimely terminated, or that have otherwise taken a turn out of line with the occupants' intentions.

Pupil careers

Pupil careers have to be seen in the first instance in the context of child development. One of the most significant sociological aspects of this is the progression from primary to secondary socialization. Primary socialization refers to the first learning that takes place within the family of basic techniques and attitudes with which to face the world. Secondary socialization, according to Berger and Luckman (1967), involves 'the internalisation of institutional or institution-based "sub-worlds" ... the acquisition of role-specific knowledge ... role-specific vocabularies ... and tacit understandings' (p.158). Some of these sub-worlds, or sub-universes of meaning as Schutz (1967) calls them, phase into each other. For example, the first lesson the child has to learn on going to school is how to become a pupil, in general terms, as distinct from 'a certain mother's child'. In the early years of infant school the boundaries between school and home are softened to ease this transition. But it is still a considerable one as children move from the confidence and certainty of primary socialization, where the world is one and indivisible and within which they are totally immersed, to a functionary world of many parts, which they quickly learn are of a different order – more distant, more utilitarian, more regulated.

A second traumatic transition of this nature occurs at age eleven, twelve or thirteen as pupils move from primary or middle to secondary or upper schools. Some indications of the meaning to pupils of this change can be gleaned from talking to pupils at the beginning of their secondary school careers (Measor and Woods 1983). What were the things that struck them most about their new school? These were, by comparison with their previous (middle) school, stricter discipline, more rules, a less 'homely' atmosphere, a greater division of labour, a move from task-oriented to time-oriented work, and larger units. This is the situation of secondary socialization. It is a difficult time for the pupil whose career at that moment is also complicated by encountering sex roles in earnest and becoming established within the informal culture.

Pupils cope with these various problems by developing strategical ability and negotiative skills, such as were outlined in chapters 6 and 7. Above all, they learn how to be 'pupils' – not the role as designated by those in authority, but as made by pupils. An instructive example of a similar adaptation from a related sphere comes from Howard Becker's study of medical students, a group with a strong commitment to a common aim – becoming doctors (Becker *et al.* 1961). His observations revealed that the students were less concerned, in the day-to-day action of their lives, with learning how to become doctors, than with learning how to become students. They had 'impossible' demands made on them in the form of extent of knowledge they were expected to absorb, and in work assignments set. The ultimate vocational call to medicine became more distant under the pressure of having to pass examinations. They were forced to devise short-term measures to cope, quite cynically, in order to qualify, but they preserved their long-term aim of becoming good practising doctors after qualification. Becker introduces the notion of 'time-perspectives' to explain this disjuncture, and argues that it is essential to see the short-term strategies as a temporary expedient to meet present contingencies against a much broader career backcloth. One might wonder, however, whether the ideal doctor *ever* emerges, any more than the ideal teacher. For constraints on action and variable resources, both personal and in the situation, follow one throughout life, and the moment is often a compromise between aspirations, possibilities and strategical knowledge. In this way, the short-term and the long-term are not as discrete as Becker suggests, but firmly related. In practice they remain inseparable. Such strategies may appear temporary, but they become part of the individual's stock of experience, which provides a resource for meeting future contingencies which are bound to arise.

Starting school, therefore, and moving from primary to secondary, are the first two stages in secondary socialization. But they are not the last. Later stages are at thirteen plus, translation from preliminary groundwork in secondary school to examination-oriented schemes; at fifteen plus, for those who stay at school, movement into sixth forms, and at seventeen plus, departure into occupations. At each such stage, there is a marked change in the status and role of pupils, the expectations required, and treatment of them. Having 'mastered' the previous stage, new problems, new situations arise in the next, making new demands on coping resources and ingenuities. The status change acts, therefore, as a stimulus to increasing strategical sophistication. During the eleven to thirteen period, new secondary school recruits learn to cope with the demands of the new senior school; during the thirteen to fifteen stage, they learn new patterns, which are superimposed upon the former, and so on. This socialization into ways of managing, solving problems, meeting demands as efficiently and economically as possible is preparation for later life, and arguably one of the most valuable lessons the pupil learns at school.

Such changes have been characterized as status passages. Glaser and Strauss (1971) have elaborated the perplexities that might be initiated: the passage may be desirable or undesirable, voluntary or involuntary; its features may not be clear, one's perceptions of them inaccurate, and control over them negligible; one might go through the passage alone, or with others, though awareness of this might be variable. In negotiating the passage and learning to cope with new situations, one might argue that behaviour might tend to take certain forms. For example, in a strange situation, the pupil might tend to be withdrawn, not active, a recipient rather than giver, consumer rather than creator. There is an initial reconnoitring phase, when those problematic elements of the passage are being worked out – what it constitutes, who else is involved, its duration, its relevance to one's own concerns, the space for manoeuvre, and so on; and when knowledge about how previous crossers of the passage coped, and similarities in one's own previous experience brought to bear.

Once again, for an example, we might look at the juncture between junior or middle school and secondary or upper school as a case in point. Pupils recognize the significance of the move: 'It's like starting a new life going to the other school.' 'It seems more grown up. You're sort of more important, and I know that happens because when I see pupils from [the upper school] in the street, you kind of look away.' 'This school just prepares you for [the upper school], that school prepares you for life.' How, then, is such a leap accomplished?

Van Gennep (1960) argued that status passages consisted of three main phases – separation, transition and aggregation or reincorporation, and this is a useful distinction, if tinctured with interactionist principles. The first phase is marked by behaviour symbolizing separation from a particular point in the social structure or a set of cultural conditions. The second is distinguished by marginality or 'liminality' (V.W. Turner 1969), wherein the characteristics of the person undergoing the passage are ambiguous, neither belonging to past nor future status. In the third phase the subject is reunited with the social order with the clearly defined rights and duties attaching to the state. As it stands, however, this is a functionalist schema, conceived from the point of view of security rather than individuals, who are seen as leaving and re-joining the system. A more appropriate model for interactionists would have a first stage of anticipation, and a third stage of 'adaptation'. This allows conceptually for the consideration of more self-system interaction from the point of view of the self (Musgrove 1977, Musgrove and Middleton 1981).

It would be a mistake to superimpose these stages on any passage – there may, for example, be no 'anticipation'. But they were certainly present in one study we made of pupil transfer from middle to comprehensive school (Measor and Woods 1983). In the first phase, we noted a great deal of emotional upheaval among pupils as they looked forward to the change. There was much excitement and anticipation, but also, and most notably, anxiety. They expressed fears of getting lost, of being late or otherwise transgressing the rules simply because they did not know their way around, of getting bullied and beaten up by older pupils. They saw the change as ultimately leading to an enhancement of status, but it was to be hard-earned, and in the short-term meant, in fact, a drop in status, as one went from the top of one school to the bottom of the next – 'silly little first years'. Teachers would be stricter and harder, especially as there were more male staff in the upper school, and it would be more difficult to develop close personal relationships with them given the size of the school and the organization of the curriculum and timetable.

Much of this fear was about not only physical security but personal identity, not only 'what was to happen to them' but 'what were they to become?' Reputations, established over the years at middle school through hard work, prowess at games or at fighting or whatever, now seemed in jeopardy. How would they cope with new forms of work, new challenges and forms of opposition? Above all, would they be split up from their friends and put in separate classes with a lot of new people? If so, their personal destruction, in the sense of the identities they had developed up till then, would be complete. They were like little fish emerging from the safety of the river into the maelstrom of the wider ocean (see also Bryan 1980).

This emotional preparation was the most prominent feature of the anticipation phase. However, aiding the transition were two highly effective agencies, one formal, provided by the school, the other informal, provided by the pupils' own culture. The upper school provided a highly effective induction programme. Pupils visited the school during the last term of middle school and were introduced to their new teachers, who explained and demonstrated new modes of working, the kinds of rules and standards they expected, and, in the process, showed pupils that they were human. Also, on the first day of term, the new first year pupils had the school to themselves. They could thus begin to familiarize themselves with the ecology of the school and the formal processes, before tackling the problems in the informal culture.

For these the second agency was a useful aid. These were pupil myths – a whole body of them which spanned the range of anxieties listed above. There were stories about getting your 'head flushed down the loo on your birthday', and other mistreatment at the hands of one's fellows, tales about impossible physical feats demanded by games' staff, of punishments, of a homosexual teacher, and of gory science lessons cutting up animals (Measor and Woods 1983). In their particulars these stories were nearly all wrong. But they seemed to serve the function of providing information of a general kind and offering a warning. They were both a proscription and prescription. Pupils were warned not to place too much of their personal identity at risk, informed about 'normal' sex roles, boys were told of the hardness and toughness expected in the male pupil subculture – these were the messages conveyed by the myths. And once the passage had been successfully negotiated, the new recruits relayed the myths on to the next intake.

'Adaptation' took place during the first year, as the pupils severed their ties with their previous school and negotiated entry to the new. There was a certain amount of 'sussing out' (see chapter 6) as pupils felt for new rules and norms, though for the most part, teachers seemed to anticipate this, and made a point of demonstrating them very clearly. Also, it seemed that on the whole pupils preferred to take a 'wait and see' attitude in initial encounters; in contrast to the pessimistic encounters noted by Ball (1980), playing the 'optimistic conformity' line, and presenting an open and friendly front to both teachers and their fellows. For a brief period, their corporate identity as new pupils was uppermost.

They had to get used to new rules in lessons. There were new restrictions about noise and movement, for example, but teacher humour was a pleasant, and unexpected compensation for this. There were differences in the pace and amount of work, but pupils were relieved to find it was not impossible, and many actually welcomed the change from an integrated day into subject disciplines. They rapidly adjusted to the size of the school, knowing their way around 'after about two weeks'.

It took rather longer to establish themselves in the informal culture. Girls, for example, had to become familiar with age-grading, which had clear rules about how much make-up it was appropriate for first-year pupils to wear – too much, though permissible for older girls, brought them the accusation of being 'tarts', too little, and they were unfeminine. Boys, brought together in new groupings, soon began to scramble for position within the informal status hierarchy. Meanwhile, boys and girls grew apart, as the old middle school groups were dissipated and new patterns formed. This gender division was matched by a gradual division of pupils into broadly 'conformist' and 'deviant' groups, clearly identified by the pupils as such, and selection of friends now took place on these bases. This invariably began with comparing notes about work, and progressed to meetings outside school, to visiting each other's home, having tea and eventually staying the night. In this way, the pupil cultures and adaptations discussed in chapter 5 took root.

However, though we can generalize about groups of pupils collectively undergoing this status passage, our data also shows that there are pupils who undergo individual status passages. Here, individuals make the passage with no particular regard to the factors mentioned above, and accomplish it in their own private way. Individuals might also undergo 'transformational episodes', catalytic moments, periods of events when the pupil undergoes significant change. They may occur during status passages, but they may occur at other times also, for there are other catalytic agents. Strauss, in speaking of 'transformations of identity' has insisted that it is change, and not just development:

> As he 'advances', his early concepts are systematically
> superseded by increasingly complex ones. The earlier ones are
> necessary for the later; each advance depends upon the child's
> understanding a number of prerequisite notions. As the newer
> classifications are grasped, the old ones become revised or
> qualified, or even drop out entirely from memory (Strauss 1969,
> p. 92).

This is remarkably similar to our conception of strategical socialization. Strauss provides a list of 'critical incidents' or 'turning-points' that can lead to such transformations, such as the 'milestone', an event that brings home to one, or crystallizes a progression or retrogression. As Berger and Luckman (1967) point out, 'bring home to one' is a peculiarly apt expression for this experience, for it strikes into the world of primary socialization. Another 'critical incident' is playing a new role well, discovering perhaps hidden and unsuspected capacities. Two that we might insert that are particularly relevant to pupils are the acquisition of new knowledge, and the influence of others, whether parents, teachers or peers.

The first is a factor which seems curiously absent from

sociological literature. Perhaps this is because sociologists have been more interested in the social construction of knowledge, and in the 'hidden curriculum'. The impact of knowledge on self-identity is but little studied. But we know, from our own experiences at least, the power of knowledge to transform selves. Thus there may be revelations for pupils along the way – indeed this is what teachers purport to provide – the discovery of an activity or area of knowledge that seizes the imagination, summons up new powers of application and ingenuity, that cuts through both the pupil's own possible undervaluing of self and the labelling prescriptive of others. This could lead to a re-routing of career, or a powerful impulsion to a new role level, from, for example, 'struggler' or 'drifter' (Dale 1972) to comparative 'expert' and 'planner'. We can speculate that, on occasions, the transformational agent is not unconnected with growing accept-ance of future responsibilities. Yet others that occur later in life do so perhaps because they are elsewhere, that is to say generated not in the sphere of public, institutional life – the world of secondary socialization – at all. Motor-cycling, stamp-collecting, hi-fi, photo-graphy, bird-watching, pigeon-fancying, fishing – these are all examples of interests that are extra-curricular. The school may have clubs and societies in some of those pursuits, but the deep, almost obsessive interest that attends hobbies derives from the complete freedom of one's own initiative, which is more common-ly experienced in the private sphere of life, the area more connected with primary socialization. The 'progressive' movement in schools could be seen as an attempt to soften the school's own blockages to 'transformational episodes', and the public-private divide; while perhaps the greater success of the primary school in this respect, and in securing the pupils' motivation generally, is related to its proximity to the complete, real world of first childhood.

The second factor that might induce one of these 'transforma-tional episodes' is an outstanding educational agent – perhaps a parent or other relative, a teacher or a friend. Most of what we learn we learn from others, be it school learning, or learning about new situations, people and tasks, and events in life generally. An outstanding teacher can transform in a truly educational sense. Some do the opposite, and cool out pupils who otherwise might have made progress educationally. Transformations are not always the result of beneficial incidents, but might arise from 'stressful situations'. Strauss suggests that these occur if 'motivations are inappropriate for further passages and when self-conceptions grate against arrangements for sequential movements' (1969, p.106).

Dale adds two more factors: 'when no clear career-line is offered by the institution, and when an institutionally discouraged but competing value system is found' (1972, p.82) – for example, a pupil counter-culture.

If pupil behaviour and attitude often appear unaccountable, erratic, inconsequential, it may well be because of the extreme marginality of their position. It might seem to be stretching a point to claim that pupilhood is marginal, since it is well established by law, custom, etc. However, at school, they are under tutelage, subordinate, directed. They are 'growing' or 'becoming', only 'arriving' when they leave. The whole period is transitional, from being unsocialized and irresponsible infants to being fully-fledged citizens. Unsurprisingly, therefore, we find the contours of many pupil careers laid down by teachers.

Pupil careers, in fact, are more noted for their continuities and channelling than for their own initiated direction. This is well illustrated by the passages undergone involving subject and occupational choice. Here, it might be thought, pupils are given the opportunity to decide which direction their careers should take. But the choices are heavily circumscribed, and non-existent for some. We saw in chapter 3 how pupils come to form different outlooks on life and judge by different criteria, some utilitarian, some social; and how these were related to social class and gender.

These pupil perspectives are matched by teachers' perspectives, and they operate with a notion of 'appropriateness'. Thus for the comprehensive school of Ball's (1981) research, teachers felt that 'O' level was appropriate for the pupils in band 1, traditional Mode 1 CSEs for band 2, and New Mode CSEs for band 3; the notion derived from the bands within which the pupils had been placed, rather than from the pupils as individuals (see also Keddie 1971). These different characterizations of pupils are reinforced by different teaching programmes. Thus 'top sets in maths follow a ... syllabus which leads on to the "O" level course, and in music, band 1 and band 2 ... don't cover the same ground, major scales go well with the first band, people don't usually try them with band 2' (Ball 1981, pp. 185–6). Even where a common examination was held, as in physics and chemistry, the 'banding' typification predominated. Results in physics, for example, showed the top ten pupils in a lower form achieving better than the bottom eleven in the one above. But only three of these pupils opted for 'O' level physics. One opted for CSE physics, and was accepted. Although his mark was above those of six out of the ten in the higher form who were accepted for 'O' level, it was not suggested to him that he opt for 'O' level (see also Ryrie, Furst and Lauder 1979).

170

If pupils, therefore, do not by themselves select the appropriate channel, it is selected for them. In my study (Woods 1979), I found there was a large number of 'pretenders' (aiming higher than they should) and 'underbidders' (not aiming high enough), and much staff time and ingenuity was spent in directing them into more 'appropriate' channels. The vast majority of those requiring rechannelling came from the lower part of the streaming structure. Teachers tried to head off pretenders and encourage underbidders by communicating to them beforehand a 'proper' notion of their ability, and of their 'rightful' place in the school structure, removing the stigma of the drop-out choice and extolling the fairness of selection techniques; and, after the choice, by persuasion based on the criteria of ability and aptitude; only as a last resort was exclusion practised. Thus were pupils encouraged to choose 'appropriate' career lines.

Cicourel and Kitsuse (1963) similarly observed how student careers in American high schools are produced by organizational activities. Students may be typed by their teachers in relation to academic, behavioural and emotional 'problems' – under-, over-, normal-achievers, opportunity students, trouble-makers, hoods, delinquents, 'nervous', 'withdrawn', 'isolates'. A syndrome of typings may precede their entry to a school, and their career as 'slow learner', 'difficult pupil' and so on, be laid down for them. Cicourel and Kitsuse show how counsellors shepherd 'typed' pupils into appropriate channels, for instance, college, vocational, and commercial types of 'academic career'; how the labelling of students might launch them into 'delinquent careers'; and how teachers, counsellors, clinical personnel and parents make diagnoses which place students in 'clinical careers'. In short the authors reveal the importance for deciding which pupils follow which school career of the interpretative rules used by the organizational personnel, who decide what forms of behaviour are to be classified as 'deviant', 'academic', etc.

None of this is to accuse teachers of conspiracy. Rather, the school is under the influence of a society that still sponsors divisions, though behind a number of masks, in Britain, of progressivism, comprehensivization, and choice. The significance of the option choice process is that it is:

a point at which school careers become firmly differentiated and at which the informal differences between pupils in terms of social reputation and their experiences of the curriculum lower down the school are formalized into separate curricular routes and examination destinations. It is here that the stratified nature of the occupation structure is directly reflected in the ability stratification within the school (Ball 1981, p. 209).

Similarly, Hurman (1978) was forced to conclude that 'options, although they do involve the making of choices, are not primarily about choosing' (p. 304). Comprehensivization amalgamated two very different curricular styles – that of the grammar school, subject-centred, examination oriented, hierarchically managed, and that of the secondary modern, topic-centred, with intuitive decision-making. It also severely modified the streaming system. Option choices got round the twin problem of selection and socialization posed by these developments in a way that seemed to accord with the spirit of comprehensivization, by giving pupils and their parents responsibility for choosing their career paths in the upper school themselves.

Two major channels for pupil careers that have been identified are those based on social class and gender. The former relates to the examination structure, the latter more to type of subject (for example, arts and languages rather than physics and chemistry, see chapter 5). These channels lead on to future careers. We have seen in chapter 5 how girls orient towards service occupations of middle or lower status, and towards family life, as opposed to the world of work. We also noted how 'working class boys choose working class jobs' with great willingness (Willis 1977). Their careers in the upper school show the same form of adaptations as in shop-floor culture, appropriating the official system for their own ends, which remain obdurately guided by that culture, despite the best efforts of teachers. They may feel that these pupils' careers are a waste of time. But for the 'lads' time is 'an aspect of their immediate identity and self-direction. Time is used for the preservation of a state – being with the "lads" – not for the achievement of a goal – qualifications' (Willis 1977, p. 29).

For middle-class and aspiring working-class pupils, their later school careers are governed by the urgency and competitiveness of examinations. Individual ambition can have relevance here. But not all ambitions can be realized where the opportunities do not exist. Schools typically indulge, therefore, in a 'warming-up' and 'cooling-out' process (Hopper 1971): 'warming-up' as many pupils as possible to achieve to maximum potential, and 'cooling-out' when the available opportunities have been exhausted. This, of course, depends on the general economic system and situation, and at times when the system is under stress, when there is, for example, high unemployment among school leavers, there are severe implications for pupil careers. Some may have to be 'kept warm', by being encouraged to continue with full-time education longer than they first anticipated, though this opportunity also may not be available. Some may therefore find this difficult. Channels are difficult to navigate if they do not appear to be leading anywhere.

Summary

The pupil's career can be represented as gaining greater strategical sophistication as one proceeds from primary to secondary socialization, that is learning how to relate to institutions and the roles within them, adapting to larger structures, and new divisions of labour and time. The pupil learns how to be a pupil, how to manage the demands that are made and problems that arise while preserving identity.

The pupil career consists of a number of steps or stages which comprise status passages. One of the most significant of these is the move from junior to secondary, or middle to upper school. In one study, there was considerable emotional preparation for the move, marked by excitement and expectation, but also a high degree of anxiety over such matters as losing one's friends, the strangeness of the new and much larger school, the prospect of rough treatment from teachers and older pupils, and the possible difficulty of new forms of work. The transition was aided, however, by the induction scheme devised by the upper school, and by the body of pupil myths that had grown up over the years around the juncture. During the first year pupils adapted to the society of the new school. Initial encounters were cautious and optimistic. Teachers took special care to make rules explicit, and also to make themselves appear human (in full accord with the pupil perspective of the 'good' teacher in chapter 3). Anxieties about the formal aspects of school were soon allayed, and the differences accommodated. New groupings within the pupil culture, which were the basis for future development, began to form on conformist/deviant and male/female lines.

There are, however, individual status passages, and there are also 'transformational episodes' when a pupil might undergo considerable personal change, perhaps through some new knowledge, and/or an outstanding educational agent. Even so, pupil careers are better noted for their continuities and for the way in which they are channelled by other forces. Two of the most powerful of these are social class and gender, and we have seen the influence they exert in the crucial processes of subject and occupational choice. Distinct career paths exist, associated with a hierarchy of knowledge which in turn is linked to the examination system. Early assignment to bands or sets, therefore, has a strong relationship to ultimate type and number of examinations taken. In option choice, if pupils do not select the correct channels for themselves, as most do through the group perspectives they have developed, teachers will redeploy them according to a principle of 'appropriateness'. Thus are pupil careers formalized in accordance with the stratified nature of the occupation structure. After this, an appropriate selection of occupation, where any exist, is almost a formality.

Chapter 9

Achievements and prospects

It is sometimes claimed that sociology is obscure, of no practical use, or that it simply tells us the obvious in convoluted language. The reader must be the judge of how far this book relates to such views, but I do believe that interactionism has much to offer the practising teacher, as well as sociology in general.

First, with regard to practical use for the teacher, I would claim that there are four major areas where interactionist studies have made distinct contributions. This is in providing information that could lead to: (1) better teaching; (2) less conflict in schools, less deviance, and hence a better situation for teaching; (3) better understanding of one's own career and those of others, possibly leading to greater satisfactions in teaching, and (4) better understanding of how both school and society are inextricably riddled with inequalities, and how they are reproduced; and an appreciation of how the heavy constraints that surround the teacher's job are acted out and in part created in the school, thus providing a sounder base for institutional and curriculum reform.

In teaching, close analysis of lessons has revealed the presence of aims and intentions of teachers other than teaching, however subconsciously held. I refer to matters such as control, survival, and coping. Pupils, especially as they grow older, complain of school being irrelevant to their concerns, and of schools being 'unreal'. Lessons oriented to non-teaching functions could be partly responsible. So, of course, could inadequate resources and an outmoded curriculum, over the first of which, at least, the teacher has little control. But though possibly forced into coping or survival, the teacher does have a degree of freedom in constructing lessons, and if 'relevance' and 'reality' are to be increased, these mechanisms must be correctly identified.

Interactionism not only induces reflexivity, and analysis of one's own thought, action and motives, but also draws attention to all participants in a situation. With its emphasis on the individual, it counter-acts the tendency to 'cohort-labelling' induced by people-processing institutions. It puts one in the position of the 'other', so that we can better appreciate alternative perspectives and strategies. We can thus better identify, perhaps, influences that are causing some pupils to underperform, that bring them to 'choose to be unequal', rather than attribute low achievement to inherent lack of ability or aptitude. We can also see, not only what strategies pupils deploy, but which ones will work, what, from their point of view, constitutes a 'good' teacher, and the importance to them of relationships in respect of work. Good teaching is nothing if it is not communicating. Conversational analysis and studies of teacher and pupil language reveal at times great distances between understandings, though appearances may be to the contrary.

As for deviance, a cure depends on a correct diagnosis. Wrong diagnosis may well aggravate the disorder. Interactionist studies have revealed the sense of order, system and rationality that lies behind much pupil behaviour, which, on the face of it, seems pointless and anarchic. Apparently unruly behaviour is shown to be strongly rule-bound. It can be culturally produced, or it could be a reaction to teachers or to the institution. It could be a necessary part of the process of discovering a working rela-tionship, as in 'sussing' or 'testing out'. But, to some extent, what is defined as deviant depends on the perspective of the teacher. Apart from how it is defined, some perspectives have been shown to be more deviance-productive than others. We have noted, too, that conformity is not always what it seems.

In teacher careers certain problems have been identified, especially in the early stages. Lacey (1977) observed an 'at risk' syndrome and proposed a strategical mode of negotiating the rough waters of those early years. We have seen how teacher cultures weigh on the new recruit, and how developments occur in the moral career. But also how the individual can make roles (as contrasted with taking or breaking them) by a judicious mixture of strategic compliance and strategic redefinition, or by developing a range of commitments and 'juggling' one's interests among them. We have seen the despair that can be caused by a spoiled career, whether it has arisen because it conflicts with one's own sense of personal development even though it might be seen as enhancing one's professionalism or through institutional change, and there are implications for policy-makers here. In the meantime, such knowledge provides teachers with a chart which might aid them to navigate these stormy seas. They can also appreciate the rough passages that pupils sometimes have to undergo, like changes between schools, and the importance this places on induction schemes and initial encounters, making rules explicit and humanizing the rough institutional edges.

Interactionist studies have also shown how inequalities are not only preserved, but also fostered in our schools, despite manifest attempts to remove them. The same divisions noted in a secondary modern and a grammar school by Hargreaves and Lacey in the 1960s have been identified by Ball in a comprehensive practising banding and mixed-ability teaching. Broadly conformist and deviant groups continue to show a strong relationship to social class. But interactionist studies go further than this in two important ways. One is that they reveal the myths and rhetorics that multiply around the reality. Close observation of the fine-grained detail that attends such concerns as progressive, mixed-ability or guided-discovery teaching, 'busyness', or subject and occupational choice reveals the obdurate influence of social class and gender factors, despite the best efforts of teachers. Future studies will no doubt engage with ethnic factors also. The other way in which interactionist studies make a distinctive contribution is that they show how these inequalities are acted out in everyday life, how they are imprinted on the minds and personalities of pupils and shape their thoughts, values and attitudes, how they form moral imperatives for action.

Not much of this is, I would have thought, 'obvious' to the casual observer, or to people involved in roles within the situation. In fact, the reverse is the case – it is the appearances that are obvious, but which, upon investigation, show signs of being illusory. For some, this may be difficult to accept, for it sometimes challenges definitions of situations participants make. To them, sociology may appear to be a threat. Burns explains why when he describes the purpose of sociology as being:

> to achieve an understanding of social behaviour and social institutions which is different from that current among the people through whose conduct the institutions exist; an understanding which is not merely different but new and better. The practice of sociology is criticism. It exists to criticize claims about the value of achievement and to question assumptions about the meaning of conduct (Burns 1967, p. 37).

Consequently, sociology is often difficult to take. It might force people to face uncomfortable realities, in that they may see themselves required to revise attitudes and motives in resolving particularly difficult problems, which they have now put behind them. However, far from spreading confusion and foreclosing on options, sociology, in offering to extend understanding, extends choices. If people stay with old realities, they can defend them with renewed vigour. But if they were at all uncertain about them, sociology offers the chance for revision.

Similarly, though some interactionists, myself included, might seem over-indulgent in specialist language at times, if it can be kept within bounds, it can be of service to teachers in that it does provide a language for discussing aspects of interaction that have not been addressed before. D. Hargreaves (1978) calls this the 'designatory' capacity of interactionism. Interactionism can, in fact, be regarded as a kind of mapping process. Schools, until recently, were largely unexplored areas. Furthermore, this was intentional policy in the early years of sociology of education in this country during the 1950s and 1960s, for researchers largely worked with an 'input-output' or 'black box' model, which assumes that 'in order to demonstrate an effect it was necessary only to show correlations between inputs and outputs. The contents of the black box (i.e. the school), the social mechanisms and process, are neglected and not without cost' (Lacey 1976, pp. 56–7). Hargreaves and Lacey in the late 1960s were like Christopher Columbuses in the new world. Many have followed them over the past decade. Thus, much of what was previously taken for granted has been exposed and identified as worthy of study, not only in its own right, but because it does have an effect upon output.

This 'charting' or 'mapping' of areas of social life within the school is a necessary task in its own right. But eventually, interactionists need to go further. Much of their work to date has been descriptive and empirical. Where theory has been addressed, it has largely been 'substantive' theory, theory developed for a particular area of inquiry. But schools have features in common with other institutions, the interactions that occur within them have similarities with others elsewhere, and the social forces surrounding schools surround all elements of society. We need, therefore, to give more thought to 'formal' theory, which Glaser and Strauss (1967, pp. 32–3) explain as 'that developed for a formal, or conceptual area of sociological enquiry, such as stigma, deviant behaviour, formal organization, socialization, status congruency, authority and power, reward systems or social mobility' (see also Denzin 1978). In other words, other 'maps' from areas such as work, medicine, handicap, deviance, youth studies, in all of which there is a growing interactionist literature, need to be superimposed on that of the school, when we might discover more fundamental processes with more general applicability. Eventually, the map-making must yield to investigation of the hinterland and identification of common elements. The opportunities are there, and occasionally have been acted upon, notably in the fields of definition of the situation, deviance theory, organizational and cultural theory, careers and status passages. The same is true for an associated, but essentially different point concerning the interactionist's apparent immersion in the 'micro' minutiae of the scene and moment, and neglect of the 'macro' forces of large-scale systems and society. The point, in fact, forms one of the crucial debates within sociology today. But while it has certainly been customary for people to work primarily in one area or the other, and hence to create the impression of distinctive and sometimes apparently oppositional forces of inquiry in some tension with each other, it is not essential for them to do so. There is another alternative, which is to take both into consideration, and there are signs that theories and arguments gather strength when this is done. Hence macro theories can be reinforced by sound ethnographic data. But the micro situation can only be understood properly if it is realized that there are sinews and filaments in it that reach out into the wider world.

We have seen several instances of where this interface is being explored. The teacher's occupational culture, for example, is the medium through which many restrictions or reforms and innovations must pass; and during the passage they may get transformed, shaped or resisted in ways completely unintended or unanticipated. The concept thus allows for consideration of both macro and micro elements. The same is true of 'coping strategies'. In fact Pollard (1982), following A. Hargreaves (1977, 1978, 1979) has elaborated a model which includes social structure and hegemony, what he calls 'institutional bias', and teacher and child biographical factors which reach back to earliest socialization. The essential feature of 'coping strategies' is that they represent the meeting point and resolution of conflict or inarticulation between external and internal forces, between constraint and creativity, determinism and volition.

Group perspectives and pupil cultures are other cases in point. They permit the identification of elements worked up in reaction to common problems and situations both inside and outside the school. Among these, social class and gender socialization have been prominent. Also running throughout the studies reported in this book is a concern for selection and socialization processes, which are also at the heart of macro considerations of the functions of the education system.

Interactionism, then, is not necessarily a-structural and a-historical, though in their eagerness to chart the basic coastline of school processes, there has to date been an underemphasis on these macro factors. A. Hargreaves (1980b) reminds us of C. Wright Mill's view that the ability and the desire to connect 'what we experience in various and specific milieux' to questions and conceptions of social structure is the core feature of the sociological imagination. The 'situation', Hargreaves argues, does not exist in a vacuum, but has political and economic origins and associations, though these may become obscured over time, or entangled with mediational factors like teacher culture, institutional bias or an individual teacher's perspectives. It is important to identify them, for upon it depends not only satisfactory sociological theory, but also proposals for reform.

This is not an easy task. It is, after all, like looking through a microscope and a telescope at the same time. To date, interactionists have favoured the microscope, and have tended to work alone on single case studies. The kind of ethnographic work they do through an extended period of participant or non-participant observation is intensely personal. Their methods, data and approaches are not as accessible as survey or experimental techniques. So a number of such studies have been conducted, quite independently of and often unbeknown to each other. This did not seem to matter while they were 'taking' problems rather than 'making' them, that is to say making no assumptions about the problem to be researched beforehand, but discovering it within the setting. What many interactionists claimed to be doing was trying to understand particular situations better. Their results might, or might not, have some wider validity. Without some attention to macro analysis, however, these studies may not have *internal* validity. Wider social factors have implications for how we interpret situations.

We might therefore regard the interactionist research in schools to date as the first stage of a process of discovery about how schools work – the first rough mappings of the hitherto dark unknown of the 'black box' interior. Stage two work will need to take stock of these earlier studies, looking for similarities, differences, inconsistencies, omissions, and plan accordingly. It will require attention to three major concerns: (1) further mapping of uncharted areas of school life; (2) formal theory; and (3) macro links. It will enhance the validity of the project if all three are conducted simultaneously. But this may be difficult, if not impossible, for one person to achieve in the traditional 'splendid isolationism' of the interactionist approach (A. Hargreaves 1980b). Hence the growing interest in some form of coordinated teamwork (ibid., Hammersley 1980b). This could take several forms. The team could address itself to an area of theory, such as that surrounding the notion of 'coping strategy' and decide to examine different, but related areas such as certain parts of teacher and pupil biographies, or the material inputs into the school and the policies associated with them, with a view to refining the overall model and advancing formal theory. Such teamwork need not take place in the same school or area. Another form of teamwork could concern itself with one area if in the first place it is looking for substantive linkages between segments of the area. In other words this team would seek to 'ground' these linkages and consequent emergent theory in the situation under study, whereas in the first kind a certain amount of 'grounding' has already been done in other studies.

Consider, for example, the subject of school 'ethos'. A study of this area would benefit from the use of interactionist techniques, for it is concerned with common understandings and with processes over time. A school 'ethos' does not just suddenly come into existence, nor is it necessarily perceived in the same way by all the inmates, nor is it bounded utterly and absolutely by the school walls. A team approach, interested in demystifying the subject of school 'ethos' or culture, could have a research worker located in each of two schools in one local authority area. Using two schools would ensure a comparative base to the study, but to aid the proper consideration of home, neighbourhood and other external factors, another member of the team could concern himself with interviewing parents and fraternizing with pupils. Another might be based in the local education authority offices, monitoring the reception of government decisions and inception of local policies. Another member might systematically study the history of the area, and of the two schools. What is happening is the recognition of several links in the chain that will lead to full understanding of the phenomenon, with acknowledgment that they cannot all be covered in the kind of detail required by one, or even two, persons. Frequent and regular meetings of the team would ensure the primacy of the overview, adequate consideration of formal theory and macro analysis, firmly grounded in the details of the area, and be a useful means of checking and cross-checking data.

Hammersley (1980b) mentions several other examples of team research. There are, for instance, parallel studies – perhaps comparing two apparently widely different forms of teaching, such as a secondary school teacher and a university academic; or a local study that examines all the various agencies that bear on deviant pupils and their careers – the pastoral organization of the school, the police, the social welfare apparatus. Willis's (1977) study would have been enriched by inputs from observation of 'ear 'oles'; and talk with the 'lads'' girlfriends and from the factory shop-floor equal to that of the 'lads'. My own study of Lowfield (Woods 1979) would have benefited from a detailed examination of the area in which the school was located, and the historical antecedents of the school as I found it. It is difficult to see how such tasks can be satisfactorily accomplished other than by a team of researchers. What a world lies at their feet:

> even within the micro-substantive quadrant there are vast tracts underinvestigated: higher/further education, primary and nursery education, private and special schools; headmaster's offices, staffrooms, pastoral organizations, playgrounds, local education authority offices, and of course the DES.
> Furthermore, settings outside the education system where selection and socialization processes occur have been almost entirely neglected by sociologists of education (for example, military and police academies, theological seminaries, religious and political sects and movements, not to mention the family) (Hammersley 1980b, p. 208).

These, of course, are by no means interactionist preserves. The full explanation of social life which includes the relationship between major systems and historical analysis on a larger scale requires other approaches. Interactionism might properly inform them, but it cannot replace them. Stage two will bring interactionism and other approaches closer together.

We have hardly begun to investigate the possibilities of methods that might help to accomplish this. The 'Life History' method, for example, popular among the Chicago School interactionists of the 1930s, has largely been forgotten since. It involves extensive and repeated interviews with one person on that person's life and career, supported by others' views and by documentation. Thus it achieves the classic interactionist perspective on the situation and the self, but in the light of how both situation and self have been historically and structurally composed. As Goodson (1980, p. 74) argues:

> Life history investigations set against the background of evolutionary patterns of schooling and teaching should provide an antidote to the depersonalized, ahistorical accounts of

schooling to which we have become accustomed. Through the life history, we gain insights into individuals' coming to terms with imperatives in the social structure.... From the collection of life histories, we discern what is general within a range of individual studies; links are thereby made with macro theories but from a base that is clearly grounded within personal biography.

Interactionists will also turn their attention to non-cognitive matters, to the emotions and to the subconscious, and these also will require new approaches. Emphasis on the 'construction of meanings' has all but obliterated these from consideration. But school is full of emotions – joy, laughter, pain, sorrow, embarrassment, shame, anxiety, excitement, happiness – no account of a school can be complete without some consideration of them.

In short, a greater flexibility, a greater openness is required if sociologists are to reap the benefits of the strengths of various approaches and shore up their weaknesses. This is not a recipe for a facile eclecticism, but rather a call for greater rigour in the exercise of the sociological imagination. In this task, interactionism has its part to play.

References

ABBS, P. (1980) 'The reconstitution of English as art', *Tract*, no. 81, pp. 4–31.

ATKINSON, P.A. (1975) 'In cold blood: bedside teaching in a medical school', in Chanan, G. and Delamont, S. (eds), *Frontiers of Classroom Research*, Slough, National Foundation for Educational Research.

ATKINSON, P.A. and DELAMONT, S. (1977) 'Mock-ups and cock-ups: the stage-management of guided discovery instruction', in Woods, P. and Hammersley, M. (eds).

BALL, D. (1972) 'Self and identity in the context of deviance: the case of criminal abortion', in Scott, R.A. and Douglas, J.D. (eds), *Theoretical Perspectives on Deviance*, New York, Basic Books.

BALL, S. (1980) 'Initial encounters in the classroom and the process of establishment', in Woods, P. (ed.), *Pupil Strategies*, London, Croom Helm.

BALL, S. (1981) *Beachside Comprehensive*, Cambridge University Press.

BALL, S. (1982) 'Competition and conflict in the teaching of English: a socio-historical analysis', *Journal of Curriculum Studies*, vol. 14, no.1, pp. 1–28.

BALL, S. and LACEY, C. (1980) 'Subject disciplines as the opportunity for group action: a measured critique of subject sub-cultures', in Woods, P. (ed.) *Teacher Strategies*, London, Croom Helm.

BARNES, D. (1969) 'Language in the secondary school classroom', in Barnes, D., Britton, J. and Rosen, H.

BARNES, D. (1976) *From Communication to Curriculum*, Harmondsworth, Penguin.

BARNES, D., BRITTEN, J. and ROSEN, H. (1969) *Language, the Learner and the School*, Harmondsworth, Penguin.

BARNES, D. and SHEMILT, D. (1974) 'Transmission and interpretation', *Educational Review*, vol. 26.

BARTON, L. and MEIGHAN, R. (eds) (1978) *Sociological Interpretations of Schooling and Classrooms: A Reappraisal*, Driffield, Nafferton Books.

BARTON, L. and WALKER, S. (eds) (1981) *Schools, Teachers and Teaching*, Lewes, Falmer Press.

BECKER, H. (1960) 'Notes on the concept of commitment', *American Journal of Sociology*, vol. 66 (July).

BECKER, H. (1963) *Outsiders: Studies in the Sociology of Deviance*, Chicago, Free Press.

BECKER, H. (1970) *Sociological Work*, Chicago, Aldine.

BECKER, H. (1976) 'The career of the Chicago public schoolteacher', in Hammersley, M. and Woods, P.(eds), *The Process of Schooling*, London, Routledge & Kegan Paul.

BECKER, H. (1977a) 'Social class variations in the teacher-pupil relationship', in Cosin, B.R. *et al.* (eds), *School and Society* (2nd ed.), London, Routledge & Kegan Paul.

BECKER, H. (1977b) 'Personal change in adult life', in Cosin, B.R. *et al.* (eds), *School and Society* (2nd ed.), London, Routledge & Kegan Paul.

BECKER, H.S., GEER, B., HUGHES, E.C. and STRAUSS, A.L. (1961) *Boys in White*, University of Chicago Press.

BELL, R. (1981) 'Approaches to Teaching', Unit 15 of *E200, Contemporary Issues in Education*, Milton Keynes, Open University Press.

BENNETT, D.J. and BENNETT, J.D. (1970) 'Making the scene', in Stone, G. and Farberman, H. (eds), *Social Psychology through Symbolic Interaction*, Waltham, Mass., Ginn-Blaisdale.

BERGER, P.L. (1969) *The Social Reality of Religion*, New York, Faber.

BERGER, P.L. and LUCKMAN, T. (1966) *The Social Construction of Reality: A Treatise in the Sociology of Knowledge*, Garden City, New York, Doubleday (Penguin 1967).

BERLAK, A. and BERLAK, H. (1981) *The Dilemmas of Schooling*, London, Methuen.

BERLAK, A.C., BERLAK, H., BAGENSTOS, N.T., MIKEL, E.R. (1976) 'Teaching and learning in English primary schools', in Hammersley, M. and Woods, P. (eds), *The Process of Schooling*, London, Routledge & Kegan Paul.

BERNSTEIN, B. (1971) 'On the classification and framing of educational knowledge', in Young, M.F.D. (ed.), *Knowledge and Control*, London, Collier Macmillan.

BERNSTEIN, B. (1973) *Class, Codes and Control, Vol. 2, Applied Studies towards a Sociology of Language*, London, Routledge & Kegan Paul.

BETHELL, A. (1980) 'Getting away from it all', *Times Educational Supplement*, 21 March.

BEYNON, H. (1975) *Working for Ford*, Wakefield, E.P. Publishing.

BEYNON, J. (1979) '"Sussing-out" teachers: pupils as data gatherers', paper presented to Conference on 'The Ethnography of Schooling', St Hilda's College, Oxford.

BEYNON, J. and DELAMONT, S. (1983) 'The sound and the fury: pupil perceptions of school violence', in Gault, H. and Frude, N. (eds), *Children's Aggression at School*, London, Wiley.

References

BIRD, C. (1980) 'Deviant labelling in school: the pupils' perspective', in Woods, P.(ed.), *Pupil Strategies*, London, Croom Helm.

BIRKSTED, I. (1975) 'School performance seen from the boys', *Sociological Review*.

BIRKSTED, I. (1976) 'School versus pop culture? A case study of adolescent adaptation', in *Research in Education*, no. 16, November.

BITTNER, E. (1967) 'The police on Skid Row: a study of peace-keeping', *American Sociological Review*, vol. 32, no. 5, October, pp. 699–715.

BLACKIE, P. (1980) 'Not quite proper', in Reedy, S. and Woodhead, M. (eds), *Family, Work and Education*, London, Hodder & Stoughton.

BLUMER, H. (1962) 'Society as Symbolic Interaction', in Rose, A.M. (ed.), *Human Behaviour and Social Processes*, London, Routledge & Kegan Paul.

BLUMER, H. (1969) *Symbolic Interactionism*, Englewood Cliffs, Prentice Hall.

BLUMER, H. (1976) 'Sociological implications of the thought of G.H. Mead', in Cosin, B.R. *et al.* (eds), *School and Society*, London, Routledge & Kegan Paul.

BRAVERMAN, H. (1974) *Labour and Monopoly Capital: The Degradation of Work in the Twentieth Century*, New York, Monthly Review Press.

BRITTAN, A. (1973) *Meanings and Situations*, London, Routledge & Kegan Paul.

BRYAN, K. (1980) 'Pupil perceptions of transfer between middle and high schools', in Hargreaves, A. and Tickle, L. (eds), *Middle Schools: Origins, Ideology and Practice*, London, Harper & Row.

BUCHER, R. and STERLING, J.D. (1977) *Becoming Professional*, London, Sage Publications.

BUCHER, R. and STRAUSS, A.L. (1976) 'Professions in process', in Hammersley, M. and Woods, P. (eds), *The Process of Schooling*, London, Routledge & Kegan Paul.

BURNS, T. (1967) 'Sociological explanation', *British Journal of Sociology*, vol. 18.

BYRNE, E.M. (1978) *Women and Education*, London, Tavistock.

CHESSUM, R. (1980) 'Teacher ideologies and pupil disaffection, in Barton, L., Meighan, R. and Walker, S. (eds), *Schooling, Ideology and the Curriculum*, Lewes, Falmer Press.

CICOUREL, A.V. (1968) *The Social Organisation of Juvenile Justice*, New York, Wiley.

CICOUREL, A.V. and KITSUSE, J.I. (1963) *The Educational Decision-Makers*, New York, Bobbs Merrill.

COHEN, A.K. (1955) *Delinquent Boys*, New York, Free Press.

COHEN, A. (1976) 'The elasticity of evil: changes in the social definition of deviance', in Hammersley, M. and Woods, P. (eds), *The Process of Schooling*, London, Routledge & Kegan Paul.

COOLEY, C.H. (1902) *Human Nature and the Social Order*, New York, Charles Scribner's Sons.

CORBISHLEY, P., EVANS, J., KENRICK, C. and DAVIES, B. (1981)

'Teacher strategies and pupil identities in mixed ability curricula: a note on concepts and some examples from maths', in Barton, L. and Walker, S. (eds), *Schools, Teachers and Teaching*, Lewes, Falmer Press.

CORRIGAN, P. (1976) 'Doing nothing', in Hall, S. and Jefferson, T. (eds), *Resistance through Ritual*, London, Hutchinson.

CORRIGAN, P. (1979) *Schooling the Smash Street Kids*, London, Macmillan.

DALE, I.R. (1972) 'The culture of the school', Unit 4 of *E282 School and Society*, Milton Keynes, Open University Press.

DALE, I.R. (1976) 'Work, career and the self', Unit 7 of *DE 351 People and Work*, Milton Keynes, Open University Press.

DALE, I.R. (1978) 'From endorsement to disintegration: progressive education from the Golden Age to the Green Paper', paper presented to the Conference of the Standing Committee for Studies in Education, King's College, London (December).

DAVIES, B. (1976) 'The culture of the child versus the culture of the teacher: an ethnomethodological study', unpublished paper, University of New England, Armidale.

DAVIES, B. (1980a) 'An analysis of primary school children's accounts of classroom interaction', in *British Journal of Sociology of Education*, vol. 1, no. 3.

DAVIES, B. (1980b) 'Friends and fights: a study of children's views on social interaction in childhood', unpublished paper, University of New England, Armidale.

DAVIES, B. (1980c) 'Pupils' attitudes to teacher organization and discipline', unpublished paper, University of New England, Armidale.

DEEM, R. (1978) *Women and Schooling*, London, Routledge & Kegan Paul.

DEEM, R. (ed.) (1980) *Schooling for Women's Work*, London, Routledge & Kegan Paul.

DELAMONT, S. (1976) *Interaction in the Classroom*, London, Methuen.

DELAMONT, S. (1980) *Sex Roles and the School*, London, Methuen.

DENSCOMBE, M. (1977) 'The social organization of teaching: a study of teaching as a practical activity in two London comprehensive schools', PhD thesis, University of Leicester.

DENSCOMBE, M. (1980a) '"Keeping 'em Quiet": the significance of noise for the practical activity of teaching', in Woods, P. (ed.), *Teacher Strategies*, London, Croom Helm.

DENSCOMBE, M. (1980b) 'Pupil strategies and the open classroom', in Woods, P. (ed.), *Pupil Strategies*, London, Croom Helm.

DENSCOMBE, M. (1980c) 'The work context of teaching', in *British Journal of Sociology of Education*, vol. 1, no. 3, September.

DENZIN, N. (1978) *The Research Act in Sociology: a Theoretical Introduction to Sociological Methods*, London, Butterworth.

DEUTSCHER, I. (1973) *What we say/What we do*, Glenview, Illinois, Scott, Foreman and Co.

DITTON, J. (1977) *Part-time Crime: an Ethnography of Fiddling and Pilferage*, London, Macmillan.

References

DOUGLAS, M. (1966) *Purity and Danger*, London, Routledge & Kegan Paul.

DUMONT, R.V. and WAX, M.L. (1971) 'Cherokee school society and the intercultural classroom', in Cosin, B.R. *et al.* (eds), *School and Society*, London, Routledge & Kegan Paul.

DUNHAM, J. (1977) 'The effects of disruptive behaviour on teachers', in *Educational Review*, vol. 29, no. 3, June, pp. 181–8.

EDWARDS, A.D. (1979) *Language in Culture and Class*, London, Heinemann.

EDWARDS, A.D. and FURLONG, V.J. (1978) *The Language of Teaching*, London, Heinemann.

EGGLESTON, J. (1977) *The Ecology of the School*, London, Methuen.

EMERSON, J.P. (1970) 'Behaviour in private places: sustaining definitions of reality in gynaecological examinations', in Dreitzel, H.P. (ed.), *Recent Sociology No.2: Patterns of Communicative Behaviour*, London, Collier Macmillan.

ESLAND, G.M. (1971) 'Teaching and learning as the organization of knowledge', in Young, M.F.D. (ed.), *Knowledge and Control*, London, Collier Macmillan.

FLANDERS, N.A. (1970) *Analyzing Teaching Behaviour*, New York, Addison-Wesley.

FRIEDSON, E. (1972) *Medical Men and their Work*, Chicago, Aldine.

FUCHS, E. (1969) *Teachers Talk*, New York, Anchor Books.

FULLER, M. (1980) 'Black girls in a London comprehensive school', in Deem, R. (ed.), *Schooling for Women's Work*, London, Routledge & Kegan Paul.

FURLONG, V.J. (1976) 'Interaction sets in the classroom', in Hammersley, M. and Woods, P. (eds), *The Process of Schooling*, London, Routledge & Kegan Paul.

FURLONG, V.J. (1977) 'Anancy goes to school: a case study of pupils' knowledge of their teachers', in Woods, P. and Hammersley, M. (eds), *School Experience*, London, Croom Helm.

GALTON, M. and DELAMONT, S. (1980) 'The first weeks of middle school', in Hargreaves, A. and Tickle, L. (eds), *Middle Schools: Origins, Ideology and Practice*, London, Harper & Row.

GANNAWAY, H. (1976), 'Making sense of school', in Stubbs, M. and Delamont, S. (eds), *Explorations in Classroom Observation*, London, Wiley.

GINSBURG, M.B., MEYENN R.J. and MILLER, H.D.R. (1980) 'Teachers' conceptions of professionalism and trades unionism: an ideological analysis', in Woods, P. (ed.) (1980a), *Teacher Strategies*, London, Croom Helm.

GLASER, B.G. and STRAUSS, A.L. (1967) *The Discovery of Grounded Theory*, London, Weidenfeld & Nicolson.

GLASER, B.S. and STRAUSS, A.L. (1971) *Status Passage*, New York, Aldine.

GOFFMAN, E. (1961) *Asylums*, Garden City, Doubleday; also in (1968) Harmondsworth, Penguin.

GOFFMAN, E. (1959) *The Presentation of Self in Everyday Life*, Garden City, Doubleday.

GOFFMAN, E. (1967) *Interaction Ritual*, New York, Doubleday.

GOFFMAN, E. (1971) *Relations in Public*, New York, Basic Books.

GOODSON, I. (1975) 'The teachers' curriculum and the new reformation', *Journal of Curriculum Studies*, vol. 7, no. 2, November.

GOODSON, I. (1980) 'Life histories and the study of schooling', *Interchange*, vol. II, no. 4.

GOODSON, I. (1981) 'Becoming an academic subject: patterns of explanation and evolution', in *British Journal of Sociology of Education*, vol. 2, no. 2.

GRACE, G. (1978) *Teachers, Ideology and Control*, London, Routledge & Kegan Paul.

GRACEY, H. (1972) *Curriculum or Craftsmanship: Elementary School Teachers in a Bureaucratic System*, University of Chicago Press.

GRACEY, H. (1976) 'The craftsman teachers', in Hammersley, M. and Woods, P. (eds), *The Process of Schooling*, London, Routledge & Kegan Paul.

GRUNDSELL, R. (1978) *Absent from School*, London, Writers and Readers.

GRUNDSELL, R. (1980) *Beyond Control: Schools and Suspension*, London, Writers and Readers.

HALL, S. and JEFFERSON, T. (1977) *Resistance through Rituals*, London, Hutchinson.

HAMMERSLEY, M. (1974) 'The organization of pupil participation', *Sociological Review*, vol. 22, no. 3, August.

HAMMERSLEY, M. (1975) 'A staffroom ideology', unpublished paper. Also in Hammersley, M. (1980) 'A peculiar world? Teaching and learning in an inner-city school', PhD thesis, University of Manchester.

HAMMERSLEY, M. (1976) 'The mobilization of pupil attention', in Hammersley, M. and Woods, P. (eds) *The Process of Schooling*, London, Routledge & Kegan Paul.

HAMMERSLEY, M. (1977a) 'Teacher perspectives', Unit 9 of *E202, Schooling and Society*, Milton Keynes, Open University Press.

HAMMERSLEY, M. (1977b) 'School learning: the cultural resources required by pupils to answer a teacher's question', in Woods, P. and Hammersley, M. (eds), *School Experience*, London, Croom Helm.

HAMMERSLEY, M. (1980a) 'A peculiar world? Teaching and learning in an inner-city school', unpublished PhD thesis, University of Manchester.

HAMMERSLEY, M. (1980b) 'On interactionist empiricism', in Woods, P. (ed.), *Pupil Strategies*, London, Croom Helm.

HAMMERSLEY, M. (1980c) 'Classroom ethnography', *Educational Analysis*, vol. 2, no. 2, winter.

HAMMERSLEY, M. (1981) 'Ideology in the staffroom? A critique of false consciousness', in Barton, L. and Walker, S. (eds), *Schools, Teachers and Teaching*, Lewes, Falmer Press.

HAMMERSLEY, M. (ed.) (1983) *The Ethnography of Schooling*, Driffield, Nafferton Books.
HAMMERSLEY, M. and TURNER, G. (1980) 'Conformist pupils?', in Woods, P. (ed.), *Pupil Strategies*, London, Croom Helm.
HAMMERSLEY, M. and WOODS, P. (eds) (1976) *The Process of Schooling*, London, Routledge & Kegan Paul.
HANNAM, C., SMYTH, P. and STEPHENSON, N. (1971) *Young Teachers and Reluctant Learners*, Harmondsworth, Penguin.
HANSON, D. and HERRINGTON, M. (1976) *From College to Classroom: the probationary year*, London, Routledge & Kegan Paul.
HARARY, F. (1966) 'Merton revisited: a new classification for deviant behaviour', *American Sociological Review*, vol. 31, no. 5.
HARGREAVES, A. (1977) 'Progressivism and pupil autonomy', *Sociological Review*, August.
HARGREAVES, A. (1978) 'Towards a theory of classroom coping strategies', in Barton, L. and Meighan, R. (eds), *Sociological Interpretations of Schooling and Classrooms*, Driffield, Nafferton Books.
HARGREAVES, A. (1979) 'Strategies, decisions and control: interaction in a middle-school classroom', in Eggleston, J. (ed.), *Teacher Decision-Making in the Classroom*, London, Routledge & Kegan Paul.
HARGREAVES, A. (1980a) 'The ideology of the middle school', in Hargreaves, A. and Tickle, L. (eds), *Middle Schools: Origins, Ideology and Practice*, London, Harper & Row.
HARGREAVES, A. (1980b) 'Synthesis and the study of strategies: a project for the sociological imagination', in Woods, P. (ed.), *Pupil Strategies*, London, Croom Helm.
HARGREAVES, A. (1981) 'Contrastive rhetoric and extremist talk', in Barton, L. and Walker, S. (eds), *Schools, Teachers and Teaching*, Lewes, Falmer Press.
HARGREAVES, D.H. (1967) *Social Relations in a Secondary School*, London, Routledge & Kegan Paul.
HARGREAVES, D.H. (1972) *Interpersonal Relations and Education*, London, Routledge & Kegan Paul.
HARGREAVES, D.H. (1977) 'The process of typification in the classroom: models and methods', *British Journal of Educational Psychology*, November.
HARGREAVES, D.H. (1978) 'Whatever happened to symbolic interactionism?', in Barton, L. and Meighan, R. (eds), *Sociological Interpretations of Schooling and Classrooms*, Driffield, Nafferton Books.
HARGREAVES, D.H. (1980) 'The occupational culture of teachers', in Woods, P. (ed.) (1980a) *Teacher Strategies*, London, Croom Helm.
HARGREAVES, D.H., HESTER, S.K. and MELLOR, F.J. (1975) *Deviance in Classrooms*, London, Routledge & Kegan Paul.
HMSO (1977) *Statistics of Education*, Home Office.
HILSUM, S. and START, K. (1974) *Promotion and Careers in Teaching*, Slough, National Foundation for Educational Research.
HIRST, P.H. and PETERS, R.S. (1970) *The Logic of Education*, London, Routledge & Kegan Paul.

HOGGART, R. (1964) 'Schools of English and contemporary society II', *Use of English*, vol. 17, no. 3.

HOLT, J. (1969) *How Children Fail*, Harmondsworth, Penguin.

HOPPER, E. (1971) 'Educational systems and selected consequences of patterns of mobility and non-mobility in industrial societies', in Hopper, E. (ed.), *Readings in the Theory of Educational Systems*, London, Hutchinson.

HUGHES, E.C. (1937) 'Institutional office and the person', in Hughes, E.C. (1958) *Men and Their Work*, New York, Free Press.

HUGHES, E.C. (1958) *Men and Their Work*, New York, Free Press.

HUNTER, C. (1980) 'The politics of participation – with specific reference to teacher-pupil relationships', in Woods, P. (ed.) (1980a) *Teacher Strategies*, London, Croom Helm.

HURMAN, A. (1978) *A Charter for Choice*, Slough, National Foundation for Educational Research.

JAMES, W. (1890) *The Principles of Psychology Vol.1*, New York, Henry Holt.

KANTER, R.M. (1974) 'Commitment and social organization', in Field, D. (ed.), *Social Psychology for Sociologists*, London, Nelson.

KEDDIE, N. (1971) 'Classroom knowledge', in Young, M.F.D. (ed.), *Knowledge and Control*, London, Collier Macmillan.

KEDDIE, N. (1973) *Tinker, Tailor ... the Myth of Cultural Deprivation*, Harmondsworth, Penguin.

KELLY, A. (1976) 'A discouraging process: how girls are eased out of science', in Hinton, K. (ed.), *Women and Science*, SISCON project.

KELLY, A. (ed.) (1981) *Missing Half: Girls and Science Education*, Manchester University Press.

KING, R.A. (1971) 'Unequal access in education – sex and social class', in *Social and Economic Administration*, vol. 5, no. 3, pp. 167–74.

KING, R.A. (1978) *All Things Bright and Beautiful*, Chichester, John Wiley.

KOUNIN, J.S. (1970) *Discipline and Group Management in Classrooms*, New York, Holt, Rinehart & Winston.

KOZOL, J. (1968) *Death at an Early Age*, Harmondsworth, Penguin.

LACEY, C. (1970) *Hightown Grammar*, Manchester University Press.

LACEY, C. (1976) 'Problems of sociological fieldwork: a review of the methodology of "Hightown Grammar"', in Hammersley, M. and Woods, P. (eds), *The Process of Schooling*, London, Routledge & Kegan Paul.

LACEY, C. (1977) *The Socialization of Teachers*, London, Methuen.

LAING, R.D. (1967) *The Politics of Experience*, Harmondsworth, Penguin.

LAMBART, A.M. (1976) 'The sisterhood', in Hammersley, M. and Woods, P. (eds), *The Process of Schooling*, London, Routledge & Kegan Paul.

LEEDS LITERATURE COLLECTIVE (1973) 'Science and girls: a study of primary science text books', in *Shrew*, vol. 5, 8 October.

LISTER, I. (ed.) (1974) *Deschooling*, Cambridge University Press.

References

LLEWELLYN, M. (1980) 'Studying girls at school: the implications of confusion', in Deem, R. (ed.), *Schooling for Women's Work*, London, Routledge & Kegan Paul.

LORTIE, D.C. (1975), *Schoolteacher*, University of Chicago Press.

LUKES, S. (1974) *Power – A Radical View*, London, Macmillan.

LYNCH, J. (1980) 'Legitimation crisis for the English middle school', in Hargreaves, A. and Tickle, L. (eds), *Middle Schools: Origins, Ideology and Practice*, London, Harper & Row.

LYONS, G. (1981) *Teacher Careers and Career Perceptions*, Slough, National Foundation for Educational Research.

MACCOBY, E.E. (1966) *The Development of Sex Differences*, California, University of Stanford Press.

MACLURE, M. and FRENCH, P. (1981) 'A comparison of talk at home and at school', in Wells, G. (ed.), *Language through Interaction*, Cambridge University Press.

MANNHEIM, K. (1952) 'The problem of generations', in *Essays on The Sociology of Knowledge*, London, Routledge & Kegan Paul.

MARDLE, G. and WALKER, M. (1980) 'Strategies and structure: some critical notes on teacher socialization', in Woods, P. (ed.), *Teacher Strategies*, London, Croom Helm.

MARSH, P., ROSSER, E. and HARRÉ R. (1978) *The Rules of Disorder*, London, Routledge & Kegan Paul.

MARTIN, W.B.W. (1975) 'Teacher-pupil interactions: a negotiation perspective', in *Canadian Review of Sociology and Anthropology*, vol. l2 (4 Part 2).

MARTIN, W.B.W. (1976) *The Negotiated Order of the School*, Toronto, Macmillan.

McROBBIE, A. (1980) 'Settling accounts with sub-cultures: a feminist critique', *Screen Education*, vol. 34, spring.

McROBBIE, A. and GARBER, J. (1976) 'Girls and subcultures', in Hall, S. and Jefferson, T. (eds), *Resistance through Rituals*, London, Hutchinson.

MEAD, G.H. (1934) *Mind, Self and Society*, University of Chicago Press.

MEAD, G.H. (1936) *Works of George Herbert Mead: Movements of Thought in the 19th Century (Volume 1)* ed. by Merritt H. Moore, University of Chicago Press.

MEASOR, L. and WOODS, P. (1983) 'The interpretation of pupil myths', in Hammersley, M. (ed.), *The Ethnography of Schooling*, Driffield, Nafferton Books.

MEHAN, H. (1978) *Learning Lessons*, New York, Harvard University Press.

MEIGHAN, R. (1981) *A Sociology of Educating*, London, Holt, Rinehart & Winston.

MERCER, N. (1981) 'Making sense of school', *New Society*, 19 February.

MERTON, R. (1957) *Social Theory and Social Structure*, Chicago, Free Press.

MEYENN, R. (1980) 'School girls' peer groups', in Woods, P. (ed.) *Teacher Strategies*, London, Croom Helm.

192

MILLER, C. and PARLETT, M. (1974) *Up to the Mark*, London, Society for Research into Higher Education.

MILLER, W.B. (1958) 'Lower class culture as a generating milieu of gang delinquency', *Journal of Social Issues*, vol. 14, pp. 5–19.

MORGAN, J., O'NEILL, C., HARRÉ, R. (1979) *Nicknames: their origins and social consequences*, London, Routledge & Kegan Paul.

MUSGROVE, F. (1974), *Ecstasy and Holiness*, London, Methuen.

MUSGROVE, F. (1977) *Margins of the Mind*, London, Methuen.

MUSGROVE, F. and TAYLOR, P.H. (1969) *Society and the Teacher's Role*, London, Routledge & Kegan Paul.

MUSGROVE, F. and MIDDLETON, R. (1981) 'Rites of passage and the meaning of age in three contrasted social groups', *British Journal of Sociology*, vol. 32, no. 1, March.

NASH, R. (1973) *Classrooms Observed*, London, Routledge & Kegan Paul.

NASH, R. (1974) 'Pupils' expectations for their teachers', *Research in Education*, no. 12, November, pp. 47–61.

NASH, R. (1976) 'Pupils' expectations of their teachers', in Stubbs, M. and Delamont, S. (eds), *Explorations in Classroom Observation*, London, Wiley.

NATANSON, M. (1973) *The Social Dynamics of George H. Mead*, The Hague, Martinus Nijhoff.

NIAS, J. (1980) 'The ideal middle school: its public image', in Hargreaves, A. and Tickle, L. (eds), *Middle Schools: Origins, Ideology and Practice*, London, Harper & Row.

NIAS, J. (1981) 'Commitment and motivation in primary school teachers', *Educational Review*, vol. 33, no. 3, pp. 181–90.

OPEN UNIVERSITY (1979) *DE304: Research Methods in Education and the Social Sciences*, Block 3, Part 5, Block 4, Part 3, and Block 6, Part I, Milton Keynes, Open University Press.

PARLETT, M.R. and HAMILTON, D. (1972) 'Evaluation as illumination: a new approach to innovatory programs', occasional paper no. 9, *Centre for Research in the Educational Sciences*, University of Edinburgh.

PARRY-JONES, W. and GAY, B.M. (1980) 'The anatomy of disruption: a preliminary consideration of interaction sequences within disruptive incidents', *Oxford Review of Education*, vol. 6, no. 3, pp. 213–20.

PERINBANAYAGAM, R.S. (1974) 'The definition of the situation: an analysis of the ethnomethodological and dramaturgical view', *The Sociological Quarterly*, vol. 15 (autumn), pp. 521–41.

PETERS, R.S. (ed.) (1967) *The Concept of Education*, London, Routledge & Kegan Paul.

PLUMMER, K. (1975) *Sexual Stigma*, London, Routledge & Kegan Paul.

POLLARD, A. (1979) 'Negotiating deviance and "getting done" in primary school classrooms', in Barton, L. and Meighan, R. (eds), *Schools, Pupils and Deviance*, Driffield, Nafferton Books.

References

POLLARD, A. (1980) 'Teacher interests and changing situations of survival threat in primary school classrooms', in Woods, P. (ed.), *Teacher Strategies*, London, Croom Helm.

POLLARD, A. (1982) 'A model of coping strategies', *British Journal of Sociology of Education*, March.

POSTMAN, N. and WEINGARTNER, C. (1969) *Teaching as a Subversive Activity*, New York, Delacorte Press. Also Penguin, 1971.

PRENDERGAST, S. and PROUST, A. (1980) 'What will I do ...? Teenage girls and the construction of motherhood', *Sociological Review*, vol. 28, no. 3.

PURVIS, J. (1973) 'Schoolteaching as a professional career', *British Journal of Sociology*, March.

QUINE, W.S. (1974) 'Polarized cultures in comprehensive schools', *Research in Education*, no. 12.

REYNOLDS, D. (1976a) 'When teachers and pupils refuse a truce', in Mungham, G. and Pearson, G. (eds), *Working Class Youth Culture*, London, Routledge & Kegan Paul.

REYNOLDS, D. (1976b) 'The delinquent school', in Hammersley, M. and Woods, P. (eds), *The Process of Schooling*, London, Routledge & Kegan Paul.

REYNOLDS, D. and SULLIVAN, M. (1979) 'Bringing schools back in', in Barton, L. and Meighan, R. (eds), *Schools, Pupils and Deviance*, Driffield, Nafferton Books.

RICHARDSON, E. (1967) *The Environment of Learning: Conflict and Understanding in the Secondary School*, London, Nelson.

RISEBOROUGH, G.F. (1981) 'Teacher careers and comprehensive schooling: an empirical study', *Sociology*, vol. 15, no. 3, pp. 352–81.

ROCK, P. (1979) *The Making of Symbolic Interaction*, London, Macmillan.

ROSE, A.M. (1962) 'A systematic summary of symbolic interaction theory', in Rose, A.M. (ed.), *Human Behaviour and Social Processes*, London, Routledge & Kegan Paul.

ROSSER, E. and HARRÉ, R. (1976) 'The meaning of disorder', in Hammersley, M. and Woods, P. (eds), *The Process of Schooling*, London, Routledge & Kegan Paul.

RUTTER, M., MAUGHAM, B., MORTIMORE, P. and OUSTON, J. (1979) *Fifteen Thousand Hours*, London, Open Books.

RYRIE, A., FURST, A. and LAUDER, M. (1979) *Choices and Chances*, Scottish Council for Research in Education.

SCHUTZ, A. (1967) *The Phenomenology of the Social World*, trans. Walsh, G. and Lehnert, F., New York, Northwestern University Press.

SHARP, R. and GREEN, A. (1975) *Education and Social Control*, London, Routledge & Kegan Paul.

SHARPE, S. (1976) *Just Like a Girl*, Harmondsworth, Penguin.

SPENDER, D. and SARAH, E. (eds) (1980) *Learning to Lose: Sexism and Education*, London, The Women's Press.

STEBBINS, R.A. (1970) 'The meaning of disorderly behaviour: teacher definitions of a classroom situation', *Sociology of Education*, vol. 44, pp. 217–36.

STEBBINS, R.A. (1974) 'The disorderly classroom: its physical and temporal conditions', *Monographs in Education No. 12*, Faculty of Education, University of Newfoundland.

STEBBINS, R.A. (1975) *Teachers and Meaning: Definitions of Classroom Situations*, Leiden, E.J. Brill.

STEBBINS, R.A. (1976) 'Physical context influences on behaviour: the case of classroom disorderliness', in Hammersley, M. and Woods, P. (eds), *The Process of Schooling*, London, Routledge & Kegan Paul.

STEBBINS, R.A. (1977) 'The meaning of academic performance: how teachers define a classroom situation', in Woods, P. and Hammersley, M. (eds), *School Experience*, London, Croom Helm.

STEBBINS, R.A. (1980) 'The role of humour in teaching', in Woods, P. (ed.), *Teacher Strategies*, London, Croom Helm.

STEBBINS, R.A. (1981) 'Classroom ethnography and the definition of the situation', in Barton, L. and Walker, S. (eds), *Schools, Teachers and Teaching*, Lewes, Falmer Press.

STRAUSS, A.L. (1969) *Mirrors and Masks*, San Francisco, Sociology Press.

STRAUSS, A.L. *et al.* (1964) *Psychiatric Ideologies and Institutions*, London, Collier Macmillan.

STUBBS, M. (1976) *Language, Schools and Classrooms*, London, Methuen.

STUBBS, M. and DELAMONT, S. (eds), (1976) *Explorations in Classroom Observation*, Chichester, Wiley.

TAYLOR, L. and COHEN, S. (1978) *Escape Attempts: The Theory and Practice of Resistance to Everyday Life*, London, Allen Lane.

THOMAS, W.I. (1928) *The Child in America*, New York, Knopf.

TORODE, B. (1977) 'Interrupting Intersubjectivity', in Woods, P. and Hammersley, M. (eds), *School Experience*, London, Croom Helm.

TOUGH, J. (1970) 'Some differences in the use of language in groups of three-year-old children', Leeds University Institute of Education.

TROPP, A. (1957) *The School Teachers*, London, Heinemann.

TUCKWELL, P. (1982) 'Pleasing teacher', in Booth, T. and Statham, J. (eds), *The Nature of Special Education*, London, Croom Helm.

TURNER, G. (1982) '"Conformist" pupils in the secondary school', PhD thesis, Open University. See also Turner, G., *Swots and Dossers: Pupil Activity in a Comprehensive School*, London, Croom Helm, forthcoming.

TURNER, G. (1983) '"Swots" and "Dossers": a decision-making approach to pupil orientation', in Furlong, V.J. (ed.), *Contemporary Research with School Pupils*, Driffield, Nafferton Books.

TURNER, R.H. (1962) 'Role-taking: process versus conformity', in Rose, A.M. (ed.), *Human Behaviour and Social Process*, London, Routledge & Kegan Paul.

TURNER, R.H. (1971) 'Sponsored and contest mobility and the school system', in Hopper, E. (ed.), *Readings in the Theory of Educational Systems*, London, Hutchinson.

TURNER, R.H. (1976) 'The real self: from institution to impulse', *American Journal of Sociology*, vol. 81, no. 5.

TURNER, V.W. (1969) *The Ritual Process*, London, Routledge & Kegan Paul.

VAN GENNEP, A. (1960) *The Rites of Passage*, London, Routledge & Kegan Paul.

VULLIAMY, G. (1979) 'Culture clash and school music: a sociological analysis', in Barton, L. and Meighan, R. (eds), *Sociological Interpretations of Schooling and Classrooms*, Driffield, Nafferton Books.

WAKEFORD, J. (1969) *The Cloistered Elite: A Sociological Analysis of the English Public Boarding School*, London, Macmillan.

WALKER, R. and ADELMAN, C. (1976) 'Strawberries', in Stubbs, M. and Delamont, S. (eds), *Explorations in Classroom Observation*, Chichester, Wiley.

WALKER, R. and GOODSON, I. (1977) 'Humour in the classroom', in Woods, P. and Hammersley, M. (eds), *School Experience*, London, Croom Helm.

WALLACE, G. (1980) 'The constraints of architecture on aims and organization in five middle schools', in Hargreaves, A. and Tickle, L. (eds), *Middle Schools: Origins, Ideology and Practice*, London, Harper & Row.

WALLER, W. (1932) *The Sociology of Teaching*, New York, Wiley.

WARWICK, D. (1974) *Bureaucracy*, London, Longman.

WEBB, J. (1962) 'The sociology of a school', *British Journal of Sociology*, vol. 13, pp. 264–72.

WEBER, M. (1930) *The Protestant Ethic and the Spirit of Capitalism*, London, Allen & Unwin.

WERTHMAN, C. (1963) 'Delinquents in schools: a test for the legitimacy of authority', *Berkeley Journal of Sociology*, vol. 8, no. 1, pp. 39–60. Reproduced in Cosin, B.R. *et al.* (eds) (1978), *School and Society*, London, Routledge & Kegan Paul.

WESTBURY, I. (1973) 'Conventional classrooms, "open" classrooms and the technology of teaching', *Journal of Curriculum Studies*, vol. 5, no. 2 (November).

WHITE, R. (1980) *Absent Without Cause*, London, Routledge & Kegan Paul.

WILENSKY, H.L. (1960) 'Work, careers and social integration', *International Social Science Journal*, vol. 12, pp. 543–74, reprinted in Burns, T. (ed.) 1969, *Industrial Man*, Harmondsworth, Penguin.

WILLIS, P. (1977) *Learning to Labour*, Farnborough, Saxon House.

WILLIS, P. (1978) *Profane Culture*, London, Routledge & Kegan Paul.

WOODS, P. (1977) 'The ethnography of the school', Units 7–8 of *E202 Schooling and Society*, Milton Keynes, Open University Press.

WOODS, P. (1978a) 'Relating to schoolwork: some pupil perceptions', *Educational Review*, vol. 30, no. 2, pp. 167–75.

WOODS, P. (1978b) 'Negotiating the demands of.schoolwork', *Journal of Curriculum Studies*, vol. 10, no. 4, pp. 309–27.

WOODS, P. (1979) *The Divided School*, London, Routledge & Kegan Paul.

WOODS, P. (ed.) (1980a) *Teacher Strategies*, London, Croom Helm.

WOODS, P. (ed.) (1980b) *Pupil Strategies*, London, Croom Helm.

WOODS, P. (1981a) 'Schools and deviance', Unit 17 of *E200 Contemporary Issues in Education*, Milton Keynes, Open University Press.

WOODS, P. (1981b) 'Strategies, commitment and identity: making and breaking the teacher role', in Barton, L. and Walker, S. (eds), *Schools, Teachers and Teaching*, Lewes, Falmer Press.

WOODS, P. and HAMMERSLEY, M. (eds) (1977), *School Experience*, London, Croom Helm.

Author index

Subject index